A STUDY OF MIXED LEGAL SYSTEMS: ENDANGERED, ENTRENCHED OR BLENDED

Juris Diversitas

Series Editor:
Seán Patrick Donlan, University of Limerick, Limerick, Ireland

Editorial Board:
Olivier Moréteau – Louisiana, US
Ignazio Castellucci – Trento, Italy/Macau, China
Lukas Heckendorn Urscheler – Swiss Institute of Comparative Law, Switzerland
Salvatore Mancuso – Cape Town, South Africa
Christa Rautenbach – North-West University, Potchefstroom, South Africa

Series Advisory Board:
Philip Bailhache – Jersey, UK
Sue Farran – Northumbria, UK
Patrick Glenn – McGill, Canada
Marie Goré – Pantheon-Assas (Paris 2), France
Werner Menski – SOAS, London, UK
Esin Örücü – Glasgow, UK (Emeritus)
Vernon Valentine Palmer – Tulane, US
Rodolfo Sacco – Turin, Italy (Emeritus)
William Twining – University College London, UK (Emeritus) and Miami, US
Jacques Vanderlinden – Free University of Brussels,
Belgium (Emeritus) and Moncton, Canada (Emeritus)

Rooted in comparative law, the *Juris Diversitas* series focuses on the interdisciplinary study of legal and normative mixtures and movements. Our interest is in comparison broadly conceived, extending beyond law narrowly understood to related fields. Titles might be geographical or temporal comparisons. They could focus on theory and methodology, substantive law, or legal cultures. They could investigate official or unofficial 'legalities', past and present and around the world. And, to effectively cross spatial, temporal, and normative boundaries, inter- and multi-disciplinary research is particularly welcome.

Published title in the series
Concepts of Law
Comparative, Jurisprudential, and Social Science Perspectives
Edited by Seán Patrick Donlan and Lukas Heckendorn Urscheler
ISBN 978 1 4094 5526 4

Forthcoming title in the series
Mixed Legal Systems, East and West
Edited by Vernon Valentine Palmer, Mohamed Y. Mattar and Anna Koppel
ISBN 978 1 4724 3106 6

For more information on this series, visit www.ashgate.com

A Study of Mixed Legal Systems: Endangered, Entrenched or Blended

SUE FARRAN
Northumbria University, UK

ESIN ÖRÜCÜ
University of Glasgow, UK

&

SEÁN PATRICK DONLAN
University of Limerick, Ireland

ASHGATE

Published by
Ashgate Publishing Limited
Wey Court East
Union Road
Farnham
Surrey, GU9 7PT
England

Ashgate Publishing Company
110 Cherry Street
Suite 3-1
Burlington, VT 05401-3818
USA

www.ashgate.com

British Library Cataloguing in Publication Data
A catalogue record for this book is available from the British Library

ISBN: 978-1-4724-4177-5 (HBK)
       978-1-4724-4178-2 (EBK)
       978-1-4724-4179-9 (EPUB)

The Library of Congress has cataloged the printed edition as follows:
Farran, Susan, author.
 A study of mixed legal systems : endangered, entrenched, or blended / by Sue Farran, Esin Örücü and Sean Patrick Donlan.
    pages cm. -- (Juris diversitas)
 Includes bibliographical references and index.
 ISBN 978-1-4724-4177-5 (hardback) -- ISBN 978-1-4724-4178-2 (ebook) --
 ISBN 978-1-4724-4179-9 (epub) 1. Legal polycentricity. 2. Comparative law. I. Örücü
E., author. II. Donlan, Sean Patrick, author. III. Title.
 K236.F37 2014
 340.5--dc23

                                                                    2014015807

MIX
Paper from
responsible sources
FSC
www.fsc.org   FSC® C013985

Printed in the United Kingdom by Henry Ling Limited,
at the Dorset Press, Dorchester, DT1 1HD

Contents

List of Tables

Notes on Contributors

Pacifico A. AGABIN studied his Bachelor of Laws at the University of the Philippines and his JSD degree at Yale University. He was formerly Dean of the University of the Philippines College of Law, and is presently Chair of the Constitutional Law Department of the Philippine Judicial Academy and a law practitioner. His publications include: *Unconstitutional Essays*, *The Political Supreme Court*, and *Mestizo: The Story of the Philippine Legal System*.

Pacifio can be contacted by email at: averheldlaw@yahoo.com.ph

Tony ANGELO is a Professor, Faculty of Law, Victoria University of Wellington, New Zealand. He has special interests in comparative and private international law, with a focus on the law of small jurisdictions. Tony's main areas of publication have been in relation to Mauritius and the islands of the South Pacific. Current research interests involve the law of Seychelles. The Mauritius connection began in 1968 and continued until 2009. During that period, the main involvement in Mauritius was as Special Advisor in the Office of the Attorney-General.

Tony can be contacted by email at: Tony.Angelo@vuw.ac.nz

Philip BAILHACHE was called to the English bar in 1968 and to the Jersey bar in 1969. He was appointed Solicitor General for Jersey in 1975 and Attorney General in 1986. In 1989 was made a Queen's Counsel. He was appointed Deputy Bailiff in 1994 and became Bailiff of Jersey the following year. He was knighted in 1996. He was made an Honorary Fellow of Pembroke College, Oxford and an Honorary Master of the Bench of the Middle Temple in October 2003. Sir Philip retired as Bailiff in June 2009 and was appointed as a Commissioner of the Royal Court in July 2009, retiring in 2011 in order to take up a political career. He founded the *Jersey Law Review* in 1997 (now the *Jersey and Guernsey Law Review*) and remains its editor. In 1998 he founded the Jersey Legal Information Board which publishes a legal information website (www.jerseylaw.je). In 2008 he founded the Institute of Law which teaches Jersey law to aspiring advocates and offers degree courses in both Jersey and English law. Sir Philip has played an active role in several Commonwealth organizations. He was a member of the group of experts responsible for the Latimer House Guidelines on Parliamentary Supremacy and Judicial Independence in 1998.

Philip can be contacted by email at: SirPhilip.bailhache@lawinstitute.ac.je

Seán Patrick DONLAN, JD (Louisiana), PhD (Trinity College, Dublin), teaches at the University of Limerick, Ireland. His research interests include comparative law, legal history and legal philosophy. He is President of Juris Diversitas, General

Secretary of the World Society of Mixed Jurisdiction Jurists, and a member of the International Academy of Comparative Law. Dr Donlan is the Editor of *Comparative Legal History* and the General Editor of the *Juris Diversitas* Book Series (Ashgate). Most recently, he co-edited (with Lukas Heckendorn Urscheler), *Concepts of Law: Comparative, Jurisprudential, and Social Science Perspectives* (Ashgate 2014).

Seán can be contacted by email at: Sean.Donlan@ul.ie

Achilles C. EMILIANIDES is Professor and Head of the Law Department of the University of Nicosia. He holds a PhD in Law from the Aristotle University of Thessaloniki, as well as an LLM in European Law and Integration from the University of Leicester and an LLM in History, Philosophy and Sociology of Law from the Aristotle University of Thessaloniki. His publications include: *Constitutional Law in Cyprus* (Kluwer 2013), *Family and Religion Law in Cyprus* (Kluwer 2012), *Religion and Law in Cyprus* (Kluwer 2011), *Religious Freedom in the European Union* (ed. Peeters 2010), *Welfare of the Child and Beliefs of the Parents* (ed. University of Nicosia Press 2010), *The New Private International Law of Contract* (Sakkoulas 2009), *Cypriot Succession Law* (Dikaionomia 2008), *Professional Law of Advocates* (Dikaionomia 2007), *Cypriot Law of Public Procurement* (Dikaionomia 2007), *Cypriot Law of Marriage and Divorce* (Sakkoulas 2006) and *Beyond the Constitution of Cyprus* (Sakkoulas 2006).

Achilles can be contacted by email at: emilianides.a@unic.ac.cy

Sue FARRAN is a Professor of Laws at Northumbria University and an Adjunct Professor at the University of the South Pacific. She lives in Scotland and was previously a Senior Lecturer at Dundee University. Her research interests use case studies from the island countries of the South Pacific region to focus on issues of human rights, legal pluralism, comparative legal studies, the challenges of development and sustainability, globalization and legal colonialism. In particular she is interested in the interface between legal systems and normative frameworks within states and between states, and the relationship between national, regional and international players in shaping and developing legal responses to contemporary issues. Sue's PhD was awarded on the basis of a collection of publications brought together under the title 'Vanuatu: Lands in a Sea of Islands'. She has published extensively in the areas of legal pluralism, comparative law, family law, human rights and property law.

Sue can be contacted by email at: sue.farran@northumbria.ac.uk

Jane MATTHEWS GLENN is Emeritus Professor of Law and Urban Planning at McGill University, Montreal, Quebec, Canada, where she is also Member of the Institute of Comparative Law and Associate Member of the McGill School of Environment. She is a graduate of Queen's University, Kingston, Ontario, Canada, in History (BA (Hons)) and Law (LLB), and was called to the Bar of British Columbia; she also received a Doctorate in public law from the Université de Strasbourg, France. Jane has been elected as an Associate Member of the International Academy of Comparative Law, and as a member of the Board of Directors (as Vice-President for North America, Central America and the Caribbean) of the Union mondiale des agraristes univeristaires; she has also been named a Miembro de honor of the Comité Americano de Derecho Agrario. Her research interests are in the general area of property law, and include agrarian law, water law, the right to housing and land tenure issues. A good portion of her research and publications has focused on the Caribbean basin.

Jane can be contacted by email at: jane.glenn@mcgill.ca

Sophie MORIN is a Professor at the University of Montreal's Faculty of Law (Québec, Canada). A graduate of Université de Montréal (LLB, LLD) and of McGill University (LLM), she specialises in civil law (civil liability and property). Her doctoral thesis entitled '*Le dommage moral et le préjudice extrapatrimonial*' was awarded the Henri Capitant prize in 2010 and was published in 2011. She is a member of the Barreau du Québec and was a law clerk at the Québec Court of Appeal and teaches the law of property and property administration. Her publications include: *Le dommage moral et le préjudice extrapatrimonial*, (Éditions Yvon Blais, 2011), *Pourquoi j'emmènerais le législateur au musée s'il voulait discuter avec moi de l'avenir du Code civil du Québec* and *Le paiement* in Pierre-Claude Lafond (ed.), *Jurisclasseur Québec – obligations et responsabilité civile* (LexisNexis 2008).

Sophie can be contacted by email at: s.morin@umontreal.ca

Esin ÖRÜCÜ has been Professor Emerita of Comparative Law, University of Glasgow, since 2005 and Honorary Senior Research Fellow, University of Glasgow since 2008. Esin is also Professor Emeritus of Comparative Law, Erasmus University Rotterdam, Visiting Professor of Turkish Family Law, Amsterdam Free University, Visiting Professor of Comparative Law, Okan University, Istanbul and a titular member of the International Academy of Comparative Law. Esin's research interests include: comparative law methodology; transmigration of laws; changing paradigms in the new world order; mixed jurisdictions; systems in transition, legal systems and legal cultures and convergence and divergence between legal systems and cultures; problems of the recipient systems in legal export/import, transpositions; core of rights; comparative jurisprudence; Turkish law, culture and language.

Esin can be contacted by email at: Esin.Orucu@glasgow.ac.uk

Christine TOPPIN-ALLAHAR is an Attorney-at-Law, specialising in environmental, planning and land law, and legislative drafting. In addition to her legal qualifications, she holds a degree in Geography, postgraduate qualifications in Geography and Planning and a Certificate in Integrated Surveys for Natural Resources Development. She has over 35 years experience in the field of planning and environmental management and over 20 years experience as a practising attorney and international consultant on environmental, planning and land law, policy and institutional arrangements, in common law, civil law and mixed jurisdictions. During 2010–2011 Christine served as Course Coordinator and Lecturer in International and Caribbean Environmental Law and Tutor in the Law of Property at the Faculty of Law, University of the West Indies, Barbados, and as External Examiner for the LLB Programme at the University of Guyana. For ten years previously, she was a part-time lecturer in planning, land and environmental law in the postgraduate programmes in Planning & Development and Land Administration at the University of the West Indies in Trinidad. She also developed the course in Environmental Law and Policy in the Masters Programme in Environmental Science & Management at the University of Trinidad & Tobago.

Mathilda TWOMEY is a native of Seychelles and a Justice of Appeal on the Seychelles Court of Appeal, the court of last resort in Seychelles. She has a BA (English and French Law) from the University of Kent and a *Diplome de Droit Francais*, *Université de Paris-Sud*. She is a Barrister-at-law (Middle Temple) and holds an LLM (Public Law) degree from the National University of Ireland, Galway. She is both a Hardiman Scholar and an Irish Research Council Scholar currently studying for a PhD at the same university; her thesis is entitled: 'Legal *métissage* in a micro-jurisdiction: the mixing of common law and civil law in Seychelles'. Her special interests include comparative law, legal history, plurality, hybridity and mixed legal systems. Mathilda has practiced as a barrister in the Oceangate Law Centre in Seychelles, as a Senior Counsel in the Attorney General's Chambers, Seychelles and was a partner in the Seychelles law firm Pardiwalla, Twomey and Lablache. She was a member of the Constitutional Commission which drafted the 1993 Constitution of Seychelles. She is currently Chair of the Committee for the Review of The Civil Code of Seychelles.

Mathilda can be contacted by email at: mattitwomey@gmail.com

Preface

The prequel to this book was a symposium held in Glasgow in June 2013. The event, entitled 'Endangered Mixed Legal Systems' was one in a calendar of activities organized to celebrate the Tercentenary of the appointment of a Regius Professor at the University of Glasgow and we were honoured to have the current incumbent of the chair, Professor James Chalmers, present at the event. Our project was generously supported with funds from the University of Glasgow Tercentenary Fund, the School of Law Research Fund and the British Association of Comparative Law, to assist with bringing our international contributors to Glasgow for the two-day workshop. The smooth running of this would not have been possible without the assistance and encouragement of the Head of the Law School, Professor Rosa Greaves and academic support staff. We are also, of course, very grateful to our authors who dedicated time and energy to revisions and responding to queries in the midst of their busy professional lives.

In looking to achieve some coherency across different jurisdictions, we initially asked contributors to consider a number of possible issues including the history of the jurisdiction to indicate when it became mixed; the events that were the cut-off point or the turning point when the system became endangered – if it was; the significance of language to the survival or decline of the system – such as the passage from bilingualism to monolingualism, both in legal language and in the population, if that was the case; legal education and professional training from the point of view of judges and lawyers including the composition of Bench and Bar; other factors such as geographic proximity to the ingredients of the system; and the impact and importance of non-legal local, regional and international influences such as membership of the European Union or other organizations or entities. The aim was to achieve broad parity of approach across diverse jurisdictions.

As will be evident to readers, each country included in this collection is unique and the final chapters brought together here provide very distinct perceptions of the past, present and future of their legal systems. Nevertheless we suggest that there are overlapping themes, concerns and strategies to which these particular case studies make an important contribution. Each contributor explores the perceived strengths and vulnerabilities of the present legal system, as well as future threats to it.

There were a number of different ways in which the chapters might have been organized. One approach might have been geographic grouping: Europe, America, Asia and the Pacific. Another would have been size and position: micro-jurisdictions and islands compared to larger less isolated countries. Yet another approach could have been to group our jurisdictions on the basis of having a Civil

Code or not; another on bilingualism and so on. We were fully aware that any sequencing could be controversial.

In the end we opted for a spectrum along which to place the jurisdictions under study, from those whose mixedness might be viewed by some to be endangered, to those whose health is not in question and where mixedness is entrenched. Along the way we also have muddled or recuperating systems and some the future mixedness of which seems to hang on a fine balance. The readers will note, however, that the sequence is partially broken in that we decided to put Mauritius and Seychelles, and Quebec and Saint Lucia as related pairs, although their natural placing in the spectrum would not correspond to this choice.

These case studies do not exist in a vacuum and in order to locate these within the wider context of academic debate and studies in mixed legal systems and comparative law discussions the volume starts with an introductory overview and finishes with an endnote written by the editors.

An Introductory Overview

The chapters in this collection are the culmination of an idea that was conceived as we strolled through the city of Valetta, Malta, on our way to a conference dinner.[1] While Malta itself appears to be a stable 'happy union' of British and Continental laws, we asked whether some mixed systems might evolve in such a way that they would appear to lose their mixed identity.[2] Were, we asked, some mixed systems in danger of disappearing or of being overwhelmed by one or other elements within them? Did certain accidents of history or contemporary events make some mixed systems more 'at risk' than others? At the time we did not pause greatly to consider that the term 'endangered' might prove contentious and evoke quite strong reactions when applied to different mixed legal systems. However, when we held a conference in June 2013 in Glasgow, to bring together colleagues to discuss this broad theme and the ways in which it did or did not apply to particular legal systems, it was soon evident that being 'endangered' is not only relative, but for some might be seen to be a positive characteristic of the evolution of legal systems. The risk of losing some aspects of a system could be a sign of healthy growth matching changing circumstances rather than something to be viewed negatively. It also became evident that because mixtures change and are reinterpreted, some mixed systems continue to be regarded as mixed although they are remodelled, while conversely some systems which appear to be becoming mixed, or have historically been so, do not embrace this as a classification.

The aim of the project was to explore different models of mixing and to consider the challenges that confront many mixed jurisdictions which may endanger their present composition as mixed systems. In particular we were interested in: the history of the jurisdiction which created a mixed system; the events that marked a cut-off point from the parent system or events which marked the point at which the system, or parts of it, became endangered; the

---

1   'Mixed Legal Systems, East and West: Newest Trends and Developments' (14–15 May 2012), organized by the World Society of Mixed Jurisdiction Jurists, the *Protection Project* of the Johns Hopkins University, the Eason Weinmann Center for Comparative Law, and the Parliament of Malta. A collection generated by that conference will be published as MY Mattar, VV Palmer and A Koppel (eds), *Mixed Legal Systems: East and West* (Ashgate forthcoming).

2   See SP Donlan, B Andò and D Zammit, '"A Happy Union"?: Malta's Legal Hybridity' (2012) 27 Tulane European and Civil Law Forum 165.

significance of language to the evolution or survival of the system; the influence of legal education and the legal profession; the role of geographical proximity or distance from other systems or parent systems; and the influence of regional or international memberships or agencies in shaping the law.

All modern legal traditions are both mixed and mixing.[3] That is, each is a hybrid; each continues to evolve over time. Modern *mixed legal systems*, where State laws of diverse origins lie in reasonably visible and frequently discrete, identifiable sections are simply the most overt mixes. The coherence and harmony in contemporary legal systems, or the appearance of such coherence and harmony, is the result of the long and complicated development of modern nations and States.[4] But if all traditions are effectively mixed, there is a meaningful division to be made between, as Joseph McKnight once put it, 'what may be termed mixed and that which has already been blended to an extent that [the] origins of rules are lost in ordinary legal practice.'[5] The distinction is 'at once ... practical and ... psychological', obvious to those both within it and without.[6] In this sense a 'blended' system or part of a system, might be regarded as one that no longer appears to be 'mixed'. Of course the system itself still remains mixed if there are new mixes or if the now blended part is only one element in a more complex mix.

Historically, this is not an unusual development. Indeed, throughout most of history a complex mix of laws and norms was typical. Only the rise of the modern nation-state makes our modern concept of a 'mixed' legal system possible, as one in which there may be multiple elements, but which all receive their authority – directly or indirectly – through the sovereign State. This process of moving from a mixed to a blended form is even true, for example, of English law. Only over the course of many centuries was the law of the courts of common law

---

3   See, for example, E Örücü, 'Mixed and Mixing Systems: A Conceptual Search' in E Örücü, E Attwooll and S Coyle (eds), *Studies in Legal Systems: Mixed and Mixing* (Kluwer Law International 1996); PH Glenn, *Legal Traditions of the World* (4th edn Oxford University Press 2010), and V Palmer, 'Mixed Legal Systems ... and the Myth of Pure Laws' (2007) 67 Louisiana Law Review 1205.

4   The transition from considerable legal complexity to greater legal unity, much of it occurring in the nineteenth century, effectively created the modern conceptual distinction between 'pure' and 'mixed' legal traditions. See P Glenn, 'Quebec: Mixité and Monism' in Örücü et al (n3) and SP Donlan, 'Remembering: Legal Hybridity and Legal History' (2011) 2 Comparative Law Review 1.

5   J McKnight, 'Some Historical Observations on Mixed Systems of Law' (1977) 22 Juridical Review (ns) 177, 186. Others might use 'blended' to suggest either a coherent or well-functioning system, whether mixed or nominally pure.

6   ibid. See I Castellucci, 'How Mixed Must a Mixed System be?' (2008) 12 Electronic Journal of Comparative Law, available at <www.ejcl.org/121/art121-4.pdf > accessed 10 December 2013.

blended together with legislation and competing jurisdictions: Equity, various commercial and urban laws, pan-European jurisdictions applying law drawn from canon law, feudal law, or the European *ius commune*, and a wide variety of summary jurisdictions of 'low justice'.[7] Modern 'mixed' systems are those that bear diverse traces of their complex construction.[8]

Indeed, determining or defining the various phases of purity and mixity is extraordinarily difficult. In an article discussing the 'hybrid' metaphor, Brian Stross wrote that:

> There are … no *pure* individuals, no *pure* cultures, no *pure* genres. All things are of necessity *hybrid*. Of course we can construct them to be relatively *pure*, and in fact we do so, which is precisely how we manage to get (new) hybrids from purebreds that are (former) hybrids.[9]

Like the evolution of species in the natural world, the process of legal change is very fluid. With legal traditions this is true, in significant part, because taxonomical judgments are subjective and conventional. Categories of classification – for example, 'common law' or 'civil law' – are the result of a process of selection that is anything but natural. This does not mean, however, that we are at a loss to discuss meaningful distinctions between different traditions. But it is a difficult task and one about which there is not necessarily consensus.

In the hope of finding greater clarity and precision, we have chosen to distinguish, in our introduction and conclusion, between systems the mixedness of which are 'entrenched', 'endangered', or 'blended' to the extent that mixity is no longer easily apparent, especially to those outside the system.[10] If these are admittedly imperfect divisions, providing a consistent definition or concept of each will, we hope, facilitate clearer discussions or debates on the subject of legal change in 'mixed' systems. In selecting the case studies for this collection we wanted to explore the risks across a wide spectrum from entrenched to highly endangered. We asked whether some mixed systems might evolve in such a way

---

7   SP Donlan, '"All This Together Make Up Our *Common* Law": Legal Hybridity in England and Ireland, 1704–1804' in E Örücü (ed.), *Mixed Legal Systems at New Frontiers* (Wildy, Simmonds and Hill 2010).

8   91 legal systems may be categorized as 'civil law', 42 as 'common law', and 94 are listed as 'mixed systems' which in turn have been arranged into ten sub-categories. For these lists see, N Mariani and G Fuentes, *World Legal Systems/Les Systeme Juridiques dans le Monde'* (Wilson and Lafleur 2000) 16–17.

9   B Stross, 'The Hybrid Metaphor: From Biology to Culture' (1999) 112 Journal of American Folklore, 254, 266–267.

10   It is important to note that nominally pure systems could also be analysed in this way.

that they would appear to lose their 'mixed' identity? Would they be reclassified, within the simplistic, dominant taxonomies of comparative law, as belonging to a single legal tradition? Were some mixed systems, or elements within such systems, more at risk than others? What strategies have been adopted to accelerate or counteract change? In addition, to what extent could the experience of these explicit mixed systems be seen as barometers of legal change more generally? What, if anything, do they tell us about legal evolution globally? We left it to the contributors to select the terms they thought appropriate and to express their own views on whether or not their particular system was at risk.

Legal traditions rarely begin with a tabula rasa. Short of revolution, even extensive legal reform is rare and more likely to be piecemeal and ad hoc. More typically, legal traditions are the products of long and complex histories. They are all 'systems in transition'.[11] The stability or instability of a legal tradition, its maintenance and preservation, may be due to a number of different factors, either singly or in combination. This includes the work of its jurists and politicians, as well as more global and shifting influences and powers. Some such systems will maintain equilibrium among their different component parts. Their legal identity, whatever it is, will be maintained. They are 'entrenched'. For our purposes, an 'entrenched' mixed system is simply one in which the various elements that compose it are stable. Such a system could be calm or contentious, but the traditions within it have achieved a sort of balance. This cycle is ongoing. Indeed, in his contribution, Achilles Emilianides notes the famous metaphor, attributed to Heraclitus that, 'you cannot step twice into the same river'. Nothing endures, that is, but change. In fact, moving from one legal categorization to another is a very rare event, not least because our taxonomies shift along with changes in the legal systems. We chose the term 'endangered' as meaning where the identity of a system appears to be changing. But such change is not easy to measure and the direction of change may be uncertain. It is rarely the result of a single event, but a process of fits and starts, of gradual accretion or decay. The bottom line here is whether the system alters so much that it leaves one classification to enter another. With such systems, one or more elements which make up the mix is being overtaken by a stronger influence either within, or possibly even from without, the system. Concerns about this type of endangerment are especially delicate in mixed systems that are hybrids of the two dominant Western legal traditions, common law (Anglo-American law) and civil law (Continental law) – although we certainly do not mean to imply that mixed systems are limited in this way. There Anglo-American global hegemony

---

11   E Örücü, 'Critical Comparative Law: Considering Paradoxes for Legal Systems in Transition' (2000) 4 (1) Electronic Journal of Comparative Law, available at <www.ejcl. org/41/abs41-1.html> accessed 11 February 2014.

has made the champions of the civil law defensive. The threat is not so much of foreign invasion, although regional and global pressures and influences may play a part – as indicated in Mathilda Twomey's contribution on the Seychelles, but a kind of legal–cultural civil war. This legal–cultural struggle may not necessarily have negative consequences. Sophie Morin, for example, locating her consideration of the present against past legal–cultural struggles, suggests that Quebec's mixed system has become entrenched and well-functioning and that there is little danger of common law dominance. Indeed, she suggests that the system may be becoming more civilian.

Our choice of the term 'endangered' might, of course, appear loaded. The word is rarely used neutrally. It is typically meant to refer to the potential loss of something viewed as valuable, as with an endangered natural species. Obviously, not all legal traditions are so precious. Legal evolution can both improve and corrupt. Indeed, even if it was possible to describe legal change without subjective bias, no single metric can prescribe the 'proper' balance within a system. This will depend on the wider, conflicting aspirations of the people involved. It will require more than a legal analysis. Those in the system, both professionals and the public, may lament change, especially where such alterations are seen to be beyond their control. This is particularly true of colonial encounters where indigenous populations had little or no choice in the introduction of foreign ideas and institutions. Indeed, neo- or post-colonial situations may also create complex problems, illustrated here by the contributions of Pacifico Agabin on the Philippines, Christine Toppin-Allahar on Guyana and Jane Matthews Glenn on Saint Lucia.

As illustrated in the chapters in this collection, context and local significance is everything. But the concerns and discussion take place against a background of well-rehearsed academic debates about mixed systems. As a result of their variety and their peripheral status in global geopolitics, mixed systems were marginalized for most of the last century. In the last two decades, however, they have drawn ever greater attention and scholars have sought to show their importance to comparative law generally.[12] Some scholars have combined the

---

12   See, for example, J du Plessis, 'Comparative Law and the Study of Mixed Legal Systems' in M Reimann and R Zimmermann (eds), *Oxford Handbook of Comparative Law* (Oxford University Press 2006). In addition to Örücü et al (1996) (n3), collections have appeared in the (2003) 78 Tulane Law Review and online collections in the (2008) 12(1) Electronic Journal of Comparative Law, available at <www.ejcl.org/121/issue121.html> accessed 11 February 2014, and the (2014) 1 European Journal of Comparative Law and Governance, available at <http://booksandjournals.brillonline.com/content/journals/22134514> accessed 11 February 2014.

general analysis of mixed systems with detailed analysis of individual traditions.[13] Some have focused attention on mixed systems similar enough to arguably constitute a 'third legal family'[14] or created collections focusing on comparisons between specific mixed systems.[15] For others, the contemporary complexity of modern laws has suggested that overtly mixed systems might provide useful information about future, more mixed, laws in Europe and beyond.[16] Still others have sought to place the study of mixed systems within a wider landscape of legal pluralism.[17] Recent scholarship on mixed systems is creating new frontiers for comparative law.[18] This is, in part, the result of a wider recognition of legal mixing across all traditions in our present globalized environment and, in part, it is the result of the new found importance of the more 'exotic' mixed systems.

Research into mixed systems must continue to be both critical and constructive. Speaking coherently about legal complexity across time and space will require an assessment of the continuing relevance of earlier models. Where possible and productive, new frameworks or vocabularies must be introduced and applied. To have any general explanatory power, these will have to be somewhat general, but cannot be so abstract that they are unhelpful or fail to communicate, however thinly, existing practices of individual traditions. It is here that we hope that this collection contributes to the existing body of

---

13   See E Örücü, especially: 'Mixed and Mixing Systems: A Conceptual Search' in Örücü et al (1996) (n3); 'A General View of Legal Families and of Mixed Systems' in E Örücü and D Nelken (eds) *Comparative Law: A Handbook* (Hart Publishing 2007); 'What is a Mixed Legal System: Exclusion or Expansion?' in Örücü (n7).

14   See VV Palmer, especially *Mixed Jurisdictions Worldwide: The Third Legal Family* (2nd edn Cambridge University Press 2012); 'Mixed Jurisdictions' in JM Smits (ed) *Elgar Encyclopedia of Comparative Law* (2nd edn Edward Elgar 2012); and 'Mixed Legal Systems' in M Bussani and U Mattei (eds), *The Cambridge Companion to Comparative Law* (Cambridge University Press 2012).

15   R Zimmermann, D Visser and K Reid (eds), *Mixed Legal Systems in Comparative Perspective: Property and Obligations in Scotland and South Africa* (Oxford University Press 2005) and VV Palmer and EC Reid (eds), *Mixed Jurisdictions Compared: Private Law in Louisiana and Scotland* (Edinburgh University Press 2009).

16   For example, JM Smits, *The Making of European Private Law: Towards a Ius Commune Europaeum as a Mixed Legal System* (Intersentia 2002) and H Kötz, 'The Value of Mixed Legal Systems' (2003) 78 Tulane Law Review 435.

17   See SP Donlan, especially, 'Comparative Law and Hybrid Legal Traditions: An Introduction' in E Cashin-Ritaine, SP Donlan and M Sychold (eds), *Comparative Law and Hybrid Legal Traditions* (Shulthess 2010) and 'Things Being Various: Normativity, Legality, State Legality' in M Adams and D Heirbaut (eds), *The Method and Culture of Comparative law: Essays in Honour of Mark Van Hoecke* (Hart forthcoming).

18   See the chapters in Örücü (n7). See also Donlan et al (n17).

knowledge and ideas. The collection treats our themes through case studies of a variety of mixed systems from around the world. All are evolving. Some are entrenched; some are endangered; some appear to have muddled aspirations, others have blended elements but remain mixed. Some are large, some small. We include European jurisdictions (Scotland), as well as systems in the Americas (Quebec) and Asia (the Philippines). By design, we have also included a large number of mixed micro-jurisdictions, both in Europe (Cyprus and Jersey) and beyond (Guyana, Mauritius, St Lucia and Seychelles). Such systems appear to be particularly sensitive to the wider, global influences on legal, and perhaps social, evolution.[19]

In the jurisdictions covered in this volume, it was important first to look at the degree of endangerment, if any, through the sequence of events, since the history and the present may tell us different things about the status of a mixed legal system. This may very well be the case in Scotland, never a colony, where common law is becoming more predominant compared to its historic roots in the civilian tradition, at least in a number of areas. Whereas in Guyana, presented as a muddled system, unsure of the direction it is taking, it is factors such as population change, loss of one of the languages, mixed use of terminology, concepts that feed into, fuse with and become part of an amalgam, that have resulted in the Roman–Dutch law becoming endangered and possibly facing extinction. In the Philippines, where one form of colonization replaced an earlier one, it is the role of American judges, the shift to English language, the case-by-case injection of common law that become the explanatory factors for the endangerment of the civil law. Here, vocabulary such as 'smothering', 'diluting', 'permeating', 'gradual' and 'imperceptible', have been used to explain the developments. These mixed legal systems are now perceived by many to be more common law oriented.

In contrast, the Channel Islands are not seen as endangered, but vulnerable. The mixture in Jersey, for example, started with Norman customary law and later both English and French influences, but changes in the composition of the population has resulted in a linguistic shift and bilingualism, with two official languages, and has become unclear in some areas. Despite this, a period

---

19   See M Bogdan, *The Law of Mauritius and Seychelles: A Study of Two Small Mixed Legal Systems* (Wallin and Dalhim Boktryckeri 1989) 9. See also A Grossman, 'Finding the Law: The Micro-States and Small Jurisdictions of Europe' (Andorra, Cyprus, Northern Cyprus, Iceland, Liechtenstein, Luxembourg, Malta, Monaco, Montenegro, San Marino, Vatican State; UK European dependencies: Channel Islands, Gibraltar, Isle of Man; Faroe Islands and Greenland) available at <www.nyulawglobal.org/Globalex/Microstates.htm> accessed 10 December 2013.

of recuperation seems to have begun with the establishment of the Institute of Law. The educational and doctrinal goals of the Institute may stabilize or even strengthen the condition of Jersey's mixed system.

In Mauritius, there is evidence not of blending where people lose sight of the mix but a further stage, in which the various parts appear to work harmoniously in a coherent, well-functioning system. The codes are in French but now the official language is English, and there is an intriguing mixture of the population and languages. The system is not endangered, the core elements of the French legal heritage still remain in French, but laws related to the economy and globalization reflect common law thinking, all operating within the droit commun of Mauritius. In contrast, in what was once a 'colony of this colony', Seychelles, where law was therefore initially a 'transplant from a transplant', the civil law operates in a context that appears to be increasingly oriented to the common law. There is an erosion of civil law tradition, not least by changes in the language of its Codes. From the perspective of those wishing to retain an earlier balance of traditions, Seychelles is not doing as well as Mauritius. The crucial question here is how to maintain that balance.

In the report here, Quebec is presented as not endangered. The concepts that came to the fore were those of language, duality, resistance and assimilation. Although knowledge of the civil law and the French language is still often lacking in the case of the judges of the Federal Supreme Court, the 1994 Civil Code has firmly anchored the civilian tradition within the province itself. In Quebec, where identity is no longer linked to nationalism, its legal confidence and autonomy indicate that the common law may be in more danger than the civil law. Closely related to Quebec in its colonial history and its Civil Code, is Saint Lucia. Just as Seychelles is not as healthy a mixture as Mauritius, Saint Lucia is doing poorly compared to Quebec. There, the Civil Code has been diluted by the insertion of common law concepts. The interpretation of the Civil Code has always been in the hands of judges trained in common law and unfamiliar with the civilian tradition. Nonetheless, Saint Lucia seems to be at a crossroads in protecting its civilian heritage. There are proposals to revise the Code drawing on the 1994 Quebec Code. If this were to happen, then some equilibrium could be restored between the two fundamental elements of this jurisdiction, at present however the future direction of the law seems somewhat uncertain.

The case of Cyprus illustrates the type of mixed system which falls outside the classical taxonomy of mixed legal systems put forward by Vernon Palmer, since here the present day private law was derived more from the common law and public law, especially administrative law, more from the civilian tradition.[20] In addition, rather then being endangered, here laws from different origins do not only seem to co-exist but also blend, with university degree courses unusually offering a mixture of Greek, English and Cypriot content in Greek and English.

---

20   See Palmer (n14).

The aim of this collection has been to provide original views on and insight into mixed legal systems in general, and some mixed legal systems, ongoing mixes and disappearing, suffocated, or muddled mixed legal systems, in particular. Whatever the label, we hope that the analyses in this volume will be helpful for scholars and students with an interest in comparative law and a special interest in mixed legal systems, and provide inspiration to pursue further inquiries.

Chapter 1

Scotland

It is important first to look at the degree of endangerment, if any, through the sequence of events, since the history and the present may tell us different things about the status of a mixed legal system. This may very well be the case in Scotland, which was never a colony, but where the English common law is becoming more predominant compared to its historic roots in the civilian tradition. In fact, Sue Farran tells us that if anything is surprising about Scots law, it is perhaps that it has survived as a distinct system for so long. It has been under siege from England, with its common law, and more recently, European Union (EU) laws, it does not have a distinct language of its own (although it has a number of obscure legal terms, as she puts it), and it does not have a Civil Code. Yet, purists and comparatists continue to celebrate the unique features of Scots law as a distinct mixed legal system. Pragmatists and sceptics on the other hand, adopt a somewhat different view. Nonetheless, the fact that there is still a debate between the two must be evidence of a surviving species. Since law does not exist in a vacuum, one should consider other things going on, which may either endanger or strengthen the position of Scots law as a mixed legal system.

In this chapter, Farran draws attention to the external and internal forces that may, in the end, have much more bearing on the survival of Scots law as a mixed legal system than any laws. The reader could regard this legal system as one where its mixedness may be under threat, with strengthening common law content and a near suffocation of the civilian component, save in some specific and limited areas. When the different elements that gave birth to Scotland as a mixed legal system are weighed up, it is easy to come to the conclusion that now it is more common law oriented. There is both theoretical and empirical data in this chapter to support this view. However, there is also every likelihood that Scots law will remain mixed although the nature of that mixture may change.

Among the issues discussed the reader will find information as to the influence of history as a forming factor for the mix, the present possibilities following the referendum for independence to be held in September 2014, and the factors that maintain the legal system such as language, legal education, the personnel of the law – in academia, legal practice and courts of appeal – and legal literature. The chapter pays specific attention to events that have threatened the survival of Scots law as a distinct legal system.

Scotland: 'Is the Tartan Fading?'

Sue Farran

Introduction

The legal system of Scotland reflects much of the political history of Scots–English relationships, from outright and bloody warfare, to wary truce, and in more recent times, new assertions of sovereignty for Scotland following devolution in 1999 with a current movement towards independence from the United Kingdom (UK) by the Scottish National Party which will be the subject of a referendum in 2014. Despite or perhaps because of this uneasy relationship between Scotland and England, historically and today, the Scottish legal system has been regarded as distinct, if not always independent. Frequently regarded as a classical mixed legal system, the future of the Scottish system faces various possibilities. One is that the national referendum results in a political divorce between Scotland and the rest of the UK and therefore an opportunity to develop an increasingly distinct legal system – which may not necessarily be a classical mix but might, for example, be dominated by the demands of separate membership of the EU – as indeed is increasingly the case today within the UK. Alternatively, and possibly regardless of the outcome of the vote on Scottish independence under the referendum, the next decade might see an increasingly strong assertion of Scottish national identity and legal sovereignty as a stand against Westminster, globalization and its related general loss of autonomy, and a strengthening of the distinctiveness of the Scottish legal system to address its own domestic agenda.

A further possibility is that the referendum result is 'no', with a strengthening of ties between Scotland and the rest of the UK especially through the decisions of the Supreme Court, shared work by the English and Scottish Law Commissions and increasing trans-border law firms being established with branches in the 'Central Belt' (Glasgow and Edinburgh, and to a lesser extent, Stirling and Perth) and Aberdeen, providing a service largely to the commercial sector. In order to examine the strengths and weaknesses of these various possibilities this chapter considers the role of history, language, legal education, the courts and links with other members of the mixed legal family to determine the extent to which the Scottish legal system, as a mixed system, might be regarded as endangered if it was perceived that its civil law and mixed elements were in danger of being swamped by common law ones.

The Influence of History

Although there had been a number of attempts to bring the Scots under English rule, the major turning point for Scotland was when James V of Scotland became James I of England following the death of the childless English queen, Elizabeth I. King of Scotland before he was King of England and Wales, James' ascension to the English throne 'united' the two countries, and the present Queen continues the tradition.[1]

The nature of Scots law prior to the 1707 Act of Union is the subject of debate among legal historians and not the subject matter of this chapter.[2] What is significant, however, is that until the Act of Union, the Scottish courts, and to a lesser extent the Scottish Parliament, were free to borrow or reject English common law ideas and institutions, just as they could do with those from the civil law systems of the Continent.[3] Scots law was also open to the reception of Roman and canon law from the Continent over a period of several centuries, although the influence of canon law seems to have waned from the Reformation in 1560 onwards – as indeed it did in England and Wales. Moreover Scots law developed its own common law through the cases,[4] as well as retaining elements of Scots folk or customary law.[5]

Following Union the influence of English law accelerated in two ways. First as regards legislation which was made in Westminster, and secondly as regards

---

* I am extremely grateful to Lindsay Farmer for his helpful and constructive comments. The opinions expressed remain my own.

1 Even if Scotland votes 'yes' for independence from the UK in the 2014 referendum it appears that the Queen will remain head of state. Other members of the royal family hold distinct Scottish titles which they assume once they cross the border.

2 W Sellar, for example, suggests that by the end of the thirteenth century one could talk of a *lex anglicana* but thereafter divergence occurred 'Scots Law: Mixed from the Very Beginning? A Tale of Two Receptions' (2000) 4 Edinburgh Law Review 3, 7. See also the views of T Craig, *De Unione Regnorum Britanniae Tractatus* ed and trans C Sandford Terry (T and A Constable for the Scottish History Society 1909); R Pont,'Of the Union of Britayne' in BR Galloway and B P Levack (eds), *The Jacobean Union: Six Tracts of 1604* (Clark Constable 1985), and A Wijffels, 'A British ius commune? A Debate on the Union of the Laws of Scotland and England during the first years of James VI/I's English reign' (2002) 6 Edinburgh Law Review 315.

3 See WD Sellar, 'A Historical Perspective' in M Meston, WD Sellar and Lord Cooper, *The Scottish Legal Tradition* (Saltire Society: Stair Society 1991) 29.

4 See W Sellar, 'The Resilience of the Scottish Common Law' and other essays in D Carey Miller and R Zimmermann (eds), *The Civilian Tradition and Scots Law: Aberdeen Quincentenary Essays* (Duncker and Humblot 1997).

5 For example, Udal law in Orkney and the Shetland Islands and Birlaw – derived from Danish or Nordic law – which governed the use of commons. See also E Attwooll, *The Tapestry of the Law: Scotland, Legal Culture and Legal Theory* (Kluwer Academic 1997).

appeals of civil cases.[6] In respect of the former, rarely were the legislative needs of Scotland considered as being unique or distinct. Legislation was for the most part extended to Scotland, occasionally 'kilted' to make it appear more Scottish. As regards the latter, Article XVIII of the Treaty of Union 1707, expressly preserved Scots private law while Article XIX stated quite clearly that no causes in Scotland were to be heard in the English courts or any other court sitting at Westminster Hall. However, there was no reference in the Treaty to the Scots role of the Judicial Committee of the House of Lords or provision as to what was to happen to those appeals from the Inner House of the Court of Session which had previously been heard by the Scots Parliament – now abolished. Following test cases in 1707 and 1709, the appeal jurisdiction of the House of Lords, for Scots civil cases, emerged.[7] This created considerably bad feeling as not only were Scots law cases being heard by non-Scots judges (in fact until 1844 frequently by peers who had no legal training at all let alone any knowledge of Scots law) but also, pending appeal to the Judicial Committee of the House of Lords, the execution of any judgment of the Court of Session was suspended (thereby undermining its authority). Appeal to the House of Lords, therefore, necessarily caused delays and was expensive.[8] At its height over 20 cases a year were proceeding to the House of Lords from the Court of Session in Scotland.[9] In almost all of them the House of Lords either overturned the Court of Session decision or remitted the case back to Scotland. Rarely were the decisions of the Scottish court upheld. Until the mid-nineteenth century there was little attempt to apply any Scots law and when it was raised the court often ignored it or assumed it must be the same as English law. For example, Lord Hope quotes Lord Chancellor Cranworth who stated in 1858:

> But if such be the law of England, on what ground can it be argued not to be the law of Scotland? The law as established in England is founded on principles of universal application'.[10]

While this type of assumption must have been tiresome for litigants, perversely it may have been beneficial to the survival of Scots law. Walker, for example, has

---

6   For a detailed review of the development of Scots law from 1701 to the end of the nineteenth century see A Gibb, *Law from over the Border: A Short Account of a Strange Jurisdiction* (W Green 1950).

7   *Earl of Roseberrie v St John Inglis* (1707) and *Greenshields v Magistrates of Edinburgh* (1709).

8   A consequence that persisted until 1808 Court of Session Act. See TB Smith, 'British Justice: the Scottish Contribution' *Hamlyn Lectures* (Stevens and Sons Ltd 1961).

9   In the late 1990s it was suggested that this was more usually four to six cases a year – Lord Hope, 'Taking the Case to London – Is it All Over?' (1998) Juridical Review 135, 138.

10   *Bartonshill Coal Co. v Reid* (1858) 3 Macq. 266 at 285. Quoted by Lord Hope ibid, 142.

suggested that the ignorance of English judges and the English Parliament was a positive influence on the survival of Scots law, because both 'contributed by their abstinence and non-interference to the maintenance of the distinctiveness of Scots law'.[11] By the mid-nineteenth century a little more notice was being taken of Scots law but at the same time events on the Continent in the late eighteenth and early nineteenth century – particularly the French Revolution, together with industrial and commercial development in Britain and the wider British Empire, inclined Scotland more towards the common law and away from the civil law influence of Europe. Scotland, for example, never adopted the modern civilian codified tradition, the court structure or the public administration systems of the Napoleonic era or its aftermath.

The industrial revolution of the late eighteenth and nineteenth century gave rise to an increase in case law and legislation and it was perhaps inevitable that where there were gaps in the law in the face of rapid change, and fewer reported cases in Scotland than in England, that Scots lawyers would look to the jurisprudence of England and Wales. The momentum of the nineteenth century which prompted considerable legislative activity continued into the twentieth century, especially towards the latter half of the century, and there was, consequently, just much more law – in terms of statute law, criminal prosecutions, commercial and corporate law, the use of judicial review, and the emergence of new fields of law such as intellectual property law, family law and employment law. The law also became more complex demanding specialism in legal practice,[12] so that generalists with a broad knowledge of the whole legal system found themselves increasingly marginalized, tending to have fewer commercial clients, fewer partners and were often located outside the major metropolitan areas.

While the wars of the twentieth century traversed intra-national boundaries, the use of regiments based on locality strengthened nationalism and between the wars there was a resurgence of emphasis on Scots law. In 1934 the Stair Society was established to assist in the 'rebirth of Scots law', and to engender a 'Scottish legal renaissance'.[13] Among the strongest protagonists of this movement were TB Smith and Lord Cooper, who between them advocated a Scottish legal nationalism which rejected any benefits of English law, stressing instead those of the civil law tradition.[14] Even by those who support the classification of Scots law as a mixed legal system, there has been some criticism of the 'neo-civilian and legal nationalist bias' of TB Smith and Lord Cooper, which it has been suggested

---

11   DM Walker, *A Legal History of Scotland: VII The Twentieth Century* (Lexis Nexis 2004),1157. More broadly see K Reid and R Zimmermann (eds), *A History of Private Law in Scotland Vols I and II* (Oxford University Press 2000).

12   See Walker ibid, Chapter 36.

13   H MacQueen, 'Legal Nationalism: Lord Cooper, Legal History and Comparative Law' (2004–2005) 9(3) Edinburgh Law Review 395.

14   See E Reid and D Carey Miller (eds) *A Mixed Legal System in Transition* (Edinburgh Studies in Law 2005).

warped 'their historical judgment', and 'idealized the period of the Institutional writers from 1681 till about 1800 as a golden age'.[15] Pragmatists tend to accept that there have either been periods of strong convergence between English law and Scots, or areas of law where distinctions between the constituent elements are being lost. Purists would argue that the Scottish legal system has always been distinctive even when most oppressed by English law influences, and would today point to the areas of law where it remains (although I would argue increasingly less so), such as property, succession and family law. It has also been suggested that as an inherently 'weak' mixed system,[16] Scots law has always been open to external instances. R Evans-Jones, for example, highlights the early reception of the Roman law of the glossators – itself a received and modified version of Roman law shaped by jurists at Continental universities, and that of English law in the early nineteenth century.[17] Of the latter he states:

> The reception of English law is therefore about Scots law being supplanted by English law. This process is, in the main, effected willingly by Scots lawyers. It is sometimes, but not normally, as Scots lawyers have tended to think, thrust upon Scotland by English judges in the House of Lords who approach Scots law from the perspective of English law.[18]

Not all would agree with this perspective, arguing perhaps that the Scottish legal system was already a developed and distinct one prior to English law influences. Be that as it may, over time it would appear that some of the civilian elements of Scots law have become eroded partly as a pragmatic consequence of changing legal demands and partly as a consequence of inertia on the part of Scots lawyers manifested by a tendency to be unresistant to the common law. Given the extra effort needed to maintain contact with the civilian traditions of Scots law or to engage with more contemporary developments in civil law systems this is perhaps

---

15   N Whitty, 'The Civilian Tradition and Debates on Scots Law' (1996) Tydskrif vir die Suid Afrikaanse Reg 227, 230 and 231.

16   R Evans-Jones uses this term to highlight the weak legal culture that underpinned the Scottish legal system, making it vulnerable to reception and imposition from other legal systems, hence its mixed nature, which he sees as evidence of this weakness and not a characteristic of strength or 'genius' as supporters of the system have sometimes claimed. R Evans-Jones, 'Receptions of Law, Mixed Legal Systems and the Myth of the Genius of Scots Private Law' (1998) 114 Law Quarterly Review 228, cf however N Whitty (n15). Evan-Jones' colourful language should not let us lose sight of the fact that Scots Law as a system has shown itself to be remarkably resilient in surviving the Union and continuing to develop, especially in the twentieth century and through to the present day.

17   ibid.

18   R Evans Jones ibid, 232. See also H MacQueen, 'Mixture or Muddle?' (1997) Zeitschrift für Europäisches Privatrecht 369, 374–375.

understandable and has been contributed to by a number of factors in recent decades indicated below.

Language, Legal Education and Legal Literature

Language

Örücü has stated that 'the factors in maintaining a legal tradition generally referred to are: shared language and terminology, legal education and legal literature'.[19] Tetley, too, drew attention to the contribution that universities can make 'to the enrichment of legal culture and the advancement of mixed jurisdictions and their respective linguistic heritages', drawing favourable attention to the Civil Law Centre of Aberdeen Law School, at the University of Aberdeen, which was established in 1994.[20] However, today the Scottish legal scene presents a mixed picture. The teaching and practice of Scots law is conducted in English and although Latin may have once been taught in the universities this is no longer the case and there is no requirement that law graduates study Latin or have an appropriate foreign language to access modern civil law systems. They do need to study Roman law, but only if they aspire to be advocates, not if they hope to be solicitors. Nevertheless much of the language of the law is obscurely Scots and includes many terms which are unfamiliar to an English lawyer. Despite advocacy of plain English in the law – especially in legal drafting,[21] legal language in Scotland is still in many respects obscure and inaccessible to those more familiar with the common law or to the average client.

Legal education

Many early Scottish lawyers received their legal education in civil law countries, originally in Italy, the home of the glossators and early commentators; France,

---

19   E Örücü 'Mixed and Mixing Systems: A Conceptual Search' in E Örücü, E Attwooll and S Coyle (eds) *Studies in Legal Systems: Mixed and Mixing* (1996 Kluwer Law International) 335, 349.

20   W Tetley 'Nationalism in a Mixed Jurisdiction and the Importance of Language' (2003) 78 Tulane Law Review 175, 189–190. The Centre languished in the late twentieth and early twenty-first century but was re-launched with a broader remit in 2009.

21   See, for example, the Office of the Scottish Parliamentary Counsel 2006 'Plain Language Legislation', which refers to a commission set up in Scotland in 1425 'to see and examine the bulkis (sic) of law of this realme (sic) ... and mend the laws that needs amendment' <http://www.scotland.gov.uk/Resource/Doc/93488/0022476.pdf> accessed 15 January 2014, and comments in *The Herald Scotland*, November 4, 2008, 'Scots law should use more plain English, says panel' referring to a panel of Business Experts and Law established by Justice Secretary Kenny MacAskill.

especially in Orleans and Paris;[22] and later in the Netherlands where they came under the influence of the teachings of jurists such as Grotius (de Groot), Voet and van Leeuwen.

Those wishing to practice as lawyers in Scotland today receive their legal education at universities in Scotland, as there are no universities outside of the country offering the requisite degree although it is possible for those qualifying in England and Wales to taking additional 'conversion' courses in order to qualify in Scotland and for Scots law graduates to convert to practice in England and Wales. Most Scots law students take a four-year undergraduate degree, which, while it includes a large number of compulsory courses – far more than, for example required by the LLB in England and Wales – also allows students to study a wide range of elective subjects, especially in their final two years. However, if one considers the current provision of legal education some interesting aspects emerge. While there are a number of senior academics at Scottish universities whom one might refer to as leading authorities in Scots law, this could be a dying breed.[23] Not only are academics today offering a very broad palate of non-Scots specialities and researching and writing in these diverse areas but also an increasing number of young academics at Scottish universities are not themselves graduates in Scots law. A survey in May 2013 of law staff at lecturer level (that is, early career academics) at the leading universities – Edinburgh, Aberdeen and Glasgow – using profiles on the university web pages, revealed that very few had undergraduate law degrees in Scots law (that is, the level of study which would most immerse them in Scots laws) (Table 1.1).[24] Some may have had LLMs or studied PhDs at Scottish universities but this is by no means the majority of early career academics now teaching future Scots lawyers.

One of the causes of this decline may be attributable to a shift in legal education from what was traditionally a vocationally oriented programme taught by those drawn from legal practice and indeed often by those still in practice, to a programme with greater academic focus. This in turn has been influenced

22   T Craig, author of *Jus Feudale* (Impensis Societatis Stationariorum 1655) was a Paris graduate while Viscount Stair, *Institutions of the Law of Scotland* (Privately printed by Andrew Anderson 1681) was influenced by the Roman–Dutch law of Grotius. H MacQueen (n18) 373. The writings of Stair were particularly influential in establishing Scots law as a distinct civilian influenced system of law.

23   Indeed WM Gordon addressing the Stair Society in 1999, regarded himself as 'one of the endangered species of professors of Civil Law in Scottish universities' WM Gordon, 'The Civil Law in Scotland' (2001) 5(2) Edinburgh Law Review 130.

24   These figures are of course constantly changing with the recruitment of new staff and staff leaving, and web entries may not reflect the full picture. Indeed a check on Aberdeen figures following a query in May 2014, indicated that profiles of seven staff at lecturer level did not indicate their undergraduate qualifications, of these three probably have Scots undergraduate degrees and two possibly did, that is, a total of seven staff out of 17. Were teaching fellows to be added in where these are deployed the figures would change again.

Table 1.1   Profile of early career academic staff

University	Glasgow (11)	Aberdeen (17)	Edinburgh (30)
Undergraduate Scots laws degree	3	2	2
Not indicated	3	6	5

by the changing funding model for universities, notably the generation of funds through student fees, especially for those coming from outside Scotland, and the quality ranking of universities through an assessment of their published research. Although the criteria for this latter has altered over time, essentially published outputs have to go beyond the practitioner notes and case-comments historically produced by practice led lecturers. So the staff recruitment practices of universities have changed. Early career lecturers today will invariably have a PhD which can be converted into one or several published outputs, as well perhaps as other publications produced during their doctoral studies. This shift is now being addressed through the appointment of 'Teaching Fellows' which opens the door again for practitioner–lecturers who are not expected to produce research of the same quantity or quality and this may, in turn, address the imbalance of Scottish qualified academics. Of course if Scotland becomes independent it would no longer need to worry about the research assessment ranking of its universities except in so far as this might be usefully used as a marketing tool for recruiting students outwith Scotland. Indeed the pressure on all universities to attract fee-paying international students at undergraduate and post-graduate level, and the opportunity for EU Member State students to study in Scotland has had considerable influence on the design and delivery of law programmes.

The present noticeable recruitment of non-Scots academics may, in this respect and in others, have positive benefits. In particular it may provide a strong environment for the nurture of comparative and international law of greater relevance to the twenty-first century than national law and could provide a platform for a broader diet of Continental or foreign law for undergraduates although not necessarily from similarly mixed systems. It may also give rise to new champions of Scots law, who approach this not from a nationalistic perspective, but as an interesting comparative model.

Historically comparative legal education has been an important dimension of Scottish legal education, as evidenced by the first chair in comparative law being established in Aberdeen University in 1947 followed only months later by one in Edinburgh. Indeed Lord Cooper is quoted as stating that 'the Scottish lawyer has been first and foremost a comparative lawyer since the thirteenth century, and when he ceases to be a comparative lawyer Scots law will die'.[25] In the 1950s TB Smith – one of the great advocates of the distinctiveness of Scots law – brought

25   Quoted by MacQueen (n13) 402.

over jurists from Quebec, Louisiana, the Netherlands and South Africa to teach at Edinburgh and gave a complete collection of South African Law Reports to the library of the Faculty of Advocates. However, despite a valuable body of late twentieth and early twenty-first century literature on comparative law and mixed legal systems coming out of Scottish universities,[26] relatively little comparative or civil law is taught today and what is taught is usually an option as demonstrated in Table 1.2.[27]

Table 1.2   Undergraduate provision for the study of comparative/ foreign law

University	Foreign Law (Civil)	Comparative Law	Other
Aberdeen	French law German law	Comparative law Comparative constitutional law	American constitutional law
Edinburgh			Civil law
Glasgow			Mixed jurisdictions

Despite the changes in the academic stage of legal education, the professional stage of legal training in Scotland is regulated by Scottish authorities – the Society of Advocates for those wishing to be advocates,[28] and the Law Society of Scotland, for solicitors.[29] Both are involved in approving and accrediting the academic stage of legal training offered by universities but only the Law Society is involved in approving the Diploma in Legal Education for solicitors which is offered by some universities at post-graduate level. Whether the potential difference between the two stages of legal education creates problems is not clear, but it may be that

26   See for example, R Zimmermann, D. Visser and K Reid (eds) *Mixed Legal Systems in Comparative Perspective* (Oxford University Press 2004).

27   Whitty (n15) 455, for example, highlights the failure of Scots law to pay greater attention to South African law, 'The Civilian Tradition and Debates of Scots law', a view shared by P du Plessis 'Innkeeper's Liability for Loss Suffered by Guests' (2007) 11 EdinLR 89. This does not diminish however the importance of the work of D Carey Miller, K Reid and E Reid or Whitty himself, nor the contribution of R Zimmerman, S Visser and J du Plessis, all of whom have drawn on South African/Scots comparisons.

28   This dates back to pre-1535 (which is the earliest date of existing records). Judges of the high court (of which there are currently 34 (four are women)) are drawn almost entirely from the Society of Advocates and almost all have had careers as advocates in Scotland although a number are also admitted to the English bar.

29   The category of solicitor–advocates is also recognized for certain solicitors who have rights of audience before the highest courts – the High Court of Justiciary (Criminal) and the Court of Sessions (Civil).

pragmatism when it comes to practice may be more significant than the purism traditionally found in academia. Indeed, in an interesting comment made in the *Edinburgh Law Review* in 2012, it was stated:

> as solicitors well know, the majority of law actually practiced has hardly ever been the subject of a judicial decision that is helpful. Far less may there be any legislative basis for what they do.[30]

This may be a questionable generalization, but may at least provide further evidence that suggests that in some areas of legal practice, pragmatism wins the day.

Legal writing

Historically legal education and the close proximity of jurists and practitioners has been key to the development and indeed survival of Scots law as a distinct mixed legal system. Indeed, it has been suggested that 'The distinctness of Scots law ... has been mainly the work of a number of distinguished judges and a handful of scholarly jurists'.[31] In particular it was the work of the institutional writers of the seventeenth, eighteenth and nineteenth century which shaped the Scots law of the day and continues to be relevant.[32] These in turn determined the sources and authorities of Scots law and informed the teaching and practice of law. The eminence of these jurists is attributable to various characteristics of the Scottish legal system, such as the reluctance of Scots law to accept the precedent of single cases – preferring instead the Continental approach of *jurisprudence constante*; the paucity of reported cases from Scottish courts in the eighteenth and nineteenth centuries; and a greater willingness to refer to the work of jurists in court (even while they were alive).[33] However, the production and use of law texts fell considerably in the period 1918–1960.[34] Even towards the end of the twentieth century the outlook seemed bleak. In 1985 Walker wrote:

---

30   RG Anderson 'Case Comment: Scottish Share Pledges' (2012) Edinburgh Law Review 99, 100.

31   Walker (n11) 1157.

32   For example, Craig, Stair, Hope, Mackenzie, Bankton, Erskine and Bell. Some of these recognized the influence of English law – such as Bell and Bankton, while others placed greater focus on Roman and civil law – such as Stair and Mackenzie, with Justinian's Institutes being an influential model for their own 'Institutes'. On the institutional writers see DM Walker, *The Scottish Jurists* (W Green 1985).

33   In English law in contrast there has been a convention – not always observed – that an author cannot be quoted from until he or she is dead. This convention appears to have originated from a judgment of Lord Eldon in 1814.

34   Reid, quotes DM Walker's comment that since 1918 'only half a dozen works of any consequence had been produced'. K Reid, 'The Third Branch of the Profession' in H

In the twentieth century the Parliamentary imposition of the same rules on Scotland as on England and the tendency to assimilate the rules in the two jurisdictions has led to increasing reference in Scotland to English books, which frequently ignore Scottish decisions and specialities in Scots law. The same reasons frequently made it not worthwhile for a Scottish writer to seek to write a distinctively Scottish book.[35]

However, in 1960 the Scottish Universities Law Institute (SULI), underwritten by the Carnegie Trust for Scottish Universities, was established to promote the writing and publication of Scots law texts.[36] Key among these has been the *Stair Encyclopaedia of the Laws of Scotland*, which is more of a digest in the civilian tradition, or a set of definitive texts, than an encyclopaedia, and over the years has allowed its various contributing authors to review and revise the law strengthening, in some instances, its civilian orientation.[37]

Indeed it was stated at the end of the twentieth century, 'Fifty years ago there was rather a dearth of Scots law books, a profusion in England. Since then there has been a veritable renaissance of Scottish legal writing'.[38] Today this may be more debateable.[39] Certainly there are still publishers producing Scottish law texts, but several of these are now merged under larger corporations,[40] and some produce a very limited number of new titles a year.[41] Specialist journals however remain,

---

MacQueen (ed), *Scots Law into the 21ˢᵗ Century* (W Green/Sweet and Maxwell 1996) 43. He points out that in the period 1961–1965 only 14 books on Scots law were published, compared to 43 in the period 1991–1995.

35   DM Walker, *The Scottish Jurists* (W Green 1985), 421.

36   The publication supported by the Law Society of Scotland of *The Laws of Scotland: Stair Memorial Encyclopaedia* was also a significant publication in the latter part of the twentieth century, and indeed remains so today, as was the establishment of the Law Reform Committee established in a part-time capacity in 1954 and then as a permanent body in 1965 under the Law Commissions Act 1965.

37   See, for example, the contribution of K Reid on property law in volume 18.

38   T Weir, 'Divergent Legal Systems in a Single Member State' (1998) Zeitschrift für Europäisches Privatrecht 564, 572.

39   For comment on the rise and fall of Scots law journals however see R Zimmermann, 'Law Journals in Nineteenth Century Scotland' (2008) 12(1) Edinburgh Law Review 9, and M Cherry 'Law Publishing in Scotland' (2009) 9(1) Legal Information Management 47–49.

40   Tottel, for example, has been taken over by Bloomsbury Professional and Green Ltd is part of the large Sweet and Maxwell publishing house. Although the University of Dundee is a newcomer to the field, its output is very small.

41   Avizandum, publishing under its own label, for example, had only 13 Scots law texts listed in its online catalogue in May 2013. Publishing under the Stair Society Titles it has more (30 titles) but only six of these are post 2009. Green Ltd lists 151 Scots titles but 60 of these date back to the last century, only six post-date 2010 (plus three forthcoming 2013/2014). (Web based research carried out 31 May 2013).

focusing primarily on Scots law, but are also increasingly looking outward. For example, the editorial policy statement of the *Juridical Review* states (*inter alia*):

> The primary focus will remain Scots law in all its aspects. However, we also recognize the critical role of the Juridical Review to inform Scots lawyers of important legal developments in other jurisdictions and for Scots lawyers to use the vehicle of the Juridical Review to explain the Scottish legal system to a wide readership.[42]

This open borders communication is of course necessary, not only because of the movement of legal ideas and issue but also to meet the needs of those servicing a diverse client base and to reflect the intellectual interests of academics.[43]

Legal practice

In the 1990s a number of English law firms established branch offices in Scotland, not to practice Scots law but to service the needs of clients based in Scotland. In recent years the practice of lawyering has changed further, especially for solicitors. While there are still a number of small high street lawyers servicing the needs of local clients, the large law firms, which are located primarily in a limited geographical area (the Central Belt referred to earlier), are having to adapt. Today, leading Scots law firms frequently have law offices outside Scotland and indeed, as a result of economic pressure in recent years, a number of Scots law firms have either merged with English law firms or gone into liquidation.[44] These larger law firms seek to offer an international legal service, primarily to commercial and corporate clients trading in the UK and globally. For example, although six Scottish law firms were listed in the UK top 100 in 2012,[45] all but one have offices outside Scotland,[46] and it may well be the case that the bulk of their work is not carried out in Scotland or under Scots law, but elsewhere.

---

42   See Juridical Review: The Law Journal of the Scottish Universities, Editorial Policy on the publisher's page <http://www.sweetandmaxwell.co.uk/Catalogue/ ProductDetails.aspx?recordid=475> accessed 15 January 2014.

43   Here it might be added that the nature of quality assessment of research outputs in universities in the UK (the Research Excellence Framework) may well be relevant in informing the nature and publication of research, despite promises that Scottish specialists will sit on panels of assessment.

44   See, for example, mergers between McGrigors and Pinsent Mason (London) 2012, and Archibald Campbell and Harley with Shoosmiths (London) 2012.

45   *Herald Scotland* referring to survey undertaken by the magazine *Legal Business*, 4 September 2012.

46   Dundas Wilson have offices in London, Edinburgh and Glasgow; Brodies have offices in Aberdeen, Edinburgh. Glasgow and Brussels; Shepherd and Wedderburn have offices in Aberdeen, Glasgow, Edinburgh and London, Dickson Minot has offices in

This is hardly surprising given that English is the language of international commerce so that, as the client base of lawyers becomes more outward looking and less localized, the nuances of Scots law (and indeed other national systems) may be undermined. Similarly as new areas of law emerge, for example cyber law, e-commerce, space law, it is likely that boundaries between legal systems will break down – as is already happening where EU law moves towards harmonization.[47]

The Role and Function of Courts of Appeal

Prior to the union between Scotland and England in 1707 appeals to the Inner House of the Court of Session went to the Scottish Parliament. When that was abolished these appeals went to the Judicial Committee of the House of Lords. This only extended to civil matters and numerically represented a very small proportion of Scottish case law. The Scots legal system retained (and still retains) a system of courts which are distinct from those of England and Wales. Nevertheless the jurisprudence of the English courts has been influential. Indeed some academic writers have suggested that what makes the influence of English law so insidious is that it creeps in by way of case citation, whereby the jurists use cases in which judges in the Court of Sessions have referred to English law.[48] Apart from decisions of the UK Supreme Court, there is no formal reason why Scots lawyers should cite English case law, and in theory the civil law dimension of Scots law could be strengthened through reference to decisions of other mixed or civil legal systems (especially as Scots law is more cautious about the rule of precedent). However, research by Esin Örücü involving the statistical analysis of the frequency with which Scots courts refer to other legal systems,[49] revealed that these references are predominantly to English decisions – although these were not always or invariably approved or followed.[50] Even where Scots courts do consider other legal systems, it was found that these tend to be predominantly common law ones rather than civilian or mixed jurisdictions. This, Örücü argues,

---

London and Edinburgh, and Turcan Connell have offices in Edinburgh, Glasgow, London and Guernsey.

47   Indeed it is evident from the publications lists of Scottish publishers than many titles are what might be described as practice manuals in the fields of contemporary legal concerns, for example, banking, finance, taxation and bankruptcy.

48   DM Walker, 'The Province of Jurists Determined' (1991) Juridical Review 20, 40.

49   C McDiarmid undertook a similar study 'Scots Law: The Turning of the Tide' (1999) Juridical Review 156–169. In 1949 D Walker found that over half the precedents cited in the first half of the twentieth century in Scots courts derived from English case law. 'A Note on Precedent' (1949) Juridical Review 283, at 288 cited in McDiarmid, 161.

50   E Örücü, 'Comparative Law as a Tool of Construction in Scottish Courts' (2000) Juridical Review 27.

'raises concerns as to unnecessary or ill conceived anglicisation of the law'.[51] Contrary perhaps to Walker's claim, however, her research also found that most Scots court decisions were decided on the basis of previous Scots cases,[52] which themselves may contain common law principles and precedents depending on the subject area.

While it is clear that appeal to the House of Lords in the eighteen and nineteenth century did not always have a positive impact on the integrity of Scots law, the presence of two Scots Law Lords on the Judicial Committee from the late nineteenth century onwards, was one way of ensuring that where Scots appeals were heard (which was only in civil cases) then the law of Scotland could be applied.[53] This tradition has prevailed and was demonstrated in the case of *Burnett's Trustee v Grainger* [2004] UKHL 8.

In 1998 when Scotland acquired greater powers to legislate for itself under the Scotland Act, two matters were referable south of the border. The first was questions of devolution, that is, issues relating to the constitutional power of the Scottish Parliament which were referable to the Judicial Committee of the Privy Council. Secondly, civil appeals continued to go from the Inner House of the Court of Session to the House of Lords Judicial Committee. In 2009 the judicial powers of the House of Lords were removed and assumed by the Supreme Court,[54] which also became the court of appeal for the Inner House of the Court of Session in Scotland.[55] The Supreme Court also took over the constitutional powers of review of the Privy Council in respect of issues concerning devolved matters.[56] Lord Hope, who until recently sat in the Supreme Court as one of two Scottish judges, has stated in respect of civil appeals:

> Many of these appeals do not raise any Scottish issues of pure Scots law at all. This is because much of the law which applies in Scotland is common to the whole of the United Kingdom. Or, as it was put by Professor Neil Walker in his review of the Supreme Court's jurisdiction in Scottish appeals, although Scots

---

51   ibid, 34.

52   Although as Örücü points out, courts both sides of the border may assume that English and Scots law are the same unless evidence is brought to demonstrate otherwise.

53   According to Chalmers, in the period 1993–2002, 48 cases were referred to the House of Lords from Scotland and in 68 per cent of these the Scottish Law Lords delivered speeches. Indeed Chalmers states 'Non-Scottish law lords simply do not in current practice deliver speeches on questions of Scots common law' J Chalmers, 'Scottish Appeals and the proposed Supreme Court' (2004) 2 Edinburgh Law Review 4, 8–9.

54   Established under the Constitutional Reform Act 2003.

55   For background see H MacQueen 'Scotland and a Supreme Court for the UK? (2003) Scots Law Times 1.

56   There is some controversy about this state of affairs. See T Kelly 'Supreme Court and Special Leave' (2011) Scots Law Times 1.

law enjoys a high level of *formal* autonomy, there is a rather lower level of *substantive* autonomy.[57]

He has also drawn attention to many areas of commonality between the law of England and Wales and Scotland, either through legislation, or the adoption of Scottish law institutions in England and Wales, for example the tort of negligence, or because of commonly developed trans-border practices, for example in the field of commercial law.

At the same time as the Scotland Act became law, the UK passed the Human Rights Act 1998, which incorporated into domestic law, the UK's international obligations under the European Convention on Human Rights.[58] A consequence of this has been that the jurisdiction of the Supreme Court to hear appeals from Scottish decisions has expanded to encompass appeals from the High Court of Justiciary on criminal law matters, where these raise issues of human rights compliance, particularly due process rights. Recently and controversially the Supreme Court has held that the Scottish practice of police detention without access to a solicitor for the first six hours and the admissibility of evidence obtained during that period at trial, was a breach of Article 6(2) of the European Convention of Human Rights. This decision was contrary to that reached in Scotland by the High Court of Justiciary, but one which would have most certainly have been reached had the case proceeded to Strasbourg.[59] Given the obligation on all courts in the UK to take into account the jurisprudence of Strasbourg and the obligation on all parts of the UK to give effect to the international treaty obligations of the UK, more along this vein may be expected especially given the pervasive effect of human rights in so many aspects of life. Although the 'margin of appreciation' may allow some leeway, it is not clear to what extent this will accommodate differences within the laws of Member States (for example, the legal system of Scotland, or Wales, or Northern Ireland as opposed to laws across the UK). While some have seen the Supreme Court as an increasing threat to Scots law through a process of Anglicization, others have viewed it as being more benign and indeed Lord Young has suggested that 'the recent record of the Supreme Court in Scottish cases

---

57   Lord Hope of Craighead 'Scots law seen from south of the border '(2012) EdinLR 1, 4. The work of Walker he refers to is, N Walker, *Final Appellate Jurisdiction in the Scottish Legal System* (Scottish Government 2010) 24.

58   Given effect in Scotland by the Scotland Act.

59   *Cadder v H M Advocate* (2010) UK Supreme Court 43, 2011 SC (UKSC) 13. Although the total number of criminal cases is small there is a degree of resentment that 'the Scottish criminal justice system has been made subject – for the first time since the 1707 Union – to some degree of external scrutiny by other UK judges who are not trained and formed within the Scottish legal system' A O'Neill, 'The Englishing of Scots Criminal Law? – the Advocate–General's proposals for the appeals to the Supreme Court in criminal cases from Scotland' <http://ukscblog.com/devolution-issues-and-acts-of-the-lord-advocate-consultation-on-clauses-to-amend-the-scotland-act/> accessed 15 January 2014.

can perhaps be described as mixed'.[60] Similarly the well-known human rights advocate Helena Kennedy has suggested that 'Scottish lawyers add to the riches of that court, as do the Northern Irish judges, and I think that sometimes you need another stage and another set of thinkers to apply their brilliance to the problem'.[61]

As one of the promises of the Scottish independence lobby is that the European Convention on Human Rights would be embedded in a new Scottish constitution,[62] it would seem likely that if the referendum vote was 'yes', Strasbourg jurisprudence would continue to influence the way Scottish law develops.[63]

The Role of Geographical Proximity/Distance from Other Systems or Parent Systems and the Influence of Regional or International Memberships/ Agencies in Shaping the Law and on Legal Autonomy

There is no dispute that historically Scots law was mixed. Today, however, maintaining the civil law element of the Scottish legal system is faced by a number of challenges. Ever since 1789 and the French Revolution, Scottish links with the Continental civil law system have been attenuated. Although there are Roman law links with South Africa, that country's own political history, and the post-apartheid legal system which is emerging, is a very different mixture from the former Roman–Dutch system. Moreover, although an increasing body of material is available in translation, few law students read a foreign language and indeed a number of Scottish universities have struggled to maintain their language courses. The consequence is that few law graduates can access civil law material in other languages, or the French language materials of other mixed systems such as Quebec and Louisiana. The focus of legal education is also changing, with increasing emphasis being placed on European and International law courses – especially as electives and at post-graduate level, and this is having a corresponding influence on, and reflecting, the profiles of staff recruited to teach at Scottish universities.[64]

---

60   Lord Drummond Young, 'Scotland and the Supreme Court' (2013) 2(1) Cambridge Journal of International and Comparative Law 67, 76.

61   M Rhodes, 'Freedom Fighter' (2011) *Holyrood* 258 (27 June 2011) 14, 17.

62   Scottish Government (2013) *Scotland's Future: From the Referendum to Independence and a Written Constitution* (2013) s.2.14 Available at <http://www.scotland. gov.uk/Publications/2013> accessed 15 January 2014.

63   C Guite, 'He Who Pays the Piper: Shifting Scottish Legal Landscape' (2013) 13(3) Legal Information Management 139–147. In a similar vein it has been argued that Scots criminal law will lose its distinctiveness. See A O'Neill, 'The Europeanization of Scots Criminal Law' (2008) Scots Criminal Law 1122–1134.

64   The emphasis on employability and issues relating to student debt, shortage of training contracts, limited places on Law Diploma courses and graduate unemployment all contribute to inform student choices.

While these academics may come from other mixed or civil law systems, the majority do not appear to be coming from a Scots law mixed system.

Besides shifting trends in legal education there are other pragmatic influences at work. Although it has its own Law Commission, some of the work of the Scottish Law Commission is done conjointly with the Law Commission for England and Wales as demonstrated in Table 1.3.[65]

Table 1.3   The work of the Law Commissions

Date	Joint	Scottish
2008	2	5
2009	2	4
2010	1	6
2011	4	5
2012	4	4

Source: Data is taken from the annual reports of the Law Commission, www.scotlawcom. gov.uk

As Lady Clark of Calton, the current Chairman of the Law Commission in Scotland has explained:

> Since establishment of the Scottish Parliament by the Scotland Act 1998, we have dealt with Scots law issues in relation to both reserved and devolved matters. Much of our work is directed at areas of Scots law which are devolved but there is an overlap on many occasions with reserved matters which require to be addressed. There are also significant projects which relate to reserved matters in which the Law Commission for England and Wales may take the lead but we require to provide considerable assistance and resources to ensure that Scots law and the practical effects in Scotland are assessed and taken into account in any recommendations for change and drafting proposed legislation.[66]

On the one hand, this taking into account the practical effects of law reforms in Scotland reflects a pragmatic approach to the issue rather than a purist approach and indeed may require very little consideration of the nature or origins of Scots law as a mixed legal system. On the other hand, there are areas of law where the distinctiveness of Scots law has been retained or even enhanced though the work

---

65   The Law Commission produces a number of different publications including reports, discussion papers (which may also be reviews of the current law), consultation papers and issues papers. I have not included in the count the annual review itself. See further on the Scottish Law Commission, G Gretton, 'Of Law Commissioning' (2013) 17(2) Edinburgh Law Review 119.

66   SLC Annual Report 2012, 8.

of the Law Commission,[67] even if, as is sometimes the case, the difference is in the detail not the broad principles.

Similarly, while under the Scotland Act the Scottish Parliament at Holyrood exercises an increasingly large portfolio of devolved powers and although in a number of matters legislation has to comply with a larger agenda than that of Scotland, often the distinctions between Holyrood legislation and that of Westminster are differences of detail. Whether this reflects a truly distinct way of contemporary legal thinking, an historical legacy or merely the need to accommodate local social or economic factors rather than jurisprudential ones is unclear.[68] Certainly a review of the first ten years of the Holyrood Parliament provoked mixed responses: 'The overall thesis of the collection is that although the Scottish Parliament has been unexpectedly industrious, the reforms it has made (with some notable exceptions) have been fairly modest.[69] It should also be pointed out that like any legal system, changes in Scots law may be driven by the need to modernize in line with changing values and needs, and that while these changes may suggest convergence between systems – for example, recent proposals to abolish the corroborative evidence rule in criminal law – this may be seen as coincidental rather than as undermining the distinctiveness of the national system.

Pinpointing events which have threatened the survival of Scots law as a distinct legal system

The survival of the Scottish legal system has been something of a roller-coaster ride. The Act of Union in 1707 was clearly a significant moment but one has to remember that for many people this made little legal difference. It is also the case that there was far less legislation being passed in the early eighteenth century than later on, and the reach of the State – apart from taxation –was limited. The lives of many ordinary Scots were predominantly governed by their landlords under a feudal system of land tenure or later their employers in mines and factories.

Of more potential significance for a distinctly Scottish mixed legal system was the moment at which Scotland regained its power to legislation for itself under the Scotland Act 1998, and the re-establishment of a Scottish Parliament. Devolution gives the Scottish Parliament a high degree of autonomy over criminal and private law. Less autonomy is given as regards some areas of public law, where competence is reserved to Westminster,[70] but in others such as education, health

---

67   For example, in the area of property law.

68   For example, legislation on housing and transport.

69   S Wilson 'Publication Review: Law Making and the Scottish Parliament: The Early Years' (2012) 16(2) Edinburgh Law Review 289, 291. The work referred to is: E Sutherland, K Goodall, G Little and F Davidson (eds), *Law Making and the Scottish Parliament: The Early Years* (CUP 2013).

70   Although it is not always clear what is a reserved matter and what is not. In reserved matters the Scottish Parliament has no power to legislate, although it has been

and local government, the Scottish Parliament is less constrained and national policies can be implemented. Devolution therefore provided an opportunity for legislation to be made by the Scots for Scotland, for proposals of the Scottish Law Commission to be carefully taken into account without being curtailed for lack of parliamentary time in Westminster (or lack of priority), and for the national, Scottish, context to be afforded proper consideration when drafting legislation.[71] The political shift therefore provided the opportunity to put an end to what Whitty has described as 'spatchcocking' Scots law into English statutes,[72] and optimists believed that 'the new Parliament's potential to benefit the future development of Scots law considerably outweighs any perceived disadvantages in its relationship with Westminster.'[73] It also provided an opportunity to redress the potential imbalance between common and civil law in the Scottish legal system.

However, others believe that the opportunity for strengthening a distinctively Scottish law has not been seized.[74] A number of factors may have contributed to this, for example, the gradual and drawn out process of the devolution of powers; failure to implement many of the proposals of the Scottish Law Commission, continuing pressure from the EU for compliance legislation, and the coincidental timing of the Human Rights Act 1998 (mentioned above), and, since 2009, the role of the Supreme Court in developing a uniform approach to the UK's human rights obligations. This last point has meant that, over the last few years, a number

---

suggested that the Westminster Parliament is extremely reluctant to pass laws relevant to Scots private law (such as company law) even where it is a reserved matter under Schedule 5, of the Scotland Act 1998. See RG Anderson (2012) Edinburgh Law Review 99, 103.

71   The role of the Scottish Law Commission may be crucial. In its 1973 report it stated, 'We view with disfavour ill-considered attempts to unify the laws of England and Scotland by the applications of principles which are not consistent with Scots law' (1973) Scots Law Com No. 28, para 12, quoted by Whitty (n15) 446. However, consideration of the legislation passed since devolution suggests that less attention has been paid to Commission proposals than might have been hoped.

72   As in 'English statutes into which segments of Scots law have sometimes been spatchcocked' N Whitty, 'From Rules to Discretion: Changes in the Fabric of Scots Private Law' (2003) 7 Edinburgh Law Review 281, 228. Whitty cites for example, the Bills of Exchange Act 1882, Partnership Act 1890, Sale of Goods of 1893 and the Marine Insurance Act 1906. Whitty (n15) 444.

73   McDiarmid (n49) 168.

74   Critics of the exercise of this power suggest that SMPs spend far too much time on trivial legislation and insufficient time on major legislation. See 'A Decade after Scottish Devolution, What is the Verdict?' 3 May 2009 The Guardian <http://www.theguardian.com/uk/2009/may/03/scotland-devolution-decade-anniversary> accessed 16 January 2014, and for a more formal assessment, see the Commission on Scottish Devolution, Final Report 'Serving Scotland Better: Scotland and the UK in the 21st Century' 15 June 2009 <http://www.commissiononscottish devolution.org> accessed 16 January 2014.

of differences between Scots law and the law of England and Wales have been removed as a result of human right challenges.[75]

Although Scottish nationalism appears to be strong, with the Scottish National Party holding power in Parliament, polls at the time of writing suggest that the 'No' vote is likely to win in the proposed referendum on independence. This could of course change if 16 and 17 year olds, who are to be given the vote, exercise it, but it may not. If there is a 'No' vote, it appears that Scotland will remain part of the UK with promises of greater devolution of powers being made by the Westminster Government. What will this mean for the Scottish legal system? More devolution may result in a strengthening of a distinct Scots law, in terms of a national law rather than a distinctly mixed legal system. Alternatively the increasing influence of laws from Europe may mean that intra-national differences within the UK and indeed across Europe are erased despite greater devolution. If this happens the mixed nature of the Scots legal system may play a key role in showing how civil and common law systems can work together or, because it is invariably treated as a distinct legal system in the current European context, Scotland can bring to the table new, nationally developed, ideas for the harmonization and modernization of laws across Europe. Indeed, Professor Jan Smits has suggested that Scots law provides a potential bridge between civilian and common law tradition in the harmonizing of European law.[76]

Even if this potential is fulfilled, there are practical considerations which may influence the future of the present legal system. Within Scotland, the changing face of legal practice and legal services especially at the present time of cut-backs in legal aid,[77] may well mean that fewer people will have access to a lawyer, especially for private law matters where one might expect the distinctiveness of Scots law to be strongest, and/or lawyers may lose their monopoly on the provision of legal services – although it has been argued that the cuts in Scotland are considerable less severe than in England and Wales.[78] One consequence of the impact of economics on the provision of legal services

---

75   Examples in criminal law relate to the age of criminal responsibility for children and the right of detained persons to have access to a lawyer.

76   JM Smits, *The Making of European Private Law: Toward a Ius Commune Europaeum as a Mixed Legal System* (Intersentia 2002) and H MacQueen 'Scots Law' in JM Smits (ed) *Elgar Encyclopaedia of Comparative Law* (2nd edn Edward Elgar 2012).

77   The Law Society of Scotland has reported that 'the legal aid fund is facing a cut 7.2 per cent over the years 2012–13 to 2014–15. Following the measures introduced to cut legal aid expenditure earlier this year, this additional cut represents a huge challenge to access to justice and to the sustainability of legal aid practice.' <http://www.lawscot.org.uk/members/legal-aid--access-to-justice/civil-legal-aid> accessed 16 January 2014. The Scottish Civil Justice Council and Criminal Legal Assistance Act became law at the end of January 2013.

78   *Daily Record* January 29, 2013, <http://www.dailyrecord.co.uk/news/politics/legal-aid-changes-in-scotland-1561482> accessed 16 January 2014.

is that two major categories of client emerge: criminals – who remain entitled to legal representation as of right, and corporate commercial clients. In the case of the former a distinctly Scottish criminal law may persist in substantive law but procedurally have to give way to the demands of European human rights, which, while in part based on the civilian influences of Europe, is likely to see any distinctiveness eradicated. In the case of the latter, commercial law has always transcended national boundaries. The practical recognition of this is already evident in Scotland where the larger law firms attracting corporate clients are likely to establish branches in most major cities including beyond the Scottish border, without worrying too much about the peculiarities of Scots law. Indeed it might be argued that in Scotland and elsewhere law is losing its territoriality. So that while the Scots may remain proud of their traditions and customs, the legal system as a distinct mixed legal system (as opposed to being mixed in the general way of all legal systems or historically mixed) may be endangered, even if, as advised by Lord Hope, it looks

> 'outwards and not inwards as it adapts to the realities of modern life. One of the great virtues of Scots law, as a mixed system, was its willingness to adapt itself so as to keep pace with the way things were done elsewhere. Pride in our own system is one thing; isolationism is quite another. We have much to gain by maintaining contact with the way that law is practised in England and Wales and beyond. We have much to lose if we were to raise the drawbridge and cut ourselves off from the outside world'.[79]

Conclusion

In many respects the legal system of Scotland reflects the challenges that confront writing about mixed systems. In some areas of the law, reform, adaptation, transplants and pragmatic considerations have given rise to new hybridities which may themselves be distinctly Scots but less obviously distinctively illustrative of classical mixedness. In others, although traditionally mixed in origin, those origins have been lost or forgotten. To the outsider it would not be immediately obvious that the law was drawn from different legal families. There is also the question of whether arguments for the distinctiveness of the Scottish legal system is a product of nationalism or purism stemming largely from academia rather than practitioners, and in particular from a very small number of 'champions' of the mixed nature of Scots law. The wearing of tartan is a symbol of affiliation, for football teams, clans or place – either of origin,[80]

---

79   Lord Hope of Craighead (2012) Edinburgh Law Review 1, 10.

80   Note, for example, the number of those living out of Scotland who wear the tartan, for example in Canada, New Zealand and so on, to demonstrate their Scottish ancestry even if remote.

or residence,[81] or even education.[82] Although not all Scots embrace the wearing of tartan, it is an identifier. The question today for the Scottish legal system is whether that identifier is fading, perhaps to be replaced by something else, or is the tartan as bright and distinctively Scots as ever, merely different in content, form and composition?

---

81   Some tartans can be worn by non-Scots, and often are for weddings and so on.

82   Male graduates from Scottish Universities frequently wear tartan kilts for graduation whether they are Scots or not.

Chapter 2
Guyana

Having looked at Scotland in the previous chapter, we now turn to Guyana (sometimes referred to as a land of six peoples, where the majority of people see themselves as of mixed heritage), a Dutch colony until 1814 at which point Britain acquired sovereignty. Guyana is presented by Christine Toppin-Allahar as a muddled system, as far as the aboriginal land law is concerned, which is part of this mixed legal system. In addition, it is factors such as population change; loss of one of the languages; mixed use of terminology from both of the parent legal systems confusing issues; concepts that feed into, fuse with and become part of an amalgam; and the use of precedents from common law in the context of Roman–Dutch law, that resulted in the Roman–Dutch law becoming endangered. When the different elements that gave birth to Guyana's mixed legal system are weighed up the system is now more common law oriented.

The chapter deals with some specific issues to illustrate this muddle as far as aboriginal land title is concerned: servitudes and Amerindian lands. According to Toppin-Allahar, the mixture of Guyana may end up more as a melting pot. Customary law and aboriginal rights have emerged in Guyana as another element in the legal mixture in spite of the fact that it is presented more as a muddle than part of the mixture.

The Roman–Dutch law seems to have withered at the roots and now can be regarded as endangered with the legal practitioners administering the law being educated in common law jurisdictions in the UK and the Caribbean. References to the Roman–Dutch law of Guyana and the civil law of Saint Lucia are few and far between. However, the new law degree now on offer in the University of Guyana may revitalise the interest in Roman–Dutch law and may save it from extinction.

This chapter again shows to the reader the importance of the legal practitioners, their education and the predominant language in use in the land and in law.

Guyana: 'Mosaic or Melting-Pot?'

Christine Toppin-Allahar

Introduction

Guyana is commonly known, and is referred to in its National Anthem, as a 'land of six peoples' because its plural society is comprised of descendants of the indigenous people, known in Guyana as Amerindians; European colonists, originally Dutch and subsequently British; Africans forcibly transported from their native lands and enslaved by the European colonists; and Portuguese, Chinese and East Indians induced to immigrate voluntarily to Guyana as indentured labourers between the emancipation of the African slaves in 1834 and the end of the indenture system in 1917. Over the past five centuries the inter-mingling of these six groups has resulted in the emergence of another significant and growing group, now the third largest segment of the population comprising approximately one in every five persons, who identify themselves as being of 'mixed heritage' rather than as belonging to any of the six original peoples.[1] In effect, Guyana's heterogeneous society has over the course of its difficult history proven itself to be a dynamic melting pot, rather than a static mosaic.

Like the society, the legal system of Guyana today is mixed – the substantive law being a combination of Roman–Dutch law and English common law, with an overlay of colonial era and post-independence statute law and a written constitution. Roman–Dutch law, itself a mixture of Roman law and legal concepts taken from Dutch customary law which evolved in the seventeenth and eighteenth centuries from the work of influential Dutch scholars including Grotius, was transplanted into all the Dutch colonies, including those in the Guianas. Although Roman–Dutch law was replaced in the Netherlands by the Civil Code in 1809, during the Napoleonic Wars, this did not affect the continuation in force of Roman–Dutch law in the Dutch colonies. When the Dutch colonies of Demerara, Essequibo and Berbice were finally captured by the British in 1803, both the pre-existing Roman–Dutch legal system and the existing system of government were preserved by Article 1 of the Articles of Capitulation, which provided inter alia that:

---

1 Government of Guyana, *2002 Population and Housing Census – Guyana National Report*, available at <www.statisticsguyana.gov.gy/census.html> accessed 25 April 2013. Results of the 2012 Census conducted on 15 September 2012 are not yet available.

> The Laws and Usages of the Colony shall remain in force and be respected ... in the same manner as before the Capitulation ... The constituted Authorities and Public Officers ... shall be continued in their respective Offices and Situations until His Majesty's pleasure shall be known.[2]

The subsequent cession of these colonies from the Netherlands to Britain by the Anglo-Dutch London Convention of 1814[3] did not abrogate the terms on which Britain acquired sovereignty over them. Hence, in his still unparalleled treatise on the development of land law in British Guiana,[4] Ramsahoye concludes that:

> It was more on account of the provision in the Articles of Capitulation retaining the laws and usages of the colonies than on account of the rule in *Campbell v Hall* that Roman–Dutch law was retained in British Guiana after cession.[5]

Other than as respects numerous anachronistic place names, the Dutch language died out in Guyana well over a century ago despite its continued use in neighbouring Suriname.[6] As has been pointed out by McPherson, the existing laws in conquered countries survived only when a sufficiently large proportion of the conquered population, including enough trained lawyers, stayed on to ensure that the study and use of the existing legal system was preserved in the language in which it was written. Otherwise pre-conquest laws were progressively replaced over time by

---

2   CO 112/4 *Laws of Capitulation signed between England and the Batavian Republic, 10 September 1803*, quoted by MN Menezes, *British Policy towards the Amerindians in British Guiana 1803–1873* (OUP 1977) 7.

3   Art. I (3) of the Additional Articles to the London Convention, which was subsequently confirmed by the Peace of Paris of 1815, pursuant to which Suriname was returned to the Netherlands.

4   The colonies of Demerara, Essequibo and Berbice were united to form the Colony of British Guiana by Letters Patent issued in the UK on 4 March 1831.

5   FHW Ramsahoye, *The Development of Land Law in British Guiana* (Oceana Publications Inc, 1966) 290. The reference made is to *Campbell v Hall* (1774) Lofft 655; 98 ER 848, a case decided after the cession of the former French colony of Grenada to Britain by the 1763 Treaty of Paris, which limited the prerogative power of the Crown to legislate for a conquered territory, and elaborated on the rule in *Calvin's Case* (1608) 7 Co. Rep.1a; 77 ER 377, that when a new territory is acquired by conquest the Crown may change the laws of that place, but until then its old law remains in force.

6   Ironically, besides Dutch, the official language, the majority of Surinamese speak 'Sranan Tongo', a creole dialect of English formerly known as 'Negerengles' (Negro English). While the first verse of the National Anthem is in Dutch, the second verse is in Sraran Tongo. Suriname, originally an English colony, was ceded to the Netherlands in exchange for New York by the Treaty of Breda 1667, occupied by Britain from 1799–1815 during the Napoléonic Wars, and finally returned to the Netherlands by the Treaty of Paris in 1815. Suriname became an independent republic on 25 November 1975 and a member of the predominantly Anglophone Caribbean Community (CARICOM) on 4 July 1995.

English law, which tended to happen when the local population was supplemented or replaced by British immigrants to the stage where the society was effectively Anglicized.[7] This is certainly true of Guyana.

The process by which Roman–Dutch law was incrementally replaced by English law in Guyana in the century following cession has been explained clearly elsewhere,[8] and does not require repetition here. For the present purposes it suffices to say that the Civil Law of British Guiana Ordinance, No. 15 of 1916,[9] while saving all existing property rights[10] abrogated Roman–Dutch law[11] and introduced the English common law and doctrines of equity,[12] with effect from 1 January 1917, but excluded the application of English law of real property to immovable property.[13] The Ordinance also provided that there should continue to be one common law for both moveable and immovable property and that all questions related to immovable property should be determined 'as far as possible' according to the principles of the English common law applicable to personal property.[14] These provisions were subject to several provisos, the first being that immovable property should continue to be held in full ownership, which would be the only form of ownership of immovable property recognized by the common law and should not be subject to any rule not attached to personal property in England.[15] Additionally, it was provided that the law and practice relating to conventional mortgages or hypothecs of moveable and immovable property, and to easements, *profits à prendre*, or real servitudes and the right of opposition in the case of both transports and mortgages would remain the existing practice.[16]

Shortly thereafter, the Deeds Registry Ordinance, No. 17 of 1919,[17] was introduced to provide for the appointment of a Registrar and other staff for a Deeds Registry and to amend the law relating to the execution and registration of transports, mortgages and other deeds (including long term leases) with effect

---

7   BH McPherson, *The Reception of English Law Abroad* (Supreme Court of Queensland Library 2007) 266–267.

8   Ramsahoye (n5) 14–18; J Matthews Glenn, 'Mixed Jurisdictions in the Commonwealth Caribbean: Mixing, Unmixing, Remixing' (2008) 12(1) Electronic Journal of Comparative Law 13–14 <http://www.ejcl.org> accessed 16 April 2013.

9   Now the Civil Law of Guyana Act, Cap.6:01 (Revised Laws 2010), hereinafter referred to as 'the Civil Law Act'.

10   ibid, s2(3).

11   ibid, s3(a).

12   ibid, s3(b).

13   ibid, s3(c).

14   ibid, s3(d). It was this provision which led to many of the difficulties in the subsequent interpretation of the land law of Guyana. See Ramsahoye (n5) 292.

15   ibid, s3, proviso (i).

16   ibid, s3, proviso (ii). 'Transport' is the Roman–Dutch equivalent of 'conveyance' in respect of transfer of property title in English law.

17   Now the Deeds Registry Act, Cap.5:01 (Revised Laws 2010).

from 1 January 1920. But this was not the end of the story. As has been reported elsewhere, the co-existence of Roman–Dutch land law and English common law caused much judicial uncertainty and resulted in further ad hoc changes in land law in Guyana.[18] Persistent doubts about the law governing leases were not resolved until four decades later when the English law of landlord and tenant was retrospectively declared to have been in force since 1 January 1917 by the Landlord and Tenant Ordinance No. 26 of 1947.[19] Further substantive changes were wrought by the Land Registry Ordinance, No. 18 of 1959,[20] which, partly with a view to 'assimilating' the law of immovable property in Guyana to the English law of real property,[21] introduced a modified Torrens system of registered title and abolished the Roman–Dutch law relating to hypothecs, servitudes and opposition with respect to lands governed by that enactment, with effect from 4 January 1960.[22]

As a result of these statutory interventions, the law of Guyana relating to rights in land, their acquisition and disposition, has changed considerably over the past 100 years. Added to these changes in the law are difficulties caused by reliance on case law precedents from common law jurisdictions in interpretation of the law. This can be illustrated by reference to the evolution of the law related to servitudes. This increasingly common law orientation is particularly marked in the emergent field of litigation over Amerindian lands. Although this issue is in its infancy, unlike their counterparts in South Africa, neither the practitioners nor judges involved nor Guyanese academics appear to be questioning the applicability to Guyana of the line of modern authorities on 'native/aboriginal title' from common law jurisdictions, despite the continuance in force of Roman–Dutch land law in the context of land disputes.

Servitudes

Much of the land on the coastal plain of Guyana, where farmland and human settlements are concentrated, lies below sea level and the use and occupation of land in this area depends upon inter-related sea defence, drainage and irrigation works. In this highly engineered landscape, the existence of real servitudes is common. The Roman law of servitudes is the basis of the Roman–Dutch law on the subject. This was preserved by the Civil Law Act in 1917 and applied

---

18   Ramsahoye (n5) 291–296; M Bhagwan, '*Legal Framework Governing Land Transactions, Tenure, Titles, Use and Conservation in Guyana,*' FAO, Land Policy and Administration: Assistance in Identifying Constraints to Agrarian Reform, Volume I Part 2, TCP/GUY/4551 (August, 1995).

19   Now the Landlord and Tenant Act, Cap.61:01 (Revised Laws 2010).

20   Now the Land Registry Act, Cap.5:02 (Revised Laws 2010).

21   Ramsahoye (n5) 296.

22   Cap.5:02, s3(1).

by the courts of British Guiana without modification[23] until 1960.[24] According to Ramsahoye, before 1917 all the forms of servitudes known to Roman law could exist in Guyana. This would include prædial or real servitudes and personal servitudes, so-called 'urban' and 'rural' servitudes, and affirmative and negative servitudes.[25] Although some of the case law from that period relates to the rights and obligations of the owners of the dominant and servient lands, most cases arose from the requirement that to take effect servitudes must be endorsed on the title document of the affected land.[26]

The Civil Law Act 1917 provided inter alia that, 'the law and practice relating … to easements, *profits à prendre,* or real servitudes … shall be the law and practice now administered in those matters by the Supreme Court.'[27] The very language of this provision reveals that by or before 1917 English common law terms had intruded into the law of Guyana relating to servitudes. Moreover, the inference that *profits à prendre* are equivalent to real servitudes also suggests the existence of some conceptual confusion. In addition to the more common rights of way/access and water/drainage rights, the right to pasture and water livestock or excavate building material on a servient parcel of land could exist as real servitudes benefiting a dominant parcel of land under Roman law.[28] However, *profits à prendre* are not necessarily appurtenant to landownership[29] and generally are analogous to usufructs, which constituted personal servitudes in Roman–Dutch law.[30] Although Ramsahoye opines that personal servitudes, including usufruct, were impliedly abolished by the first subsection of the Ordinance abrogating Roman–Dutch law in general,[31] the reference to *profits à prendre* in this provision raises a question as to whether usufructs could have been preserved inadvertently. Certainly, the law would be clearer if the English common law terms easements and *profits à prendre* had been omitted from the subsection.

As is the case in Civil and Scottish law, under Roman–Dutch law in Guyana servitudes can be acquired in various ways. Although many servitudes today, for example way-leaves to facilitate the provision and maintenance of public utilities, are created by statute, generally servitudes in Guyana are created by express grant or reservation and are mentioned in the deeds of transport of the dominant and servient lands respectively, but servitudes in the nature of 'ways of necessity'

---

23   Ramsahoye (n5) 27.

24   When the Roman–Dutch law relating to hypothecs, servitudes and opposition was abolished with respect to lands governed by the Land Registry Act, see (n20).

25   Ramsahoye (n5) 27.

26   ibid, 27 and 30.

27   Cap.6:01, s3 proviso (ii).

28   C Anderson, *Law Essentials: Roman Law* (Dundee University Press 2009) 41.

29   R Megarry and HWR Wade, *The Law of Real Property* (5th edn Stevens and Sons 1984) 850.

30   Anderson (n28) 41; Ramsahoye (n5) 26.

31   Ramsahoye (n5) 27 and 30.

appurtenant to a land-locked parcel of land can be recognized as having been created by implied grant.[32] In addition, servitudes can be acquired by prescription through continuous use and enjoyment over a long period of time. In Guyana this is provided for by the Title to Land (Prescription and Limitation) Act,[33] which defines 'land' as inclusive of 'any easement, *profit à prendre*, servitude or other right over immovable property or connected therewith.'[34]

The Act provides that title to land (including State or Government land)[35] may be acquired by sole and undisturbed possession, use or enjoyment for 30 years, if such possession is established to the satisfaction of the court and was not taken or enjoyed by fraud or consent. It is also provided that title to private land may be acquired by 12 years possession, use and enjoyment, if the court is satisfied that the right of every other person to recover the land or interest has expired or been barred and their title has been extinguished.[36] This proviso is a cross reference to the limitation provisions of the Act, which stipulate that no action for the recovery of any land may be brought by any person after the expiry of 12 years from the date on which it accrues.[37] The Act also provides that no right of action to recover land accrues or can continue to exist unless the land is in possession of someone in whose favour the period of limitation can run, which is expressly referred to in the Act as a requirement that the land be in 'adverse possession.'[38] This is another instance in which the mixed use of Roman–Dutch and common law terminology in a statute has muddied the waters for legal practitioners in Guyana.

In practice, applications for the acquisition of title by prescription pursuant to the Act filed in the High Court are assigned by the Chief Justice to be heard

---

32   See the Civil Law case of *Michel v Augier* (1997) UKPC 16 (Saint Lucia).

33   Cap.60:02 [Laws of Guyana 2010].

34   ibid, s2.

35   During the colonial era in Guyana, a distinction was made between 'Crown' and 'Colony' lands. As explained by Ramsahoye (n5) 119, the distinction was originally made between lands vested in the Crown by virtue of sovereignty and lands granted by the Crown to or purchased from other persons by the Government of the Colony. Upon the transformation of Guyana into a Republic in 1970, following the attainment of political independence in 1966, the terminology for distinguishing between these two types of land was changed to 'State' and 'Government' lands. In the author's opinion, the distinction between these two classes of land was abolished by s6(1) of the 1970 Republic Act, Cap.1:02, and it is now preferable to use the term 'public land', which is defined by s5 of the Interpretation and General Clauses Act, Cap.2:01 as inclusive of both State and Government land. In practice, the only important distinction between these two types of land are that, while 'Government' land is held by the State under title documents identical to those applicable to private land, the State has no documentary title to 'State' land, its claim to which is founded solely upon sovereignty.

36   Cap.60:02, s3.

37   ibid, s5.

38   ibid, s10.

by the Land Court established by the Land Registry Act.[39] In the 1989 case of *Cole v Eccles Ramsburg District Council et al*,[40] the petitioner claimed to have acquired title by prescription to a parcel of land vested in the District Council, by a deed of transport, as a road/drainage reserve.[41] Based on the facts in evidence, the judge found that the petitioner, not having been in possession of the land for the applicable limitation period of 12 years,[42] had not acquired the title by prescription. Additionally, despite acknowledging the need for legislation stipulating clearly that reserves cannot be acquired by adverse possession, in a lengthy *obiter dicta* the judge went on to propound a general rule that, in light of various provisions of later statutes for the social control of land, public policy prohibits the granting to private persons of title by adverse possession to such reserves.

Further, as the petitioner was a trespasser, the judge relied on the decision of the English Court of Appeal in the case of *Hanning v Top Deck Travel Group Ltd*[43] as authority for the principle that a court cannot grant *title by adverse possession* when the claim is based on criminal acts prohibited by statute. Actually, the ruling in that case was that a person whose exercise of a right of way would otherwise have been sufficient to acquire an *easement by prescription*, cannot not acquire an easement by virtue of conduct which is prohibited by a public statute. The key to understanding the decision in *Hanning v Top Deck Travel Group Ltd* seems to be that, under the common law, the acquisition of an easement by prescription is based on the legal fiction of a 'lost grant'.[44] In other words, an easement claimed by prescription is presumed to have been exercised as of right. Since a right cannot be founded on a wrong, the court would not recognize the acquisition of an easement by prescription which was based on conduct that involved the commission of an offence.

This highlights an important distinction between the common law doctrine of prescription, which applies to the acquisition of incorporeal rights over land, analogous to servitudes, and the common law doctrine of adverse possession, which applies to the acquisition of title to land. Adverse possession necessarily always begins with the commission of a wrong, the tort and offence of trespass, by a squatter. A squatter has been defined by Lord Denning MR as 'One who, without any colour of right enters upon an unoccupied house or land, intending to stay

---

39   Bhagwan (n20) 33.

40   Petition No. 2554/89 (Demerara), Decision of Gerald O. Brooms, Commissioner of Title/Judge of the Land Court.

41   Squatting on reserves is rife in Guyana. See: HTSPE Ltd, 'Land Tenure Problems' *Guyana National Land Use Plan* (10th EDF Technical Assistance for Development of Land Use Planning, EuropeAid/128780/D/SER/GY December 2012) s3.3.3, 103.

42   Presumably, the period of 30 years would not have been applicable because the land in question was owned by the local government body, not the State per se, but this was not an issue in the case.

43   (1993) 68 P&CR 14.

44   Megarry and Wade (n29) 875 *et seq.*

there as long as he can,'[45] and at least one legal commentator has asked whether 'squatter's title' with its undertones of 'land stealing' has any place in a civilized society.[46] Hence, a possessory title to land is acquired by virtue of the extinction of the right of the original owner to retake possession of the land upon expiry of the limitation period, not on the basis of some implied right on the part of the person in adverse possession.

By contrast, under Roman–Dutch law both the processes of acquiring servitudes by use and enjoyment and of acquiring title to land by possession are known as 'acquisitive prescription'. This is reflected in the marginal note to the operative section in the Guyanese Title to Land (Prescription and Limitation) Act,[47] which reads, 'Title to land by prescription', but as regards title to land this cannot be equated with prescription in the common law sense of that term. Hence, the decision in *Hanning v Top Deck Travel Group Ltd* concerning the acquisition of an easement by prescription under the common law cannot be applied to limit the right of a squatter to claim title to land by prescription in Guyana on the grounds that squatting is an offence. This part of the decision of the Land Court in *Cole v Eccles Ramsburg District Council* is therefore illustrative of the subtle pitfalls that await Guyanese lawyers trying to apply precedents from common law jurisdictions in the context of Roman–Dutch land law.

As mentioned previously, in 1960 the Land Registry Act[48] abolished the Roman–Dutch law relating to servitudes with respect to lands governed by that enactment. Part VII of that Act makes provision for the acquisition of registered title by adverse possession and Part VIII provides for the registration of easements, restrictive covenants and other rights and interests. Part IV of the Act provides for both the systematic registration of land in declared registration areas and the sporadic registration of parcels of land outside of registration areas. Moreover, even within registration areas, it is not mandatory to bring land within the system of land registration, as provision is made for the annotation of the parcel number on the existing deed and the recording in the parcel folio in the land register of the fact that the parcel is unregistered land and a cross reference to the transport deed for the land registered in the Deeds Registry.[49] Hence, the landscape of Guyana is now covered with a patchwork of Roman–Dutch servitudes and common law easements and restrictive covenants, depending on the nature of the title documents to the dominant and servient land.

---

45   *McPhail v Persons Unknown* (1973) Ch. 447, 456 B.

46   MJ Goodman, 'Adverse Possession of Land – Morality and Motive' (1970) 33 Modern Law Review 281.

47   Cap.60:02, s3.

48   Cap.5:02, s3(1).

49   ibid, ss30 and 33. This expedient was adopted because Guyanese believe that Roman–Dutch transport deeds, which must be executed 'in the face of the Court', provide a very secure form of title and few were initially prepared to accept registered Certificates of Title instead.

Amerindian Lands

In the Commonwealth Caribbean context, Guyana at 83,000 square miles (215,000 sq km) is a large country, comparable in size to Ireland or Austria,[50] with a relatively small resident population of about 750,000 persons,[51] or less than 10 persons per square mile (3.5/sq km). However, even this figure is misleading, as some 90 per cent of the population live and work in the towns and farmlands on the coastlands, which constitute about 10 per cent of the country's land area. As observed by VS Naipaul on his first visit there, 'For most Guianese the coast is Guiana; everything beyond is bush ... And so it is.'[52] This situation has not changed much in the ensuing 50 years. In the interior, the population density falls to less than 1.25 persons per square mile (0.5/sq km)[53] and the nine distinct indigenous Amerindian groups,[54] who together constitute less than 10 per cent of the national population, comprise the majority of the resident population of the tropical forests and savannahs.[55] Apart from its forest resources, which have been commercially exploited from the earliest years of the colonial era, the interior is rich in mineral resources,[56] especially gold and diamonds which both occur as alluvial deposits in and along the rivers and creeks that traditionally serve as communication routes within the interior and near which Amerindian villages are most often sited.

By an amendment made in 2003, the Constitution of Guyana now declares that 'Indigenous people shall have the right to the protection, preservation and promulgation of their languages, cultural heritage and way of life'.[57] This is backed up by the establishment of an Indigenous Peoples' Commission whose task

50   Equivalent to the States of Minnesota, Utah, Idaho or Kansas in the USA, or in Canada to the Provinces of New Brunswick and Prince Edward Island combined.

51   A large number of Guyanese live abroad. The growth of the population slowed as a result of emigration after Independence in 1966 and actually fell in the 1980s, at the height of the PNC dictatorship. Since the restoration of democracy in 1992, the population has gradually built back up to the level it had attained in 1980. It is claimed that there is at least one Guyanese living abroad for every person in Guyana.

52   VS Naipaul, *The Middle Passage* (Penguin Books 1969) 103.

53   This figure has been calculated based on the geographic size and population of Regions 1, 7, 8 and 9.

54   The Akawaio, Arawak, Arecuna, Carib, Machushi, Patamona, Wai Wai, Wapishana and Warrau.

55   International Human Rights Clinic, Human Rights Program, *All That Glitters: Gold Mining In Guyana, The Failure of Government Oversight and the Human Rights of Amerindian Communities* (Harvard Law School March 2007) 2.

56   Guyana lies on the northern flank of the Guiana Shield, a geologically ancient mineral rich region which stretches from Brazil to Venezuela, through French Guiana, Suriname and Guyana.

57   Art. 149G of the Constitution of the Cooperative Republic of Guyana, as amended by Act 10 of 2003. This Article is within Part II Title I of the constitution which deals with Protection of the Fundamental Rights and Freedoms of the Individual.

it is 'to enhance the status of indigenous peoples and respond to their legitimate demands and needs'.[58] The specific functions assigned to the Commission include promoting and protecting the rights of indigenous people and promoting their empowerment.[59] Although this can possibly be read into phrases such as 'preservation of their way of life' and 'legitimate demands', the lack of express reference to the land rights of the indigenous people of Guyana is conspicuous in its absence from these provisions of the constitution. Nevertheless Amerindian land rights are a significant and contentious issue for Guyana, both domestically and internationally.

At the 1965 British Guiana Independence Conference, the Government of Guyana undertook to grant legal ownership or rights of occupancy over areas where Amerindian communities were ordinarily resident or settled, and other legal rights, such as rights of passage, in respect of other lands where Amerindians by tradition or custom de facto enjoyed freedoms and permissions corresponding to rights of that nature. Consequently, in 1966 an Amerindian Lands Commission (ALC) was established by the Amerindian Lands Commission Act,[60] to implement that decision and determine the areas referred to with as much particularity as practicable, and the nature and extent of the rights which the Amerindians de facto enjoyed in respect of those areas; to make recommendations regarding whether grants should be made and the nature of the rights to be granted, as well as to whom and subject to what terms and conditions land should be vested; and to determine what other freedoms and permissions should be granted. It is evident from the language of the Act that in 1966 the Government did not regard the Amerindians as having any de jure claims of right to or over the lands they used and occupied in Guyana.

In their 1969 report, the ALC identified 128 large and small Amerindian communities; of these 116 made requests for land titles, but the ALC also made recommendations for the other 12 communities. In all the indigenous people laid claim to some 43,000 square miles (111,370 sq km), just over half of the country. Most of these claims were rejected by the ALC as 'excessive', but the areas allocated by the ALC totalled 24,000 square miles (62,160 sq km) or just less than 30 per cent of the land area of Guyana.[61] In 1976 individual land titles were granted to the residents of eight Amerindian communities, because of the high degree of alienation, and communal titles were conferred on 65 Amerindian Villages and Districts by the Amerindian Act.[62] In 1991 titles were conferred by State grant on 12 other communities who had not been granted titles in 1976 because of a proposed

---

58   ibid, Art.212S.

59   ibid, Art.212T.

60   Cap.59:03 [Revised Laws 2010].

61   A Bulkan, 'Amerindian Land Rights: Is the "Struggle for Equality" Really Over?' (2002) 3(1) Guyana Law Review 30–57, 40.

62   Cap.29:01 [Revised Laws 1973].

hydro-electric project on the upper Mazaruni River which never materialized.[63] Under the Amerindian Act all rights, title and interest of the State in and over the lands situated within the boundaries of the 65 named Amerindian Villages and Districts, the general boundaries of which were described in the Schedule to the Act, were vested in their respective Amerindian Councils for and on behalf of the Amerindian communities by operation of law, with the exception of rivers, land within 66 feet of the mean low water mark, minerals or mining rights, airfields and existing State-owned structures.[64]

As a result of continuing Amerindian concern about the insecurity of their titles to the lands vested in them by the Amerindian Act, during the 1990s the Government of Guyana embarked upon a programme, which is still ongoing, of having the geographical boundaries of these Amerindian Villages and Districts accurately surveyed and title documents issued under the State Lands Act.[65] Such State land grants recite that the lands granted to the Amerindian communities have been occupied by them from time immemorial;[66] however, as noted by Matthews Glenn, the very existence of this process casts doubt on the nature of the Amerindian communities' title to such lands.[67] Indeed, in response to criticisms of the new Amerindian Act 2006,[68] arising out of the judgment in recent litigation over the exercise of mining rights under Amerindian lands,[69] the drafter of that legislation stated that 'Many critics of the Amerindian Act seem unaware that State lands are owned by the State, not by any Amerindian community. There is not, and never has been, any such thing as ancestral or traditional lands in Guyana'.[70] This opinion undoubtedly reflects the State's position on the question of Amerindian title, which is generally accepted in Guyana as reflected in the constitutional amendments concerning Amerindian rights made in 2003, but is contested by

---

63   C Toppin-Allahar, *A Report on Forest Law and Policy* (Guyana Forestry Commission and UK Overseas Development Administration November 1995) 14.

64   Cap.29:01, s22.

65   Cap.62:01 [Revised Laws 2010].

66   For example, the 1991 State Land Grant to the Arau Village Council quoted in *Arau Village Council* case (n73) 3.

67   Matthews Glenn (n8) 18.

68   Act No.6 of 2006.

69   *Chang v Guyana Geology & Mines Commission & Isseneru Village Council*, oral judgment of Justice Diane Insanally, delivered 17 January 2013.

70   M Janki, Director, Justice Institute Guyana, 'The Grant of land to Amerindian communities is made under the State Lands Act not the Amerindian Act' Letter to the Editor, *Stabroek News*, 10 March 2013. Accessible at: <http://www.stabroeknews.com/2013/opinion/letters/03/10/-> accessed 10 March 2013.

Amerindian non-governmental organizations, notably the Amerindian People's Association (APA), and their international partners[71] and Guyanese supporters.[72]

In 2009, *Devroy Thomas & The Arau Village Council v The Attorney General of Guyana & The Guyana Geology and Mines Commission*,[73] the first case of a claim of indigenous title to land based on the occupation of land from time immemorial by Amerindians, was decided by the High Court of Guyana.[74] The facts in this case are that the Arau Village Council had received a grant of State land in 1991; however, the Arau village was not situated within the area granted to them, but on adjacent land. The Guyana Geology and Mines Commission (GGMC) had issued concessions for mining activities on several blocks of land outside the titled area, but in the vicinity of the area where the Amerindian village was actually located, to which the Amerindian community was objecting on the grounds that these mining activities were taking place on their ancestral lands. The trial judge accused the Amerindian community of trying to 'blow hot and cold' for having accepted a grant of State lands on the basis of occupation from time immemorial then claiming another area on the same grounds, but he went on to consider at length the salient question as to whether the Arau community had any proprietary or occupational right to the area of land in contention. After brief observations (devoid of reference to any evidence or authority) about the status of Amerindians' land rights under Dutch rule, the impact of cession to the British and the abolition of Roman–Dutch law, the judge embarked on a lengthy discussion of the common law jurisprudence with respect to indigenous title, and eventually dismissed the claim to indigenous title on the basis of a lack of concrete evidence of occupation of the area by the Arau community from time immemorial and of their customary laws and practices in relation to land tenure.[75]

---

71   The Forest Peoples Programme. See <http://www.forestpeoples.org/sites/fpp/files/publication/2013/02/urgent-communicationakawaioissenerukakoguyanafeb2013.pdf. > accessed 10 March 2013.

72   Notably, Dr Janet Bulkan formerly of the Amerindian Research Unit, University of Guyana. See 'The Protection for Amerindian Rights in the Laws of Guyana – the Case of Isseneru Amerindian Village', *Stabroek News*, In the Diaspora Column, 4 February 2013. <http://www.stabroeknews.com/2013/features/02/04/-> accessed 10 March 2013; and 'Kako people entirely within their constitutional rights to resist the issue of mining concessions over their lands', Stabroek News, 27 March 2013. <http://www.stabroeknews. com/2013/opinion/letters/03/27/-> accessed 16 April 2013.

73   High Court Civil Action No. 166-M 2007.

74   Judgment of Justice Ian Chang, Acting Chief Justice, 30 April 2009 [Unreported].

75   ibid, 33. The judge then turned to consider whether the constitutional rights of the Amerindian community had been violated. After finding that the Amerindian way of life involves communal usufructuary uses of the forests, rivers and creeks, which would be *sui generis* property rights existing as burden on the legal and beneficial title of the State to the land, he concluded that the Arau people's property rights under Art. 142 of the constitution had not in fact been infringed. However, he found that, Art. 142G affords protection against the impairment of lands occupied by Amerindians to the extent that such lands are essential

With respect to the situation under Dutch rule, the effect of cession and the abolition of Roman–Dutch law, the judge stated that, although the Dutch colonial administration made a deliberate effort to prevent dispossession of the indigenous people by settlers, they never gave de jure recognition to any indigenous sovereign right or system of customary law; hence, when the British acquired sovereignty, indigenous customary rights survived the act of cession, but only as de facto rights. Although private property rights existing before 1803 were specifically preserved by the Articles of Capitulation, this only applied to de jure rights and all property for which no subject could show legal title became Crown land.[76] Turning to the effect of the Civil Law Act, the judge opined that because the feudal concept of allodial ownership has never been part of the law of immoveable property in Guyana, the Crown was the *absolute* owner of all lands other than privately-owned lands, but with the introduction of the English common law in 1917 the courts became bound to recognize rights which are recognized by the English common law, even if they are not derived from the common law. Hence, he concluded, 'In so far as the English common law gives recognition to native rights and interests in and over land, the courts [of Guyana] must view such rights as de jure and not de facto.'[77]

The main pitfall in this analysis is that the common law doctrine of indigenous title is based upon the equitable principle of constitutional common law that colonization per se did not destroy indigenous rights to land[78] and recognition that, under common law, the Crown/State's title to unalienated land is not an absolute, beneficial title.[79] As explained by McPherson – referring to aboriginal title claims in Australia:

> Current legal theory is that the ultimate or 'radical title' to all land over which sovereignty is asserted, *which is not to be equated with beneficial ownership*, is vested in the Crown subject to the rights of the native owners or occupiers, which continue to subsist as a burden on that title until validly extinguished by legislation or by surrender to the Crown … *Considered from the perspective of the common law, recognition of the rights of indigenous people in the soil*

---

to their way of life, even if no 'native rights' in or over such lands are established. Hence, he granted a declaration that the Respondents had a constitutional duty to ensure that mining activities did not adversely impact the usufructuary value of the land and affect the Arau people's way of life.

76   On this point, the judge cited statements made by Ramsahoye (n5) 113, and the Australian case of *Williams v A,G of New South Wales* (1915) CLR 409, quoted by Ramsahoye, which are no longer regarded as good law, to show that the Crown is the absolute owner of all land from first settlement.

77   Judgment of Justice Ian Chang (n74).

78   B Slattery, 'Understanding Aboriginal Rights' (1987) 66 Canadian Bar Review 727, 736–740.

79   *Mabo and Others v Queensland (No .2)* (1992) 175 Commonwealth Law Reports 1, per Brennan, 69.

rests upon their continuing possession of it from the time when sovereignty and radical title was first asserted by the Crown ... Attempting to define native title in terms of English law conceptions of interests in land is erroneous. It is now correctly regarded as *sui generis* and as extending to all rights of the indigenous inhabitants in land, whether community, group or individual, possessed under traditional laws and customs ... *it operates as a burden on the radical title capable of being extinguished* only by surrender to the Crown, or by some form of sovereign act showing a clear intention to do so, ... *but not by the bare act of acquiring territorial sovereignty or radical title to the land.* [Emphasis added] [80]

As noted by Slattery, the Crown's ultimate title to the soil 'flowed from the feudal character of the British constitution, whereby the Crown was not only sovereign but the ultimate landlord. Once a British court recognized the assertion of sovereignty, it also attributed to the Crown a *notional title* to the lands claimed'.[81] However, although both feudal obligations and land held allodially were known to Roman–Dutch law in the Netherlands,[82] even in the early stages of the Dutch colonization of Guyana there was never a feudal relationship between *patroons*[83] and a higher authority, and Dutch land grants in Guyana conveyed full ownership.[84] With the preservation of Roman–Dutch law and Dutch colonial constitutional arrangement[85] by the Articles of Capitulation in 1803[86] and the continuance in force of Roman–Dutch land law by the Civil Law Act in 1917,[87] including an express provision preserving full ownership of immovable property,[88] there can be no doubt that this feudal principle has never been part of the land law of Guyana and the State does not hold an ultimate or radical title to private land in Guyana, whether the title stems from Dutch or British colonial land grants or land grants issued after independence.

What then of the unalienated lands to which the State lays claim as the successor in title to the Crown? Under the English common law, the Crown's claim to ownership of all 'vacant' or 'waste' land in the colonies, by virtue of territorial sovereignty, also stems from the feudal rights of the monarch as lord

---

80   McPherson (n7) 53, 54 and 55.

81   Slattery (n78) 742.

82   The former being subject to feudal law which was administered in the feudal courts and the latter to the ordinary principles of the Roman–Dutch common law administered in the ordinary courts.

83   Leaders of the Dutch settlements.

84   Ramsahoye (n5) 146.

85   This 'constitutional anomaly' continued in being until 1928 when British Guiana became a Crown Colony. See Menezes (n2) 5 and 7–12.

86   ibid, 7.

87   See (n9).

88   ibid, s3(d)(i).

paramount.[89] It is evident from the Civil Law Act, that prior to 1917 the nature of the Royal Prerogative as enjoyed by the British Crown in Guyana was determined by Roman–Dutch law;[90] hence, unless this is also the position under Roman–Dutch law, it cannot be assumed that in British Guiana the Crown had beneficial ownership of all 'vacant' or 'waste' land, including lands occupied by Amerindians, simply by virtue of British territorial sovereignty. Further, if at cession the Crown did acquire all unalienated land by virtue of the Dutch Royal Prerogative, was the Crown's ownership of that land under Roman–Dutch law absolute? If it was absolute, indigenous 'title' per se cannot co-exist with the State's absolute beneficial title, other than as a dismemberment of ownership; hence, occupation from time immemorial could at best confer on Amerindians only a lesser real right in the land. Bearing in mind that usufructuary rights were impliedly abolished in Guyana by the Civil Law Act, is indigenous 'title' capable of existing as a *sui generis* real right, analogous to a public servitude,[91] burdening the State's absolute title to the land? And, if the Crown's title was not absolute, what then is the nature of indigenous title? Based on the available scholarly literature and decided cases from Suriname and South Africa, it appears that there is a divergence of legal opinion on these points.

In Suriname, the State's claim to absolute ownership of all unalienated land is based on the so-called 'domain principle' set out in the L-Decrees,[92] relatively

---

89   McPherson (n7) 66.

90   Cap.6:01, s.22, provides that, 'Except as specifically enacted, nothing in this Act contained shall be deemed to limit or restrict the royal prerogative as hitherto enjoyed by the British Crown under the Roman–Dutch law of Guyana, and except as aforesaid that prerogative shall as from the date aforesaid [1 January 1917] comprehend all the pre-eminence and all the special dignities, liberties, privileges, and powers conferred on the Crown by the common law of England.' The phrases 'except as specifically enacted/aforesaid' appear to be a cross reference to s5(6) substituting the passing of immovable property to the Crown as *bona vacantia* (in the absence of persons entitled to succeed in cases of intestacy) 'in lieu of any right to escheat'.

91   A public servitude is a servitude (equivalent to a common law easement in gross) that grants certain rights in favour of the public at large or some class of indeterminate individuals over a particular immoveable property. It is interesting to note that in the Richtersveld case (n111), as an alternative to their claim to indigenous title, the plaintiffs applied for a declaration that the Richtersveld people held a public servitude over the land acquired by immemorial use, which entitled them to exclusive beneficial occupation and use of the land.

92   There were 7 L-Decrees made in 1982. L-1, Decree on the Principles of Land Policy; L-2, Decree on the Issuance of Domain Land,; L-3 Decree on the Legal Position of Land Issued before 1 July 1982; L-4 Decree on the Land Chamber; L-5 Decree on the Development Corporation Suriname; L-6 Decree on Penalizing Squatting; and L-7 Decree on Amendment of the Stamp Act. Decree L-8, Decree Against Illegal Subdivision, was made in 1984. Buursink International Consultants in association with Wisconsin Land Tenure Centre, *Proposal for Suriname Land Management Project: Diagnosis of Land Management Issues* (Ministry of Natural Resources, Republic of Suriname May 2002) 11.

recent legislation made by Presidential decree in 1982, during the military dictatorship. As stated therein, the domain principle is that 'All land to which others have not proven their right of ownership, is the domain of the State'.[93] Opinion amongst Surinamese and Dutch experts as to whether this is simply a codification of the Roman–Dutch common law or new law is divided. In the opinion of Quintus Bosz,[94] the domain principle has always been the basis of land law in Suriname. If various Dutch Governors refused to incorporate it into colonial legislation, this was because it was never in dispute.[95] This opinion is assumed to be correct by van Velthuizen,[96] who points out that this principle has also been incorporated into the 1987 constitution.[97] However, Quintus Bosz' view is vigorously contested by Kambel and McKay,[98] who contend that it does not correspond with the historical evidence.[99] Further, they rely on the opinion of Professor E. H. s'Jacob on national domain and Indonesian customary law[100] to argue that the effect of Article 1 of Decree L-1 is simply to reverse the burden of proving its title to land imposed on the State by Article 576 of the Civil Code, which has always provided that 'lands and immovable property which are unmanaged and have no owner ... belong to the State'.[101]

---

93   Decreet L-1 Beginselen Grondbelied (Decree on the Principles of Land Policy) SB 1982 no.10 e.v., Art. 1.

94   Reference is made to the opinion of Professor Quintus Bosz by both T van Velthuizen, *The Land Rights of the Indigenous Peoples and Descendants of the Maroons in Suriname* (Paramaribo 2008), and ER Kambel and F McKay, *The Rights of Indigenous Peoples and Maroons in Suriname* (International Work Group for Indigenous Affairs 1999) however, it appears that his writings on the subject are not available in English.

95   The view that, before the British occupation of the Cape Colony, the Crown remained the owner of all land until a grant of absolute title had been made to another, is shared by the South African scholars Botha and Nathan quoted by the Land Claims Court in the first *Richtersveld* case, (n111), s43, but it is admitted therein that this view is not shared by all South African scholars.

96   van Velthuizen (n94) 24–28.

97   This appears to be a reference to Art.41 of the 1987 Constitution of the Republic of Suriname, which provides that 'Natural riches and resources are property of the nation and shall be used to promote economic, social and cultural development. The nation has the inalienable right to take complete possession of its natural resources in order to utilize them to the benefit of the economic, social and cultural development of Suriname'.

98   Kambel and McKay (n94) 88.

99   One of the critical pieces of historical evidence on which their argument relies is Art. 14 of the 1629 *Ordre van Regieringe* (Order of Government) that applied to all Dutch colonies in the West Indies, including Essequibo, Demerara and Berbice, which provides that 'the Spaniards, Portuguese and Naturals of the land who subject themselves to the government and obedience of the Lords States General will keep their *ingenios*, lands and houses and other goods and will remain free and protected in the free possession and use thereof ...'.

100   Jacob, EH *Landsdomein en Adat Recht* (Kemink en Zoon 1945).

101   Kambel and McKay (n94) 89.

Kambel and McKay conclude that, in Suriname, the State only has absolute ownership (*BW-eigendom*)[102] of land that belongs to its *private domain*, as the English and Dutch acquired only public law rights over lands occupied by the indigenous people, so that these areas are part of the *public domain* of the State.[103] A similar distinction between State land in the private and public domain is also to be found in the civil law[104] and has a parallel in Scottish law [105] which implies that the public trust doctrine[106] could be applicable to such lands. In 2007 an indigenous community in Suriname succeeded in obtaining a ruling in the Inter-American Court of Human Rights[107] that its right to property under Article 21[108]

---

102   BW stands for the Surinamese Civil Code (*Suirnaams Burgerlijk Wetboek*) of 1860. The BW provides for two types of land title, private property (*privé or 'BW' eigendom*) and 75-year leases (*erfpacht*), which appear to be the equivalent of emphyteutic leases in Roman and civil law. Prior to the introduction of the BW, and continuing until 1937, when provision for implementing the relevant provisions of the BW was made by the Agrarian Law, land was issued by both the British and the Dutch colonial governments on conditional grants of a kind unknown to Dutch law. Such land, which forms the majority of alienated land in Suriname, is called allodial property (*allodiaal eigendom*). A new form of title, the 40-year land lease (*grondhuur*) was created by the L-Decrees in 1982. These are the only legal forms of real title in Suriname, as simple tenancies (*hurr*) and use rights (*gebruik tot wederopzegging*) are personal rights. See: Buursink (n92).

103   Kambel and McKay (n94) 39 and 88.

104   The French Civil Code in force in French Guiana (Cayenne), like the Civil Codes in Belgium and many other countries, makes a distinction between State land in the private domain (which may be alienated, or otherwise dealt with by the State, and is susceptible to prescriptive acquisition) and State land in the public domain (which has no commercial properties and cannot be alienated or acquired by prescription), special legislation being required to transfer land from the public to the private domain. See: R Dekkers, *Précis de droit civil Belge* (É. Bruylant 1954–1955) Vol.1, Bk.2, Tit.1, Ch.1 '*Biens nationaux*', s791 *et seq*.

105   According to Erskine's *Institute of the Law of Scotland* (Bell and Bradfute 1824), under Scottish law the *res publicæ* of Roman law are known as *inter reglia* (things appropriated to the sovereign) and 'the King's right to them is truly no more than a trust for the behoof of his people.' The regalia were divided into '*regalia minora*', rights of which the Crown could dispose, and the '*regalia majora*', including forests, not alienable by the Crown without the consent of Parliament. Provisions were made to save this aspect of Scottish law when the Abolition of Feudal Tenure, etc (Scotland) Act was enacted in 2000.

106   LVM Bento, 'Searching for Intergenerational Green Solutions: The Relevance of the Public Trust Doctrine to Environmental Preservation' (2009) 11 Common Law Review 7; Available at <www.commonlawreview.cz.> accessed 22 February 2011.

107   *Case of the Saramaka People v Suriname*, Judgment of November 28, 2007, Series C-185, s87–116. The Saramaka are one of the six Maroon peoples of Suriname (formerly known as 'Bush Negroes') descended from escaped African slaves, who comprise 10 per cent of the population of Suriname and are now regarded as indigenous people. The indigenous Amerindian peoples of Suriname comprise less than 4 per cent of the population.

108   Art. 21 establishes, *inter alia*, that: '1. Everyone has the right to the use and enjoyment of his property. The law may subordinate such use and enjoyment to the

of the American Convention on Human Rights has been violated by the State, because Suriname's domestic law does not recognize the communal property rights of its indigenous communities as de jure rights, but the judgment does not address the issue of the nature of the State's title to the land in question.

The issue of the applicability of the doctrine of indigenous title to South Africa received some examination by academic writers[109] before a claim to indigenous title first arose in the *Richtersveld* case. This case concerned a claim by the inhabitants of four villages within the Richtersveld Reserve for restitution of their rights to ancestral lands outside the Reserve, under the Restitution of Land Rights Act, No. 22 of 1994. This Act provides for the restoration of the land rights of any community dispossessed of a right in land, including a customary law interest in land, after 15 June 1913,[110] as a result of racially discriminatory laws or practices. In 1920, a decade before the establishment of the Richtersveld Reserve, alluvial deposits of diamonds were discovered on the subject land, which the colonial government considered to be unalienated Crown lands, and the Government awarded claims for diggings from 1926 onwards. In 1994, the Government of South Africa granted the land, including all mineral rights, to Alexkor Limited a wholly State-owned mining corporation. In 1998, the Richtersveld community applied for restitution of the land based on ownership by appropriation, or alternatively indigenous title to the land, or alternatively a right acquired by beneficial occupation of the land for more than 10 years before the date of their eventual dispossession.[111]

At first instance, the Land Claims Court (LCC) held that the Richtersveld community constituted a community for the purposes of the Act and had beneficially occupied the subject land for a continuous period of not less than 10 years prior to its dispossession after 19 June 1913; but the community had failed to prove that this dispossession was the result of discriminatory laws or practices. Additionally, the LCC held that it did not have jurisdiction to develop the common law so as to realize the doctrine of indigenous title in South Africa.[112] On appeal, the Supreme Court of Appeal (SCA) overturned that judgment.[113] Finding that the Richtersveld community had been in exclusive possession of the whole of the

---

interest of society. 2. No one shall be deprived of his property except upon payment of just compensation, for reasons of public utility or social interest, and in the cases and according to the forms established by law.'

109   TW Bennett, 'Redistribution of Land and the Doctrine of Aboriginal Title in South Africa' (1993) 9 S. Afr. J. on Hum. Rts. 443; TW Bennett and CH Powell, 'Aboriginal Title in South Africa Revisited' (1999) 15 S. Afr. J on Hum. Rts. 449.

110   The date on which the Native Land Act, No. 27 of 1913, the first of the laws called the pillars of apartheid, came into force.

111   *Richtersveld Community & Others v Alexkor Limited & Another* (2001) (3) SA 1293 (LCC), s6.

112   ibid, s44–47.

113   *Richtersveld Community & Others v Alexkor Limited & Another* (2003) (6) BCLR 583 (SCA).

Richtersveld prior to and after its annexation by the British in 1847, it held that the community had rights to the subject land (including minerals and precious stones) that constituted a customary law interest as defined in the Act, the substantive content of that interest being a right to exclusive beneficial occupation and use, akin to that held under Roman–Dutch common law ownership. As respects the doctrine of indigenous title, the court observed that:

> All aspects of the doctrine do not fit comfortably into our [Roman–Dutch] common law. For instance, the idea that the State or Crown possesses radical title to all land may have its origin in English feudal laws and be foreign to our law. In view of [the] conclusion that a customary law interest, for which the law expressly provides, has been established in the present case, it is not necessary to pursue the matter any further and it becomes unnecessary to decide whether the doctrine forms part of our common law or whether our common law should be developed to recognize [indigenous] rights.[114]

Alexkor Limited then appealed to the Constitutional Court (CC), which accepted jurisdiction to decide the case because the Restitution of Land Rights Act was enacted in 1994 to implement specific provisions of the interim constitution of 1993.[115] Based on specific provisions of the South African Constitution, the court held that indigenous law (African customary law) is now part of the South African legal system.[116] The court then upheld the decision of the SCA that the Richtersveld community had title to the land prior to annexation and that this title had survived annexation, and they departed from the decision of the SCA only with respect to the characterization of the title that the Richtersveld community had prior to annexation. As stated by the court:

> We are of the view that the real character of the title that the Richtersveld community possessed in the subject land was a right of communal ownership under indigenous law. The content of that right included the right to exclusive

---

114   ibid, s43.

115   *Alexcor Limited v Richtersveld Community* (2004) (5) SA 469 (CC).

116   As stated by the court, 'While in the past indigenous law was seen through the common law lens, it must now be seen as an integral part of our law. Like all law it depends for its ultimate force and validity on the Constitution. Its validity must be determined not by reference to the common law, but to the Constitution. … [T]he Constitution acknowledges the originality and distinctiveness of indigenous law as an independent source of norms within the legal system. At the same time the Constitution, while giving force to indigenous law makes it clear that such law is subject to the Constitution and has to be interpreted in light of its values. Furthermore, like the common law, indigenous law is subject to any legislation consistent with the Constitution that deals specifically with it. In the result, indigenous law feeds into, nourishes, fuses with and becomes part of the amalgam of South African law.' ibid, s51.

occupation and use of the land by members of the community. The community had the right to use its water, to use its land for grazing and hunting and to exploit its natural resources, above and beneath the surface. It follows therefore that prior to annexation the Richtersveld community has a right of ownership in the subject land under indigenous law.[117]

Although the ultimate decision in the Richtersveld case is based upon specific statutory and constitutional provisions expressly referring to customary law, rather than on Roman–Dutch legal principles,[118] some of the dicta in the judgments of the South African courts in this litigation are applicable to Guyana. Of particular note is the following passage from the judgment of the SCA in which the court cast doubt on the validity under Roman–Dutch law of the proposition that all unalienated land belongs to the Crown/State, and held that the enactment of the Crown Lands Acts was not effective to extinguish the Richtersveld community's prior interest in the land:

> The LCC held that in terms of the law in force in the Cape Colony at the time of annexation all land not granted under some form of tenure belonged to the Crown … This view, no doubt, is based upon English feudal law and to the extent that Roman–Dutch law had some remnants of feudal law, that law was never introduced in South Africa. In support of this finding the LCC held further that the Colonial government made laws under which non-issued land (considered to be Crown land) could be disposed of … At best for them it can be said that the Legislature assumed that all land not allocated by means of the grant of title deeds belonged to the Crown, but the implied assumption cannot be elevated to a legislative act with that consequence.[119]

Several cases concerning Amerindian lands are currently before the courts of Guyana; hence, it would be premature to predict the eventual outcome of Amerindian claims to indigenous title in Guyana; however, it is arguable that in the absence of constitutional recognition of Amerindian land rights in Guyana, the continuation in force of Roman–Dutch land law should to be taken into account in the application of the common law doctrine of indigenous title to Guyana. As McPherson warns:

> It is wrong to suppose from what has been said about native title in settled colonies that English conceptions of land law were received or superimposed on all territories under British rule … The common law travelled across the world, but did not carry all of its baggage everywhere it went.[120]

---

117   ibid, s62.
118   G Pinaar, 'The Methodology Used to Interpret Customary Land Tenure' (2012) 15(3) *Potchefstroom Elektroniese Regsblad/ Potchefstroom Electronic Law Journal* 153, 168.
119   ibid, s63–66.
120   McPherson (n7) 57.

Conclusion

In her 2008 paper on mixed jurisdictions in the Commonwealth Caribbean, Professor Matthews Glenn rightly predicted that the doctrine of aboriginal rights, implying as it does the recognition of the customary law of indigenous peoples alongside the formal legal system, would emerge as another form of legal mixture in Guyana.[121] Actually, as the foregoing look at the law relating to servitudes and indigenous title illustrates, at this point calling the land law of Guyana a 'mixture' is generous – 'muddle' might be a far more appropriate word! Certainly, like Guyanese society. the present legal mixture resembles a melting pot more than a mosaic. Apart from the facts that Roman–Dutch law has withered at the root and that the Guyanese branch was severed from the thriving branches long ago, the major factors accounting for the endangered status of Roman–Dutch law in Guyana have been the structure of the judicial system and the influence of legal education in common law jurisdictions on Guyanese legal practitioners.

During the colonial era, the Judicial Committee of the Privy Council was the final court of appeal from Guyana, like other British Commonwealth countries. Although composed of Law Lords drawn from the House of Lords, the UK's court of last resort, the Privy Council had to handle appeals from all three jurisdictions in the Commonwealth with a heritage of Roman–Dutch law until 1950, when South Africa withdrew.[122] Guyana remained subject to the jurisdiction of the Privy Council after attaining independence in 1966, but terminated the right of appeal to the Privy Council when it became a republic in 1970. From 1970 until 2005, when Guyana acceded to the appellate jurisdiction of the Caribbean Court of Justice (CCJ) established in 2001, the local Guyana Court of Appeal was the court of last resort. Although the three non-Common law jurisdictions in CARICOM[123] subscribe to the original jurisdictions of the CCJ,[124] and there is a Dutch jurist on the CCJ,[125] none of these countries yet subscribes to the appellate jurisdiction of the CCJ; moreover, they are all civilian jurisdictions. Hence, Guyana's court of last resort remains a body dominated by judges schooled and practiced in the

---

121   Matthews Glenn (n68) 17.

122   Despite attaining independence as a Dominion within the Commonwealth in 1948, Sri Lanka (formerly Ceylon), the third former British colony where Roman–Dutch law was preserved, did not withdraw from the jurisdiction of the Privy Council until it became a republic in 1972.

123   Haiti, Saint Lucia and Suriname.

124   In its original jurisdiction the CCJ is an international court that interprets the revised Treaty of Chaguaramas which established CARICOM.

125   Justice Jacob Wit, formerly a judge of the Joint Court of Justice of Aruba and the Netherlands Antilles. See: <http://www.caribbeancourtofjustice.org/about-the-ccj/judges/wit> accessed 28 January 2014.

common law who, with the exception of the eminent Guyanese judge on the CCJ,[126] would have little or no knowledge of Roman–Dutch law.

Until recently the members of the Bar and Bench of Guyana[127] were trained abroad in common law jurisdictions in the UK and Caribbean. Before the Law Faculty of the University of the West Indies (UWI) was established in Barbados in 1970, all lawyers in the region had to obtain British qualifications as solicitors or barristers. From 1970 until 1993, when a full law degree progamme was established at the University of Guyana (UG), Guyanese students could only take the first year of UWI's Bachelor of Laws programme, which did not include the study of land law, at UG. Although the UG Department of Law now has a LLB degree programme, the only comprehensive text on the land laws of Guyana[128] is very dated and out of print, and both of the current text books on land or property law in the Commonwealth Caribbean make only passing reference to the Roman–Dutch law of Guyana (and the Civil Law of St. Lucia).[129] Hence, it remains to be seen whether the teaching of land law at UG will revitalize interest in and understanding of Roman–Dutch land law amongst legal practitioners in Guyana and help preserve it from extinction.

---

126   Justice Désirée Bernard, formerly the Chancellor of the Judiciary in Guyana. See: <http://www.caribbeancourtofjustice.org/about-the-ccj/judges/bernard> accessed 28 January 2014.

127   Including Justice Désirée Bernard ibid.

128   Ramsahoye (n5).

129   G Kodilinye, *Commonwealth Caribbean Property Law* (Cavendish 2006); S Owusu, *Commonwealth Caribbean Land Law* (Routledge Cavendish 2007).

Chapter 3
Philippines

In the Philippines, the industrial coloniser, the United States of America, replaced the feudal coloniser, Spain; and as Pacifico Agabin demonstrates, it is the role of the US judges, coupled with the shift to English language and the case-by-case injection of common law whereby the common law slowly strangled civil law concepts. These developments can be regarded as the explanatory factors for the endangerment of the civil law element in the Philippines. In this chapter the author introduces terms such as smothering, diluting, permeating, gradual and imperceptible, that have all been used to explain the process of this overtake by the common law, which Agabin regards generally as a phenomenon of the twentieth century. He also sees a connection with globalization and capitalism in the process of the common law winning over civil law. In fact he names the twentieth century as the 'common law's century'.

This endangerment of Philippines' status as a mixed legal system can definitely be tied to the triumph of the common law over the civilian tradition, thus this mixed legal system is, when the different elements that gave birth to it are weighed up, now more common law oriented. The process of this happening was gradual, almost imperceptible. The Civil Code was diluted and this hybrid was smothered. Earlier, Spanish law was transformed through the role of the US judges, and the US trained judges, who injected common law into civil law, using the case-by-case approach that overwhelmed the abstract principles of the civilian tradition. Later still, the fact that the 1950 Civil Code was in English and the overall shift from Spanish to English, appear to be the most important factors for the common law influence.

As Roman–Dutch law has withered in Guyana, so did Spanish law wither in the Philippines.

Philippines: 'The Twentieth Century as the Common Law's Century'

Pacifico A. Agabin

Introduction

In the Philippines, the last century was the common law's century. It was the legal system's good fortune that the period was dominated by *Pax Americana*, and the country was colonized by the US at the turn of the century. Before America's hegemony, much of the world was ruled by *Pax Britannia*, and, like its former colony, Britain wielded power also in the form of the common law. Law is essentially a function of power. When the world was ruled by *Pax Romana*, the Roman empire likewise imposed its law on its colonies. With the decline and fall of the Roman Empire in the West, the medieval world was ruled by *Pax Canonica*, as the power vacuum left by the Roman emperors was filled by the Papacy. The Islamic world, which stretched from the Atlantic to North Africa and to the Western Mediterranean down to the Indies and up to the Malay archipelago in the later medieval period, was governed by the *Sharia*.

Before the coming of the Americans, the Philippines, having been a Spanish colony for more than 300 years, was placed under the unadulterated civil law system of Spain. As early as 1530, the old compilations, *Fuero Juzgo*,[1] *Fuero Viejo*, *Fuero Real*, *Las Leyes de Toro*,[2] and the *Siete Partidas*,[3] were extended to the Philippines by the *Leyes de las Indias*. In 1567, the *Ordenamiento de Alcala* and *La Nueva Recopilacion*[4] were extended to the colony by the *Recopilacion de las Leyes de Indias*. On 8 September 1884 the Spanish Penal Code of 1870 was extended to the Philippines. Two years later, in 1888, the Spanish Code of Commerce of

---

1   Cited in *Legarda v Valdez* (1905) 1 Phil. Reports 148.

2   *Llorente v Rodriguez* (1904) 3 Phil. Reports 701; *Mijares v Nery* (1903) 3 Phil. Reports 197; *Ebreo v Sichon* (1905) 4 Phil. Reports 706; *Pineda v Gasataya* (1905) 5 Phil. Reports 140; *Araneta v Garrido* (1905) 5 Phil. Reports 139; *Capistrano v Gavino* (1907) 8 Phil. Reports 135; *Siguiong v Siguiong* (1907) 8 Phil. Reports 9; *Cosio v Pili* (1908) 10 Phil. Reports 72; *Matias v Alvarez* (1908) 10 Phil. Reports 402.

3   *Benedicto v De la Rama* (1906) 3 Phil. Reports 34; *Ker v Cauden*, 6 Phil. Reports 735.

4   *Orozco v Heirs of Henares* (1901) 1 Phil. Reports 77; *US v Mendezona* (1903) 2 Phil. Reports 377; *Mijares v Nery* (1903) (n2); *Benedicto v De la Rama* (1903) (n3).

1829, the *Ley de Enjuicimiento Civil*, *Ley de Enjuicimiento Criminal*, and the *Ley Provisional para la Aplicacion de las Disposiciones del Codigo Penal en las Islas Pilipinas* were also imposed on the Philippines. Finally, in July of 1889, the Spanish Civil Code, as well as the law on mortgages, on mines and minerals, on waters, on intellectual property, notarial law, railway law, code of military justice, and on administrative law and procedure, were extended to the Philippines.

The Spanish–American War: Birth of the Hybrid

When war broke out between the US and Spain in April 1898, Admiral George Dewey, whose small force was in Japan, was ordered to show the flag in the neighbourhood of the Philippines so as to catch the attention of the Spaniards in a diversion to the action in Cuba.[5] On 24 April 1898 the US Congress passed a resolution declaring war with Spain, and the Secretary of the Navy, with McKinley's approval, cabled Dewey, 'Proceed at once to the Philippines. Commence operations against the Spanish squadron. You must capture or destroy. Use utmost endeavors.'[6] After midnight on 1 May 1898, Dewey proceeded to the Philippines and destroyed the aging Spanish fleet after a mock two-hour battle. On 13 August 1898, the elements of the US Army captured Manila, and the following day, the commander of the army, General Wesley Merritt, proclaimed to the Filipinos that:

> The government established among you by the US Army is a government of military occupation, and, for the present, it is ordered that the municipal laws such as affect private rights of persons and property, regulate local institutions, and provide for the punishment of crime, shall be considered as continuing in force, so far as compatible with the purpose of the military government, and that they be administered through the ordinary courts substantially as before the occupation, but by officials appointed by the government of occupation.[7]

On 10 December 1898, the Treaty of Paris between the US and Spain was signed, granting independence to Cuba but making the Philippines, Guam and Puerto Rico American possessions. A military government, placed under the War Department of the US, was installed over the Philippines, which exercised executive, judicial and legislative power.[8] The military authorities issued General Orders re-establishing the Supreme Court of the Philippines Islands along the lines of the old Spanish *Real*

---

5   S Karnow, *In Our Image: America's Empire in the Philippines* (Pocketbook ed.1989) 95.

6   ibid, 102.

7   JP Laurel, 'What Lessons May Be Derived by the Philippine Islands From the Legal History of Louisiana' (Part Two) (1913) 2 Philippine Law Journal 63, 80.

8   E Root, *Report of the Secretary of War to the President* (Kindle e-book, first published 1901).

Audiencia, reopening of the courts of first instance, and providing for a new law on criminal procedure.[9] The American occupation threatened the survival of the newly-established Philippine revolutionary Government in 1899.

When the Philippine–American war erupted in Manila in February 1899, the responsibility for the governance of the Philippines was transferred from the State department to the War department. This department was headed by Elihu Root, a Harvard-trained lawyer, who was also transferred from the US State department to Secretary of War. At the time of his appointment as Secretary of War, the most urgent question was that of the administration of the new possessions, involving as it did the preservation of order and the substitution of an American system of government for the medieval systems which had prevailed for centuries under Spain.[10] One of his first official acts was to justify the expansionist policy of the US as regards the Philippines and, in the instructions he drafted for McKinley addressed to the Philippine Commission, which was the lawmaking body formed to govern the new colony, he emphasized that America would civilize the natives according to the standards of the US Constitution.[11] The War department, through Root, reminded the members of the Commission that certain principles of government are essential to the rule of law and the maintenance of freedom, and the natives must adhere to these standards for their own liberty and happiness.[12]

In 1901, the US Congress began to enact laws to govern the Philippines. The task of crafting the necessary legislation was given to Senator John Spooner, who looked at the acquisition of the Islands as 'one of the bitter fruits of war'.[13] He authored the Spooner Amendment, which created the principal organ of legislation and administration of the new colony: the Philippine Commission, composed of Filipino and American commissioners. In the same year, the military government was put to an end, and a civil government was instituted. When McKinley looked around for an honest and able figure to head the Second Philippine Commission, he chose William Howard Taft, who was then a federal judge in Ohio.

The role of William Howard Taft

Before William Howard Taft came to the Philippines in 1900 as Civil Governor, he had been trained, educated and worked as a judge in the common law tradition. Early in his career, he already carried the institutions of the common law as his intellectual baggage. He advocated judicial activism, the rule of law, independence of the judiciary and primacy of property rights. As a federal judge, he had

---

9   Laurel (n7) 81.

10   LA Coolidge, *Elihu Root, Secretary of War* (Kindle e-book 2012) 17–21.

11   Karnow (n5) 95, 170.

12   See McKinley's Instructions to the Second Philippine Commission, which was ratified by the US Congress on 1 July 1902. See MM Kalaw, *The Development of Philippine Politics 1872–1920* (Oriental Commercial 1926) 10.

13   Karnow (n5) 166.

established his credentials in the US as champion of property rights, critic of social democracy, and a believer of the role of the US Supreme Court as guardian of the rights of property through the instrument of judicial review.[14]

Taft was shrewd enough to see that the Philippines could never be developed as a market for American goods if there was bad blood between Americans and Filipinos. Taft therefore launched a policy of attraction in the Philippines: he attracted the elite, the *ilustrado* class, by perpetuating the feudal oligarchy or by holding out promises of liberal tariffs for Philippine agricultural exports to the US, or of public utility franchises; he attracted the middle class by promising government positions as municipal officers, provincial board members, members of the civil service and members of the colonial legislature. But, knowing the power of judicial review, he stopped giving out positions to Filipinos at the judiciary on the stated grounds that, 'It is the basis of all civil right and liberty, and no Filipino judiciary could have any adequate conception of what practical civil liberty is.'[15] Thus was born the policy of the colonial administrators which led to the wholesale importation of American judges bred and trained in the common law tradition.

The role of American judges

It is perhaps fortunate, from the viewpoint of the Philippine judiciary, that the military commander of the American forces in 1899 was Major General Elwell Otis, who graduated from Harvard Law School. Not only did he prescribe municipal elections so that the local officials would cooperate in the pacification campaign, he also renovated the Spanish-created judiciary, putting native magistrates in the trial courts, and he created the Supreme Court, placing Cayetano Arellano, a Filipino jurist, as the Chief Justice.[16] However, this policy of appointing native magistrates was reversed by Taft, who distrusted the Filipinos.

The new colonial masters soon appointed American judges at all levels of the Philippine judiciary, and they imported American statutes wholesale into the Philippines. The Americans superimposed common-law principles of judicial process on the existing civil-law tradition, and made sure that the former would prevail. Further, it was provided in the organic law of the Philippines that decisions of the Philippine Supreme Court might be reviewed by certiorari by the Federal Supreme Court of the US. In that environment, there was no escape from the grip of stare decisis, as the American judges had to look to American decisions for authorities, especially those in jurisdictions from where statutes were borrowed wholesale, as well as to decisions of the US Supreme Court.

The rules on interpretation of statutes used by American common law judges began to reshape the law of the land in the Philippines. When the provisions of

---

14   AT Mason, *William Howard Taft: Chief Justice* (Simon Schuster 1965) 15.

15   BS Salamanca, *The Filipino Reaction to American Rule, 1901–1913* (New Day Publishers 1984) 60.

16   Karnow (n5) 153.

a statute needed to be interpreted, all the techniques and guidelines followed in common-law courts were to be employed by the judges in an attempt to elicit the intent of the legislature. Philippine courts began to resort to American common-law jurisprudence to understand the meaning of the terms employed in the borrowed statutes. The same rules were even applied to statutes that dated back to the Spanish colonial period. By way of consolation to the civil law, the views of civilian commentators, text writers and Spanish courts were also sometimes consulted, at least during the first three years of the existence of the Supreme Court, from 1900 to 1903.

By 1935 the Philippine Supreme Court was dominated by Americans and justified its reliance on American authorities on the grounds that:

> ... many of the rules, principles, and doctrines of the common law have, to all intents and purposes, been imported into this jurisdiction, as a result of the enactment of new laws and the organization and establishment of new institutions by the Congress of the United States or under its authority; for it will be found that many of these laws can only be construed and applied through the aid of the common law from which they are derived, and that, to breathe the breath of life into many of these institutions, recourse must be had to the rules, principles and doctrines of the common law under whose protecting aegis the prototypes of these institutions had their birth.[17]

How did the common law effectively strangle the civilian system? Roscoe Pound provides the answer: 'Whenever the administration of justice is mediately or immediately in the hands of common law judges their habit of applying to the cause in hand the judicial experience of the past rather than attempting to fit the cause into its exact logical pigeonhole in an abstract system gradually undermines the competing body of law and makes for a slow but persistent invasion of the common law.'[18]

The observation of Pound certainly holds true in the case of the Philippines. William Howard Taft, after assuming office in 1900, noted that he could count with the fingers of one hand the number of Filipino judges who were honest. 'The administration of justice though the native judges in Manila stinks to Heaven,' he wrote to Elihu Root, complaining that 'with a few notable exceptions, there is not a single Filipino lawyer who could be trusted to resist the temptation of a bribe were he raised to the bench.'[19] As indicated above, Taft decided to substitute American judges for the Filipino bribe-loving jurists.[20] He reorganized the Supreme Court

17   *Alzua v Johnson* (1912) 21 Phil. Reports 308.

18   RR Pound, *The Spirit Of The Common Law* (Dartmouth Alumni Lectureship Series 1921) 3.

19   Salamanca (n15) 191.

20   HF Pringle, *The Life and Times of William Howard Taft, Vol. I* (Archon Books 1939) 206.

by reducing its membership from nine to seven, and reducing the Filipinos to a minority of three, with four Americans in the majority. This reversed the ratio set during the military regime of General Otis and General MacArthur when there were six Filipinos against three Americans in the court.[21] Taft also controlled the influence of Filipinos in Government through his policy of only appointing Filipinos to the Government who were members of the Federal Party, a political party formed by Filipinos advocating statehood with the US, 'We can select the men who will be as orthodox in matters of importance as we are,' he wrote.[22] Later, a former Governor-General, W Cameron Forbes, writing of the facility with which American judicial ideas were readily acquired and practised by the judiciary in the Philippines, enthused, 'The spirit infused by the American Administration in the whole judicial system was little short of marvelous.'[23]

The power of judicial review during the colonial era was lodged not only in the American-dominated Supreme Court of the Philippines but also in the Federal Supreme Court of the US. Thus, Section 10 of the Philippine Bill of 1902 provided:

> That the Supreme Court of the US shall have jurisdiction to review, revise, reverse, modify or affirm the final judgments and decrees of the Supreme Court of the Philippine Islands in all actions, cases, causes and proceedings now pending therein or hereafter determined thereby in which the constitution or any statute, treaty, title, right, or privilege of the US is involved or bought into question.[24]

The tenacity of habits of thought among common law judges referred to by Pound can be gauged by looking at the decisions of the Philippine Supreme Court in the first few years of its existence. For example, in the first volume of the Philippine Reports – the national court reporter system, covering decisions from 1901 to 1902 – the Philippine Supreme Court cited only 48 federal and State decisions in the US, while it relied on 64 decisions of the Spanish Supreme Court. The following year, reliance on US precedents increased, the High Court citing 103 American decisions but only 37 decisions of the Spanish Supreme Court. This trend continued progressively until the Philippine Court stopped citing Spanish cases by the time the Philippines was granted independence by the US in 1946.

Consciously or unconsciously, the American judges who dominated the judiciary from 1901 up to 1935 injected common law concepts even in areas of the law reserved for the civil law. For instance, American judges sometimes misapplied common law principles to cases involving breach of contract, cases

---

21   Salamanca (n15) 62.

22   Pringle (n20) 205.

23   WC Forbes, *The Philippine Islands* (Harvard University Press 1945) 307; cited in Salamanca (n15) 63.

24   Act of Congress of the USA of 1 July, 1902, s10, 32 stat., part 1.

arising from violation of provisions of the Spanish Civil Code[25] or misused tort doctrines in *quasi-delict* situations.[26] Even the validity of local laws and ordinances affirmed on historical grounds cited the experience, not of the Philippines, but that of common law countries like England and the US.[27]

Importation of American Statutes

The second Philippine Commission set up by the US in 1900 was vested with legislative and executive functions, while the judicial functions were exercised by a judiciary with an American-dominated Supreme Court at its apex.[28] The grant of legislative power to the Philippine Commission, which lasted until 1916, led to the influx of American laws as well as of common law doctrines. The dearth of public laws at the beginning of the American regime greatly stimulated legislative activity on the part of the Commission. The almost indiscriminate borrowing from American models made it inevitable for the Philippine Supreme Court to interpret the provisions of those laws in line with American precedents.[29] Subsequently, the US Supreme Court stamped its *imprimatur* on this practice in line with the rule of construction that the provisions of borrowed laws must be construed with reference to the parent statute.[30] Then the Philippine Court laid down the rule that all provisions of the US Constitution for the protection of the rights and privileges of individuals which were extended to the Philippines must be interpreted as meaning what similar provisions meant when the US Congress made them applicable to the Philippines.[31]

The exigencies of asserting American authority against the Filipino rebels and of setting up a civil government made it imperative for the Philippine Supreme Court to use common law concepts in public law to assert authority. Initially, the court subordinated property rights to police power, using American precedents. 'police power' is, of course, a term borrowed from Chief Justice Marshall of the US Supreme Court, who first used it in 1824. The first decision of the Philippine Supreme Court where the issue of due process was raised affirmed the supremacy of police power especially where the property involved is invested with a social function, a doctrine borrowed from the common law.[32] In another case that cropped

---

25 For example, *De la Cruz v Seminary of Manila* (1910) 18 Phil. Reports 330.

26 *Rakes v Atlantic, Gulf and Pacific Co.* (1906) 7 Phil. Reports 366.

27 *US v Pompeya* (1915) 31 Phil. Reports 275.

28 Act No. 136 s18 (1901).

29 *Alzua v Johnson* (1912) 21 Phil. Reports 308.

30 See *Kepner v US* (1904) 195 US 100, 24 S. Ct. 797, 49 L. Ed. 114; *Serra v Mortiga* (1907) 204 US 470, 27 S. Ct. 343, 51 L. Ed. 571.

31 *US v Bull* (1910) 16 Phil. Reports 7.

32 *US v Ling Su Fan* (1908) 10 Phil. Reports 104; affirmed by the US Supreme Court, in *Ling Su Fan v US* (1910) 218 US, 302, 31 S. Ct. 21, 54 L. Ed. 1049.

up in 1915, the court upheld the validity of the law prohibiting the slaughter of carabaos for human consumption.[33]

The court pointed to the emergency caused by the rinderpest of 1902 as the basis for the remedial legislation, and declared that police power rested upon necessity and the right of self-protection, another principle drawn from the common law.[34]

It was in the regulation of shipping and in the imposition of burdens on shipowners that the common law doctrines applicable to businesses clothed with public interest were excessively used by the Supreme Court. In *De Villata v Stanley*,[35] the court went to the extreme and held that the Government may require shipping companies which are common carriers to carry mail free of charge. The court reasoned that the business of common carriers is a quasi-public employment and it is only when the owner of a vessel enters the business that additional burdens may be imposed upon him.

Procedural law: from inquisitorial to accusatorial

It is in this area of remedial law that the American common law immediately superseded Spanish procedural law. This started immediately upon the Americans' entry into Manila after the signing of the Treaty of Paris in 1898. In fact, the Spanish Codes of Procedure were repealed by General Orders of the military, purportedly 'to cover omissions of the Spanish legal system'. General Order No. 68, promulgated on 18 December 1899, displaced the provisions of the *Siete Partidas* on marriage, securing liberty of marriage and instituting civil marriages. The new Code of Civil Procedure, based upon the California, Vermont and Ohio Codes, departed radically from the Spanish rules by abrogating the challenging of judges, the civil liability of judges and by requiring public trials. General Order No. 58, promulgated on 23 April 1900, as the new Code of Criminal Procedure, was issued 'to safeguard the civil liberties of the inhabitants', abolishing the inquisitorial procedure and adopting the accusatorial system in the investigation and trial of crimes. Thus, the Code had to secure all the rights of an accused under American common law rules except the trial by jury, retaining trial by a single judge. The Philippine Commission, which was the sole legislative organ of the colonial government from 1900 to 1907, passed 1,800 laws of public character, the most important of which were: the Municipal Code, the Provincial Government Act, the Manila Charter, the Special Provincial Government Act, the Township Government Act, the Government Reorganization Act, the Civil Service Law, the Election Law, the Charter of Baguio City, the Organic Act for Mindanao and Sulu, the Organization of Courts Act and the Code of Civil Procedure.[36] These were all copied from American common law models.

---

33   *US v Toribio* (1910) 15 Phil. Reports 85.
34   ibid.
35   *De Villata v Stanley* (1915) 32 Phil. Reports 541.
36   P Ylagan, 'Philippine Law' (1917) III Philippine Law Journal 237, 239.

Retention of the Civil Code

The Americans decided to retain the Spanish-imposed Civil Code of 1889 based on the *Code Napoléon*. However, this was made subject, to a large extent, to the principles and institutions recognized in the US Constitution. In a 1920 Philippine Supreme Court decision, the tribunal justified this action, and said that:

> This retention of the local private law was merely in accordance with the principles of International Law in that regard. However, by the mere fact of the change in sovereignty, all portions of that statute law which might be termed political law were abrogated immediately by the change in sovereignty. *Also, all Spanish laws, customs and rights of property inconsistent with the Constitution and American principles and institutions were thereupon superseded.*[37]

Thus, although the Spanish Civil Code of 1889 was described by a former American Governor General as 'admirable and, in later years, was to a great extent based on the *Code of Napoléon*',[38] those parts of the Civil Code which were found inconsistent with American principles and institutions were immediately superseded. Understandably, Title I of the Code on citizenship was repealed. Title II on status of natural and juridical persons was modified by the Code of Civil Procedure and the Corporation Law. Title IV on marriage was modified by the military administrator, General Wesley Meritt, in the form of General Order No. 68, which recognized civil marriages. Title V on paternity and filiation as well as Title VII on parental authority, Title VIII on absence, Title IX on guardianship, Title X on the family council and Title XI on emancipation on majority age, were either repealed or modified by the Code of Civil Procedure. On the law of property, which is Book Two and Book Three of the Civil Code, the concepts of property, ownership, possession, usufruct, wills, inheritance, intestate succession and executors, were slightly modified by the Code of Civil Procedure. Likewise, in Book IV of the Code, the law on partition, obligations, contracts, purchase and sale, lease, labour, carriers, partnership, agency, loan, deposit, bailments, insurance, gambling, arbitration, pledge, mortgage, preference of credit and prescription were either repealed or modified by the Code of Civil Procedure or by American common law compilations.

It can be seen that the most significant changes in the then existing Civil Code were provisions on property, obligations, contracts, business organizations, credit transactions, transportation, and banking and insurance transactions, all core activities of a business civilization like that of America. The obsolete and antiquated civilian concepts born out of feudal Spain had to be overhauled to accommodate new legal notions evolved out of a newly-industrialized US. An example would be the interest in land shown by the Americans. The interest of a feudal colonizer, like

37   *In re Shoop* (1921) 43 Phil. Reports 213; emphasis added by author.
38   WC Forbes, *The Philippine Islands* (Cacho Hermanos 1945) 143.

Spain, would certainly differ from the interest of a liberal capitalist country like the US. Before the imposition of the Civil Code of 1889, what really interested the Spaniards in land was its political importance, which reflected the feudal mentality of the old colonizer. This was not so with the Americans. By the time they decided to annex the Philippines in 1898, their interest in land was not so much political as it was economic. Thus, the so-called 'Sugar Trust' in the US was the primary lobbyist which goaded President McKinley to redefine his notion of Manifest Destiny, the American policy of westward expansion from Texas to California, which was conveniently revised to include territories beyond the North American continent. The sugar lobby had properly focused on using the sugar estates in the Philippines as their prospective plantations. The mining interests had heard of tales of gold from the ornithologist Dean Worcester, who had earlier familiarized himself with the location of mineral deposits in the Islands, and both added their voice for annexation, while the trading merchants looked at Luzon as a springboard for trade with China.

So land laws had to be modified from their civilian roots to make the law more consistent with the ruling ideas of a business civilization. For this purpose, the tools of the common law served the colonialists in good stead. The civilian classification of property into movables and immovables had to be modified, so that the new law derived from the Anglo-American system would divide it into property rights in land and property rights in movables. This distinction recognizes the difference between property and the *subject matter* of property so as to lay the foundation for exchange, sale or alienation of the subjects of property.

Criminal law: lone civilian survivor in public law

The Penal Code imposed by Spain in 1884 remained the sole survivor in public law in the onslaught of the common law in 1900. The old Penal Code, which was based on the Spanish Penal Code of 1870, was not superseded by any common law code imposed by the occupying American colonial administrators. However, it was altered by the Americans not only to make it consistent with the political and civil rights enumerated in the organic laws, but also to serve the political purposes of the new sovereign. Thus, most of the crimes defined under Book II, Title II of the old Penal Code, which are crimes against the fundamental laws of the State, had to be either abrogated or modified. In the course of pacifying the rebellious *indios* and setting up the colonial government, the Philippine Commission passed the Treason, Insurrection and Sedition Law (Act No. 292), the Libel Law (Act No. 277), the Law on Perjury (Act No. 1697), the Customs Administrative Act (Act No. 1180).[39] Most of these laws were later incorporated into the Penal Code when it was revised in 1930.

---

39   AE Cuyugan, 'Origin and Development of Philippine Jurisprudence' (1917) 3(6) Philippine Law Journal 191, 208.

The role of language

The shift to English as the official language from Spanish, which took place immediately when the Americans supplanted the Spaniards in 1898, was the primary factor that led to the dominance of the common law system in the Philippines. Initially, the Americans had insisted by 1900 that the language of the law should be English. This led the Filipino lawyers to protest against this policy that the Philippine Commission sought to implement. Because of the intensity of the protests, the Commission was forced to retreat, and it allowed a transition period, up to 1906, to implement this language policy.

Needless to say, the adoption of English as the language of the law also paved the way for the hegemony of the common law over the civilian system. Even the traditional civil law concepts, when translated from Spanish to English, acquired common law connotations. Some of these connotations were carried over into the Supreme Court decisions, and became precedents. Thus, civil law concepts, like *bienes inmuebles, bienes muebles, servidumbres, obligaciones mancomunadas, pena, pago, acreedor* and *cuasi-contratos*, were translated freely as 'real property', 'personal property', 'easements', 'joint obligations', 'penalty', 'payment', 'debtor', 'creditor' and 'quasi-contracts', respectively. Common lawyers who speak Spanish will readily discern that the civil law concepts have been diluted in translation and their English equivalents have acquired, through misuse, a meaning more akin to Anglo-American law.

The influence of legal education

The coming of American lawyers and judges to the Philippines and the introduction of the common law system led to changes in the methods of instruction in the law schools. Before this, the study of law was undertaken by a priestly class of scholars who derived this tradition from the Continental universities in Europe and who, in turn, inherited this from the medieval monks. Thus, law study was a ritualistic and mystical exercise which consisted of memorizing codal provisions and laws taught *ex catedra* by monkish professors. Here the relationship between law and religion was emphasized by the law teachers compelling obedience to law through the threats of hellfire and brim-stone. By contrast, the American teachers brought with them the case method of instruction, which is adapted to the common law. This was the current teaching fad in the US law schools before the turn of the twentieth century, hence it is no surprise that this method was quickly imported in the Philippines to hasten the absorption of the common law into the Philippine legal system.

In the Philippines, an American colonial official, George Malcolm, established a law school in the State University of the Philippines in 1911, which became a model for the existing law schools in the country to follow. From its founding, the College of Law of the public university used the case method of study, and the other colleges of law followed.

Smothering the Hybrid: The Advent of Constitutionalism

The common law method of judicial review is the most convenient instrument to reconcile the political and social changes with the text and history of a written constitution. This can be seen from the constitutional history of the US. The beginning of the twentieth century saw the rise of constitutionalism and judicial activism in the US. It was the common law practice of judicial legislation which impregnated the 'due process' clause of the American Constitution, a procedural guarantee of fair and even-handed hearing before a neutral arbiter or judge, with a substantive aspect, that is, a guarantee that any law or rule seeking to deprive a person of his life, liberty or property must meet substantive requirements of rationality and non-oppressiveness. This mutant notion of 'substantive' due process paved the way for the so-called 'Lochner' era in American jurisprudence, a reference to the period in the US from the turn of the twentieth century to the 1920s, named after the ruling of the Supreme Court in *Lochner v New York*,[40] which invalidated the New York statute setting maximum working hours for bakers, as in violation of liberty of contract.

The political mood of the twenties in the US profoundly affected the course of judicial thought in the Philippines at about the same time. The change of administration in Washington also meant a change in economic policies. The pull of gravity exerted by a business civilization began to influence judicial thought. President Harding, and later President Coolidge, made the economic philosophy of laissez faire a plan for dynamic policy of the American Government.[41] By that time, William Howard Taft had been nominated to the US Supreme Court as Chief Justice, and he saw no greater domestic issue in the 1920 election 'than the maintenance of the Supreme Court as the bulwark to enforce the guaranty that no man shall be deprived of his property without due process of law'.[42] President Harding, whose guiding slogan was 'less government in business and more business in government',[43] did not spare the Philippines, which at that time was known for its numerous Government-owned development and marketing corporations.[44] Appointed Governor-General of the Philippines was Leonard Wood, a trusted Harding lieutenant who, upon his induction into office in 1921, pursued Harding's policy of 'keeping the government out of business in order to encourage private enterprise'.[45] He thus reversed the policy laid down by his predecessors, and sold

---

40   198 US 45 (1905).

41   AT Mason, *Security Through Freedom: American Political Thought and Practice* (Cornell University Press 1959) 56.

42   WH Taft, 'Mr. Wilson and the Campaign' (1920) 10 Yale Review 19–20.

43   Mason (n41) 38.

44   JP Apostol, *The Economic Policy of the Philippine Government; Ownership and Control of Business* (University of the Philippines 1927) 93.

45   ibid.

to private firms almost all Governmental operations.[46] He strongly opposed the grant of Philippine independence on the grounds that the country did not have a stable government, and he defined a stable government as 'one where public and private funds are abundant and readily seek investment at moderate rates of interest'.[47] The colonial government's partiality to American businessman can be seen from the fact that federal taxes supposed to be paid by American businessmen doing business in the Philippines were not collected during the Harding, Coolidge and Hoover administrations as a result of strong representations made by Chief Justice Taft, Governor General Wood, and even President Hoover himself.[48]

It was at this stage of Philippine economic development that the common law began to demolish the ramparts of the hybrid legal system. The American-dominated judiciary became a model of what a court should be in protecting property interests against the assaults of what was then the establishment of the newly-installed Filipino legislature, which acted as the lower house in a bicameral lawmaking body, with the Philippine Commission as the checking upper house from 1907 until 1916. Suddenly, it dawned on the American-dominated judiciary that an all-Filipino legislative body might pass laws destructive of property rights, and the Supreme Court began to act as a super-legislature to protect property rights and freedom of contract. The Philippine Supreme Court thus became the apex of what Justice Scalia of the US Supreme Court calls 'common law courts in a civil law system'.

In 1920, four years after the Philippine Supreme Court ruled adversely against a shipping company which petitioned against the forced carriage of mail, another shipping firm challenged the same statute on the same grounds, that is, deprivation of property without due process. The Federal Supreme Court reversed the earlier ruling of the Philippine Supreme Court and held the law invalid as repugnant to the due process clause.[49] In another Philippine case, an order of the Board of Public Utilities Commissioners, which required an operator of a steamship company to maintain and publish a fixed schedule of the arrival and departure of ships, was challenged as violative of due process. Again, the Philippine Court upheld the contention of the petitioner.[50] At this juncture, the Philippine Supreme Court, the majority of whom were Americans, began to veer away from established doctrines of hegemony of police power in the area of constitutional law, and began a process of eroding police power and enshrining liberty of contract and property rights.

Thus, new meaning came to be infused into the due process clause of the Organic Act when, in 1922, an Act of Congress and an implementing executive order of the previous Governor General fixing the price of rice was challenged before the

---

46   ibid.

47   WMH Anderson, *The Philippine Problem* (GP Putnam and Sons 1939) 139.

48   ibid, 49.

49   *Board of Public Utility Commissioners v Ynchausti* (1920) 251 US 401, 40 S. Ct. 277, 64 L. Ed. 327.

50   *Yangco v Board of Public Utility Commissioners* (1917) 36 Phil. Reports 116, 126.

courts.[51] In declaring both the executive order and the statute unconstitutional, the Supreme Court adopted a rigid and absolutist approach to the constitution, and in ringing tones, exhorted:

> The Constitution is something solid, permanent and substantial. Its stability protects the life, liberty and property rights of the rich and poor alike, and that protection ought not to change with the wind or any emergency condition. The fundamental question involved in this case is the right of the people of the Philippine Islands to be and live under a republican form of government. We make the broad statement that no state or nation, living under a republican form of government, under the terms and conditions specified in Act. No. 2868, has ever enacted a law delegating the power to any one to fix the price at which rice should be sold.[52]

Coupled with this far-reaching decision in favour of private property, the court adopted from the US the doctrine of 'liberty of contract' to complete the cult of laissez faire. The constitutional challenge was thrown at the Women and Child Labor Law,[53] which required employers to give maternity leave pay to women employees. An employer who refused to comply with the statute was indicted for violation of the law and, as a defence, he challenged the law as violative of his freedom to contract.[54] In declaring the law unconstitutional, the court, speaking through Justice E Finley Johnson, said:

> The law has deprived every person, firm or corporation owning or managing a factory, shop or place of labor of any description within the Philippine Islands, of his right to enter into contracts of employment upon such terms as he and the employee may agree upon. The law creates a term in every such contract, without the consent of the parties. Such persons are, therefore, deprived of their liberty to contract. The Constitution of the Philippine Islands guarantees to every citizen his liberty and one of his liberties is the liberty to contract.[55]

The influence of Chief Justice William Howard Taft as high priest of the new constitutionalism was not limited to the US. An opportunity for him to write his notion of what was fair and reasonable in the regulation of business cropped up with the *Yu Cong Eng* case,[56] which involved the Chinese Bookkeeping Act. Sometime in 1920, the Philippine Legislature, seeking to prevent tax evasion among the Chinese businessmen, passed an Act which made it unlawful for any

---

51   Apostol (n44) 23.
52   *US v Ang Tang Ho* (1932) 43 Phil. Reports 1, 17.
53   Act No. 3071 (1916).
54   *People v Pomar* (1924) 46 Phil. Reports 440.
55   ibid 454.
56   *Yu Cong Eng v Trinidad* (1926) 271 US 500, 46 S. Ct. 619, 70 L. Ed. 1059.

person engaged in commerce, industry or any other activity for the purpose of profit to keep its account books in any language other than English, Spanish or any local dialect.[57] As expected, the Chinese merchants brought the case to court on the issue of constitutionality. The Philippine Supreme Court, attempting to give every intendment possible to uphold the validity of the Act, indulged in semantics by defining 'account books' to mean only those that are necessary for purposes of taxation. The court limited the meaning of the phrase by way of compromise between upholding the law and safeguarding the property rights of the Chinese merchants.

On review, the US Supreme Court, speaking through Chief Justice Taft, rejected the construction given by the Philippine Court and instead took the view that the law by its plain terms forbade the Chinese from keeping their account books in any language except English, Spanish or any local dialect; in short, according to the Washington Court, it forbade the Chinese to keep their account books in Chinese.[58] That court then held that to prohibit Chinese merchants from maintaining a set of books in Chinese would be 'oppressive and arbitrary' as it would prevent them from being advised of the status of their business.

These cases illustrate how the legal processes and methods of the common law system had begun to chart the course of Philippine constitutional history. They also show how historical forces and the dominant economic philosophy of an era could reshape the constitutional law of a social order.

Diluting the Civil Code with common law concepts

The Philippines was granted political independence on 4 July 1946, a year after the end of the Second World War. Decades before, the US had prepared the country for self-rule by allowing the Filipinos to elect a unicameral legislature in 1907, although real political power still resided in the Governor General appointed by the American President. In 1935, the country was given the opportunity to draft and ratify a constitution, patterned after the American Federal model, and which had to be approved by the President of the US. The Constitution adopted the presidential form of government following the tri-partite separation of powers, limited further by an American-styled bill of rights, and it provided for amendment or revision by the qualified voters. In the following year, the Philippines was granted an autonomous commonwealth status, and it was allowed to elect all of its high government officials, from the President to the lowest local government officials. As American writer Stanley Karnow has observed, the US tried to transform the Philippines into its own (US) image.[59]

While the Spanish authorities imposed their version of the *Code Napoléon* in the Philippines in 1889, and the Americans retained it with some modifications

57   Act No. 2972 (1920) s2.
58   ibid 511.
59   Karnow (n5) 3–4.

when they took over as colonial masters in 1898, the independence granted to the Philippines in 1946 goaded the new political leaders, breathing the fresh air of independence, to seek revision of the Spanish Civil Code imposed by the two colonial powers.

In 1950, the Congress of the fledgling republic approved a new Civil Code which incorporated legal concepts and techniques borrowed from the common law, such as (1) private remedies for violation of civil and political rights, not only against agents of the State but also against private individuals; (2) equity jurisprudence; (3) principles of social justice; (4) liberalization of women's rights; (5) independent civil actions against tortious conduct separate from the criminal prosecution; and (6) adopting the concept of trusts.

New remedies for violation of civil liberties enumerated in the Constitution, which may referred to as 'constitutional torts', were inserted in the New Civil Code of 1950. These provide that 'any public officer or employee, or any private individual who directly or indirectly obstructs, defeats, violates, or in any manner impedes or impairs any of the (constitutional rights and liberties) of another person shall be liable to the latter for damages'.[60] The damages referred to here include moral and exemplary damages, both of which are also imported from the common law.

The new Code also created a new right of action against unfair competition,[61] another concept borrowed from the common law, as well as against a judge who unduly delays the trial of a civil or criminal case.[62] Also included in the new Code is the concept of privacy, another common law creation from America. It provides for damages against any person for (1) prying into the privacy of another's residence; (2) meddling with or disturbing the private life or family relations of another; (3) intriguing to cause another to be alienated from his friends; and (4) vexing or humiliating another on account of his religious beliefs, lowly station in life, place of birth, physical defect or other personal condition.[63] In addition, the Code likewise adopts the common law technique of penalizing, by way of moral and exemplary damages, any person who, even if he has not violated any positive law or existing statute, willfully causes loss or injury to another in a manner that is contrary to morals, good customs or public policy.[64] The common law principle against unjust enrichment is also penalized in the new Code by means of damages.[65] Other common law imports by the new Code include an action for injunction to stop thoughtless extravagance during a period of acute public want

---

60   Art. 36, Civil Code of the Philippines.
61   Art. 31, Civil Code.
62   Art. 30, Civil Code.
63   Art. 28, Civil Code.
64   Art. 23, Civil Code.
65   Art. 24, Civil Code.

or emergency;[66] and for relief to every taxpayer suffering loss if a public servant refuses or neglects, without just cause, to perform his official duty.[67]

Another important common law intrusion into the domain of civil law is the concept of equity. The Spanish Civil Code which was imposed on the Philippines by Spain suffered from strict legalism. The drafters of the new Civil Code of the Philippines seized upon the common law concept of equity as the antidote to strict legalism. They remedied the rigidity of the Civil Code by adopting, for individual cases, the following measures: first, reformation of instruments;[68] second, the doctrine of trust;[69] third, quieting of title to real property and removal of cloud on a title,[70] fourth, the power of the court to reduce a penalty for breach of contract if such is found to be iniquitous or unconscionable.[71] And the new Code expressly adopts the common law method approximating judicial legislation where it enjoins the judge that he shall not 'decline to render judgment by reason of the silence or obscurity or insufficiency of the laws',[72] and instead commands that 'in case of doubt in the interpretation or application of laws, it is presumed that the lawmaking body intended right and justice to prevail'.[73] This provision opens the door to the common law practice of judicial legislation. Lastly, it is an irony that the common law doctrine of precedents is expressly mandated by the new Civil Code, as follows: 'Judicial decisions applying or interpreting the laws or the constitution shall form part of the legal system of the Philippines.'[74] Thus, by specific legislation in the Civil Code, the common law concept of stare decisis was given formal recognition under a civilian system.

The notion of social justice creeps into the Civil Code

The Constitution that was promulgated in 1935 for the Commonwealth of the Philippines and approved by then President Franklin Roosevelt reflected the philosophy of the welfare state. In the words of an American author and former Vice-Governor of the Philippines, Joseph Ralston Hayden, 'The constitution was

---

66 Art. 27, Civil Code.
67 Art. 29, Civil Code.
68 Art. 1365, Civil Code.
69 Art. 1475, Civil Code.
70 Arts. 476 to 481, Civil Code.
71 Art. 1229, Civil Code.
72 Art. 9, Civil Code.
73 Art. 10, Civil Code.
74 Art. 8, Civil Code.

more socialistic than capitalistic in orientation.'[75] It is not surprising then that it contained aspirational statements on social justice.[76]

A new welfarist approach was sought to be implemented in the Civil Code of 1950. For example, a new section under the heading 'Contract of Labor' seeks to protect the rights of workers and employees, and it provides for compensation of work-related ailments and accidents. Needless to say, most of these innovations were borrowed from common law jurisdictions.

Other common law concepts permeate the civil law

Only 57 per cent of the new Code's provisions came from the Civil Code of 1889. The bulk of the new provisions of the Philippine Civil Code came from doctrines built up from Anglo-American common law, like provisions for State indemnity for erroneous criminal conviction, civil action for damages after acquittal in a criminal case on reasonable doubt, actions for obstruction of civil liberties, rights of natural children by legal fiction, rights of a wife in case of maladministration of conjugal property by the husband, proof of illegitimate filiation, abatement of nuisance, sales, reformation of instruments, implied trusts, estoppel, quasi-contracts, liability of municipalities for damages, and moral and nominal damages.[77] In addition, some of the legal standards developed under the civilian system were replaced by common law standards, such as extraordinary diligence for common carriers,[78] the measure of moral, liquidated, nominal, temperate and exemplary damages,[79] as well as common law authority for judges to engage in judicial legislation in case of ambiguity or gaps in the law.[80] In addition, the new Code adopted almost wholesale the uniform commercial codes of the US, for example, the Uniform Sales Act,[81] the Uniform Partnership Act,[82] and Uniform Limited Partnership Act.[83]

---

75   JR Hayden, *The Philippines: A Study In National Development* (Macmillan 1950) 242.

76   For example, 'The Promotion of Social Justice to Insure the Well-being and Economic Security of All the People Shall be the Concern of the State.' (Art. II, s5, 1935 Constitution of the Philippines); 'The state shall afford protection to labor, especially to working women and minors, and shall regulate the relation between landowner and tenant, and between labor and capital in industry and in agriculture. The state may provide for compulsory arbitration.' (Art. XIV, s6, 1935 Constitution).

77   ibid, 547–548.

78   ibid, 613.

79   ibid, 621–626.

80   Arts 8, 10 and 11, New Civil Code of the Philippines.

81   CV Sison, *The Civil Code Reader* (UP Law Complex 2005) 701.

82   ibid, 709.

83   ibid, 710.

Lastly, but more importantly, the new Civil Code was promulgated in English, unlike the Civil Code of Spain. In translating Spanish legal terms into English, the nearest equivalents in the common law were used. Since the English common law terms are not the exact equivalents of the Spanish terms used in the Code of 1889, the Philippine Supreme Court decisions from 1951 to the present, translated terms that were sometimes understood or defined in light of American jurisprudence. For instance, *cuasi contratos* under the Civil Code of 1889 enumerated only two kinds: *negotiorum gestio*, or the administration of others' property, and *indebiti solution*, or the payment by mistake of what is not owed. In contrast, under American common law, quasi-contracts include recovery upon a record, recovery upon a duty, and recovery upon the doctrine that no person shall be allowed to unjustly enrich himself at the expense of another. Thus, in a case, the Philippine Supreme Court interpreted *cuasi-contratos* in common law terms, holding that while there was no relation of *negotiorum gestio* between the parties, as the defendants did not ratify or approve the acts of the plaintiffs' father, the fact remained that the house of the defendants was improved by the work of their father, and for this reason the defendants were liable for the obligations incurred by the plaintiffs' father for their benefit and advantage.[84]

Meanwhile, notable common law doctrines began to be accepted in the Philippines and these were blended into the civil law system by the American judges. These are the doctrines in the field of torts: proximate cause, negligence and contributory negligence, reckless negligence, last clear chance rule applicable to automobile accidents, vicarious liability, sovereign immunity, moral damages, loss of profits, speculative profits and mitigation of damages. In decided cases, Philippine courts applied American tort doctrines,[85] like last clear chance rule,[86] requirements of duty,[87] sovereign immunity,[88] and nuisance and trespass.[89]

The same observation applies with regard to contracts. For example, the Civil Code provides that 'the principles of estoppel are hereby adopted insofar as they are not in conflict with the provisions of this Code, the Code of Commerce, the Rules of Court, and special laws'.[90] As for the doctrine of laches, Philippine law now follows the common law rule that equity will not aid a plaintiff whose unexcused delay, if the suit were allowed, would be prejudicial to the defendant.[91] The Supreme Court has also held that the 'consideration' of American law and the *causa* of the civil law, although somewhat different in theory, have equivalent

---

84   *Smith v Lopez* (1905) 5 Phil. Reports 78.

85   *Rakes v Atlantic, Gulf and Pacific Co.* (1907) 7 Phil. Reports 320.

86   *Picart v Smith* (1907) 37 Phil. Reports 809.

87   *Ollendorf v Abrahamson* (1918) 38 Phil. Reports 585.

88   *Metropolitan Transportation Service v Paredes* (1947) 79 Phil. Reports 819.

89   *Hidalgo Enterprises v Balandan* (1952) 91 Phil. Reports 490.

90   Art. 1432, Civil Code.

91   *Manila Railroad Co. v Luzon Stevedoring Co.* (1956) 100 Phil. Reports 145.

effects in practical jurisprudence.[92] Although the common law 'consideration' is narrower than *causa*; consideration may consist in some benefit to the promissor or in some detriment to the promisee; *causa* is the essential reason of the contract.[93] With regard to acceptance of an offer, the new Civil Code provides that 'acceptance made by letter or telegram does not bind the offerer except from the time that it came to his knowledge. The contract, in such a case, is presumed to have been entered into the place where the offer was made'.[94] This is another common law rule adopted by the Code.

The 1950 Civil Code has also adopted the rule on 'discharge by breach' in contracts especially in sales of goods, as the Philippines borrowed from the provisions of the Uniform Sales Act of the US. For instance, it is provided that 'where the goods have not been delivered to the buyer, and the buyer has repudiated the contract sale, or has manifested his inability to perform his obligations thereunder, or has committed a breach thereof, the seller may totally rescind the contract of sale by giving notice of his election to do so to the buyer'.[95]

In the matter of setting the standard for personal conduct, there is the mixing of the concept of a judicious *pater familias* in Roman law with the common law concept of 'the reasonable man'.[96] The standard of a good father of a family, which is the standard laid down by the Roman based civil law in the matter of determining the vicarious liability of an employer, has been redefined in terms of the common-law concept of a reasonable man. For instance, in the selection of one's driver, the employer should not be satisfied with the mere possession on the part of the driver of a professional driver's licence, but he should carefully examine the applicant for employment as to his qualifications, experience and record of service, and he should examine the applicant's background and ask him to submit to police clearances and to undergo not only a physical examination but also a driving examination consisting of theoretical and practical tests.

Common law concepts found in the American-imposed Code of Civil Procedure, also modified some concepts in the civil law of succession. For instance, an 'heir' under the Civil Code means not only a relative of the deceased who takes the property of one dying intestate, but also the person, relative or not, who takes what might be called the residuary estate by will. In the Code of the Civil Procedure, 'heir' is used in the first sense only, and in connection with intestate estates. As therein used, an heir is always a relative. A person taking by will is called (whether an heir or not) a 'devisee' when real property is inherited, and 'legatee' when personalty is taken. Under the former Spanish Civil Code, an heir succeeded to the rights and obligations of the deceased and became owner of the property; under the Code of Civil Procedure, the heir is not personally liable

---

92   *Santos v Reyes* (1908) 10 Phil. Reports 125.
93   *Lui v Ocampo* (1954) 55 Official Gazette 1778.
94   Art. 1319, Civil Code.
95   Art. 1597, Civil Code.
96   *Picart v Smith* (1918) 37 Phil. Reports 768.

for the debts and obligations of the deceased so that he cannot alienate or charge it free of such debts unless these are extinguished.[97]

Forced heirship and free testation, borrowed from the common law, is also now recognized by the existing Civil Code of the Philippines (Book III, Title IV). For instance, Article 888 of the new Civil Code provides that 'the legitime of legitimate children and descendants consists of one-half of the hereditary estate of the father and of the mother. The latter may freely dispose of the remaining half, subject to the rights of illegitimate children and of the surviving spouse as hereinafter provided'.

Even the concepts of surety and guaranty in the 1950 Civil Code have been penetrated by the common law. Under the old Spanish Code, these two concepts were incorporated under the single term, *fianza*, but under the present Code, there is the concept of surety where the principal as well as his surety bind themselves in an absolute promise to pay and subrogation is made easy by the common law, while the concept of guaranty has been imported under which the guarantor is just a conditional and collateral obligor who pays only in the case of the insolvency of the principal debtor.[98]

The concept of trusts, borrowed from common law, is now embodied in Book IV, Title V of the Civil Code of the Philippines, which adopts the English trust in its original form, with a few modifications. An example of a modification is the concept of 'family trust', where the revenues from a *corpus* of properties are distributed annually, or at longer or shorter periods, among the relatives of the founder of the trust.[99]

Likewise, the principle of promissory estoppel has been fused to the concept of *causa* in contracts, as may be seen from this definition of the term by the Philippine Supreme Court, thus:

> An estoppel may arise from the making of a promise, even though without consideration, if it was intended that the promise should be relied upon, and if a refusal to enforce it would be virtually to sanction the perpetration of a fraud which would result in other injustice.[100]

The common law conquers commercial law

The commercial law of any country is always reshaped by the ideology of the dominant economy. This can be seen from the development of mercantile law during the medieval period. At that time. though the Roman Law may have been the foundation of the law merchant, this was superseded by the common mercantile law when the old caravan routes of the early Middle Ages were abandoned when

---

97   *Suiliong and Co. v Chio Taysan* (1908) 12 Phil. Reports 13.

98   Art. 2047, New Civil Code of the Philippines.

99   *Barretto v Tuason* (1927) 50 Phil. Reports 925.

100   *Ramos v Central Bank* (1971) 41 SCRA 588.

the Mediterranean and Atlantic sea routes were developed and shipping in the Baltic increased. This led to the development of new customary law to deal with the new conditions in trade. The new codes showed the increasingly maritime character of the newer mercantile law.[101] This was the nature of the Code of Commerce which Spain imposed on the Philippines in 1888.

It is in the area of commercial law that the attempt of the new colonizers to develop an economy in the image of America's business civilization is most evident. The lawmaking body, the Philippine Commission, and later from 1907, the Philippine National Assembly, borrowed wholesale American laws on corporations, negotiable instruments, securities, insurance, banking, transportation, trademarks and copyright, unfair competition, chattel mortgage, insolvency and bankruptcy, and bulk sales. Thus, the Corporation Law (Act No. 1459), the Bankruptcy Act (Act No. 1956), Negotiable Instruments Act (Act No. 2031), Warehouse Receipts Law (Act No. 2031), Public Utilities Act (Act No. 2137), Insurance Law (Act No. 2427), Usury Law (Act No. 2655), Salvage Law (Act No. 2616) and Irrigation Act (Act No. 2153) superseded the Code of Commerce of Spain and other existing mercantile laws. All of these new laws are the foundation of a capitalist economy that forms the core of a business civilization. As America tried to create a new legal culture, it had to impose its ideology and its laws even in an underdeveloped economy which was not quite ready to adjust to the needs and ethos of a modern civilization. This confirms the observation of one legal scholar on the primary theme of the goals and practices of colonizing countries from the industrialized North:

> As industrial nations such as Great Britain, Germany and the US became colonizers (displacing the feudal colonizers such as Spain and Portugal) the dominating considerations became economic. Colonies provided sources of raw materials, markets for finished goods, settlements for surplus population of the colonizers, and investments or business opportunities for colonials.[102]

It is therefore no surprise that, in the Philippines, after the turn of the twentieth century, the common law began to replace the civilian system in commercial law, as well as the law of property rights, obligations and contracts, and of business organizations and transactions. The US found the laws imposed by a feudal colonizer like Spain inappropriate for a capitalist economy. As one of Taft's aides in the Philippines observed, they had inherited a legal regime 'so antiquated and disorganized as not to admit of patching or repair'.[103] This included the laws on business and commerce imposed by the Spaniards.

---

101   E Jenks, *The Book of English Law* (Houghton Mifflin Co 1929) 26–27.

102   PV Fernandez, 'The Emergent World Federal Capitalist System and Its Implication for Constitutionalism', in MR Fernandez (ed), *Law and Society: Collected Works of Perfecto V Fernandez* (UP Law Complex 2005) 346.

103   Karnow (n5) 198.

Eventually, as observed by the then American-dominated Philippine Supreme Court, a Philippine 'common law' was evolved based on Anglo-American jurisprudence. 'The practical result is that the past twenty years have developed a Philippine Common Law or case law based exclusively, except where conflicting with local customs and institutions, upon Anglo-American Common Law,' said the high tribunal in 1920.[104] It came to a point where, by 1921, Pound, in his Dartmouth Alumni Lectures, observed that 'in the Philippines and in Porto Rico, there are many signs that common law administration of a Roman Code will result in a system Anglo-American in substance if Roman-Spanish in its terms'.[105]

Globalization: A Continuing Threat to the Hybrid System

In one sense, it can be said that what happened to the Philippines' mixed legal system after the turn of the century is now being repeated on a worldwide scale with the advent of globalization. American military and economic dominance carries with it that country's values, ideology and legal traditions. Even if the US has not really colonized the world by force of arms, its hegemony over the world's economy has influenced the development of its commercial laws and has imposed its modes of administering justice and of settling disputes. By 1921, Roscoe Pound had already observed that 'the American development of the common law doctrine of supremacy of law, in our characteristic institution of judicial power over unconstitutional legislation, is commending itself to peoples who have to administer written federal constitutions'.[106] Even a communist country like China has modelled its commercial laws on American models.

More than the rule of law and the doctrine of judicial review, America is imposing on the civilized world what many refer to as 'cultural imperialism'. Aside from the organization and style of its legal order and its basic legal attitudes and notions, the US is creating a globalized society in its own image – a business civilization based on liberal democratic capitalism.

It is the thesis of sociologists that, of all legal systems, it is American common law that is most inspired by economic rather than political referents.[107] The general conclusion is that while the Continental civil law system is a product of political referents (that is, State sovereignty), the common law responds to economic referents (that is, economic interests). Indeed a number of American legal historians point out that in their country, judges had systematically advanced the legal principles expressing the values of a society increasingly committed

---

104   *In re Shoop* (n37) 246–247.

105   Pound (n18) 2.

106   Pound (n18) 3.

107   MR Ferrarese, 'An Entrepreneurial Conception of the Law: The American Model Through Italian Eyes' in D Nelken, *Comparing Legal Cultures* (Dartmouth 1997) 157–161.

to market capitalism and economic growth. James Willard Hurst, for instance, points out that in the early phases of industrialization, law in action reflected the premise that 'it was common sense, and it was good, to use the law to multiply the productive power of the economy'.[108] Edward Corwin believes that the basic pillar of capitalism, the protection of established property rights against interference by the State, is the basic doctrine of American constitutional law.[109] 'Uses of law and disputes over uses of law are so woven into economic growth in the US that legal and economic history cannot be separated,' concludes JW Hurst.[110] In the age of globalization, the common law of America has become the common law of our globalized world.

It is no coincidence that the twin pillars of the common law, the assertion of individual rights, which includes freedom of contract and the protection of property interests, are also the hallmarks of capitalism. The great guru of classical liberalism, Nobel Prize winner Frederick Hayek, looks at the common law as the favoured instrument of capitalism because of its predilection for freedom of contract and its protection of private property.[111] The constitutional law of the US, according to one political scientist, is best understood when it is read in the light of capitalism and capitalism is best understood when it is read in the light of constitutional law.[112]

There are inherent characteristics of the common law which gives it durability even in the face of changes in intellectual movements. It fits hand in glove with the ideology of capitalism and, later, of globalization, which is nothing but mega capitalism. Globalization sustains the common law because the latter's techniques are adapted to the expansion of globalization. There is, first, the case-by-case development of its jurisprudence. In short, compared to the civil law system, which develops on the basis of abstract legal concepts, the common law system develops on the basis of rulings involving actual controversies. This enables the system to encroach upon the territory of the civilian system very gradually, almost imperceptibly. For the common law is more a mode of resolving actual cases rather than a systematic body of law classified into various subjects. It is more method than substance; it is more process than essence. It is this characteristic which fits it into capitalism, an economic system riven with controversy. Controversies on property ownership, sharing of profits, possession or repossession of chattels, interpretation of contracts, conduct in the open market, success or failure of an economic activity, accumulation of wealth and its trickle-down effect on labour,

---

108   JW Hurst, *Law and the Conditions of Freedom in the 19th Century United States* (University of Wisconsin Press 1956) 33.

109   E Corwin, 'The Basic Doctrine of American Constitutional Law' (1914) 12 Michigan Law Review 247.

110   JW Hurst, *Law and Social Process in US History* (Da Capo Press 1972) 9.

111   FA Hayek, *The Constitution of Liberty* (Routledge 1960) 156.

112   HE Willis, 'Capitalism, the United States Constitution, and the Supreme Court' (1934) XXII Kentucky Law Journal 343, 350.

are the recurring controversies in a capitalist economy which can be resolved better on a case-by-case basis rather than on general and abstract principles of law. General principles do not resolve concrete cases, as Holmes aptly observes.[113] In this respect, common law tends to overwhelm the general principles of the civilian system using the case-by-case approach, the rule on precedents and the rules of statutory construction. It is the methods and the processes of the common law, which impregnates jurisprudence on a global scale, overwhelming the abstract concepts of the civil law.

---

113   OW Homes, 'The Path of the Law' (1879) Harvard Law Review 457, 465.

Chapter 4
Jersey

The first three chapters in this volume, Scotland, Guyana and the Philippines, can be regarded as being at one end of a spectrum where the common law element of the mixed legal system has strengthened and the civil law ingredient become endangered to varying degrees. Whereas Sir Philip Bailhache presents Jersey not as really endangered, but recuperating. Although, the legal system started with civilian customary law and French law, the linguistic shift to English with a new population has led to the birth of a mixed legal system. Criminal law was the first to be influenced and became thoroughly mixed, then gradually yielding to English law.

In Jersey, bilingualism with two official languages got muddled in some areas and yet recently the recuperation seems to have begun with the establishment of the Institute of Law in 2008, with proactive initiatives being made to retain the local version of civil law. This is an important development since the prior legal education in France had given way to legal education in England and we know that this is one of the factors that can lead to suffocation of the earlier element. Now that the Institute of Law has been established, recuperation starts. Sir Philip indicates that recently a rediscovery of the civilian roots is taking place such as in contracts, although tort remains more in the realm of common law. Commercial law is English similar to that found in many other mixed legal systems, but succession and property are close to the customary roots.

The health of this mixed legal system appears to be getting better and recuperation is indeed the proper diagnosis, possibly to be labelled as entrenched. It is the appellate judges that help in the development of civilian concepts, again pointing to the importance of legal education and the role of the legal actors in preserving a mixed legal system.

Jersey: 'Avoiding the Fate of the Dodo'

Philip Bailhache

Introduction

The dodo is the emblem of what used to be called the Jersey Wildlife Conservation Trust,[1] founded by the late Gerald Durrell in 1963. The dodo, a flightless bird that was once endemic to Mauritius, became extinct in the seventeenth century. It has become the symbol of the Trust which has a mission to take in endangered species and to breed them for ultimate return to the wild. An integral part of the Trust's work is to educate people and governments about the conservation of habitats and the means of protecting the environment so as to ensure the sustainability of the habitats concerned. The Education Centre at the Durrell Wildlife Park is at the heart of the Trust's work.

To what extent does the experience of the natural world, and man's destruction of the earth's biodiversity, translate into the world of law and legal systems? In the natural world, the loss of different species is of course part of the process of evolution; but man's interventions over the last half-century have caused the destruction of species on an unprecedented scale. It will be submitted that in the sphere of law, the challenges to the integrity of Jersey's legal system have been equally intense in the last 60 years since the Liberation from German occupation in 1945, but that so far Jersey law is avoiding the fate of the dodo.

Potted Constitutional History

The constitutional history of the Channel Islands as autonomous States begins in 1204. At the beginning of the tenth century they were part of Brittany, but they were annexed by William 'Longsword', Duke of Normandy, in 933. In 1066, William the Conqueror, a successor Duke of Normandy, conquered England at the Battle of Hastings, and the Channel Islands became part of the growing Norman Empire, but remaining attached in an administrative and ecclesiastical sense to the mainland of Normandy.[2] Few documents relating to the history of

---

1   Now the Durrell Wildlife Conservation Trust.

2   The Islands formed part of the diocese of Coutances with two established rural deaneries, one for each Island. See JH Le Patourel, *Medieval Administration of the Channel Islands* (first published OUP 1937, reprinted by Guernsey Bar 2004) 26 *et seq*: G White,

the Islands prior to 1200 have been published, but it is clear that Jersey must have been subject to the customary law of Normandy, as well as certain local customs. In 1204 King John lost Normandy to Philip Augustus of France.[3] An invasion force reached Jersey but could not consolidate its success and withdrew. The Islanders were faced with an agonizing choice. Their familial, religious, linguistic and commercial relations were with Normandy. Yet their Duke was the King of England. For a number of complex reasons the leading men of the Islands chose to remain loyal to the Plantagenet King. Their loyalty was rewarded by the grant of a number of constitutional privileges, including the right to establish their own administration separate from that of England, and the right to be governed by their own laws, essentially the customary law of Normandy. These rights were embodied in the eponymous constitutions of King John, issued at some time before the end of his reign in 1216,[4] which decreed *inter alia* that there were to be chosen in each Bailiwick 12 good men to be sworn to administer justice.[5] These *coronatores* (only later to be known as Jurats or *Jurés justiciers*) were there to support the Bailiff in the jurisdiction conferred by the constitutions to deal with the Petty Assizes without writ.[6] The court constituted by the Bailiff sitting with Jurats became known as the Royal Court, and Jersey law as a separate legal system came into existence. In the beginning, therefore, Jersey law was essentially the customary law of Normandy, augmented by certain local customs. In 1333 the inhabitants of Guernsey and Jersey submitted a petition to the King which begins:

> To our Lord the King and to his Council show his liege people the community of the Islands of Guernsey and Jersey, that whereas the islands are, from old, a parcel of the Duchy of Normandy, and in such manner hold of our lord the King as duke, and in the said islands they hold and use and have always used the custom of Normandy which is called Summa of Maukael, together with certain other customs used in the islands time out of mind ...[7]

'The Ecclesiastical Court of Jersey: the Court of the Dean or of the Bishop?' (2013) 17 Jersey and Guernsey Law Review 374.

3   JA Everard and JC Holt, *Jersey 1204: The Forging of an Island Community* (Thames and Hudson 2004) 34 *et seq*.

4   *Constitutiones et provisiones constitute pr Johannem regem postquam Normannia alienate fuit*, a document which survives in a return to a royal writ of 11 September 1248 addressed to Drew de Barentin, Warden, (*custos* or bailiff) of the Islands of Jersey and Guernsey. The return is at C145/22 in the National Archives at Kew.

5   JC Holt, 'Jersey 1204: The Origins of Unity' in *A Celebration of Autonomy 1204– 2004: 800 Years of Channel Islands Law* (Jersey Law Review 2005) 121 *et seq*.

6   ibid, 122.

7   In the translation to be found in F de L Bois, *A Constitutional History of Jersey* (States Greffe, Jersey 1970) 4, 16.

The Summa of Maukael is generally considered to be the Latin text of the *Grand coutumier de Normandie* and not the earlier text of *Le très ancien coutumier*.[8] Customary law was defined by Routier in the opening words of his *Principes généraux du droit civil et coutumier de la Province de Normandie:*

> *La Coutume n'est autre chose qu'un droit non écrit, qui s'est introduit par un tacite consentement du Souverain et du Peuple, pour avoir été observée pendant un tems considérable.*[9]

To the extent that the *Grand coutumier* was silent upon certain areas of law, the interstitial gaps were filled by the other customary laws of France, or the civil law, the whole being subject of course to the Ordinances of the Sovereign.[10]

Early challenges to Jersey law

It is interesting that the earliest challenge to the territorial integrity of the fledgling system of Jersey law came not from the law of the sovereign State (England), but from France. The customary law at the time of the separation in 1204 continued to evolve in Normandy. The independence of Norman law itself was clearly under threat following the French conquest, but the Normans were determined that their legal system should survive. In 1315 they exacted from King Louis X a charter known as *La Charte aux Normands*[11] granting a number of concessions to its judicial independence, including an assurance that no Norman cause should be tried outside the Duchy, and that no appeal should lie from the Court of Exchequer of Normandy to the King's court in Paris. Other documents show that Norman law was continuing to evolve during the fourteenth and fifteenth centuries. *L'Ancien Style de Procéder*, published at the end of the fourteenth century, and *Le Nouveau Style*, published around 1460, contain a mass of information not only about procedure but also about substantive law.[12] A further revision, known as *Le style*

---

8   According to S Nicolle, *The Origin and Development of Jersey Law* (Jersey and Guernsey Law Review Ltd, 1998 edition, s4) the academic consensus is that the *Très Ancien Coutumier* appeared at the turn of the twelfth and thirteenth centuries. The date of the *Grand coutumier* is generally put at 1254–1258.

9   'Custom is nothing other than an unwritten law, which has been introduced by the tacit consent of the Sovereign and the people having been observed for a considerable time.' C Routier, *Principes généraux du droit civil et coutumier de la Province de Normandie* (2nd edn Pierre Le Boucher 1748) 1.

10   ibid, 2.

11   The *Charte aux Normands* is published in Le Rouille's edition of the *Grand Coutumier,* and that text would no doubt have been known to Jersey lawyers. See also John Kelleher, '*The Charte aux Normands*' (2007) 11 Jersey and Guernsey Law Review 167.

12   R Besnier, *La Coutume de Normandie, Histoire Externe* (Sirey 1935) 112, wrote of *L'Ancien Style* : '*Cet ouvrage est d'un grand intérêt, il fournit pour le XIVe siècle une*

de 1515, was published as an annexe to *Le Rouillé*, and would equally have been known in Jersey.[13]

In 1453 Charles VII of France ordered the revision and redaction of all customary law systems in France. In Normandy the reaction to that Royal Ordinance was slow, but in 1583 a revised text of *Le grand coutumier* had been completed, and it was approved as *La coutume reformée* in 1585. The *Coutume*, having been enacted by royal decree, could no longer evolve as custom.

In the meantime, across the water in Jersey, there is little doubt that many of these evolutionary changes were adopted by the Royal Court. When Jean Poingdestre wrote his *Commentaires sur l'ancienne coutume de Normandie* in the latter half of the seventeenth century, he lamented the uncertainties that had crept into the law over the previous 400 years. How happy our ancestors were, he wrote, to be able to assert with one voice that the laws by which they were governed were the customs of Normandy. Now that the Normans had constructed a new *Coutume*, based on the Custom of Paris, '*nos Practiciens sont demeurés en suspends entre la vieille et la nouvelle, sans scavoir laquelle suyvre*'.[14] Poingdestre set out, page by page, his assessment of the extent to which the *Grand coutumier* was no longer followed.

In a later work, which remains unpublished, Poingdestre set out his *Commentaires sur la coutume reformée*,[15] identifying those parts of the reformed custom that had been absorbed into the law of Jersey. He urged that a code should be enacted setting out what remained of the customary law and what had been changed by Orders in Council and regulations approved by the King. The Code was never to come to pass, but the works of Poingdestre and his successor as Lieutenant Bailiff, Philippe Le Geyt,[16] constituted a substantial body of *doctrine*.[17]

---

masse de renseignements de première valeur non seulement pour la procédure, mais aussi pour le fonds de droit, il permet de suivre l'évolution de la Coutume, du XIIIe à la fin du XIVe siècle.' [This work is of great interest. It provides for the fourteenth century a mass of information of the greatest value, not only in respect of procedure but also in respect of substantive law. It makes it possible to follow the evolution of the Custom, from the thirteenth to the end of the fourteenth century.]

13   Both the *Nouveau Style* and the *Style* of 1515 appear in the 1534 and 1539 editions of *G Le Rouillé, Le Grand Coustumier du pays et duché de Normandie* (F Regnault) and would have been known to Jersey practitioners at the time of Le Geyt and Poingdestre.

14   'Our practitioners remain suspended between the old and the new, without knowing which to follow'. J Poingdestre, *Les Commentaires sur l'Ancienne Coutume de Normandie* (The Law Society of Jersey 1907) 1.

15   A manuscript copy of this work has been placed on the website of the Jersey Legal Information Board at <www.jerseylaw.je.> accessed 6 January 2014.

16   Philippe Le Geyt was sworn to office as Lieutenant Bailiff on 15 June 1676 and held that office until 1694. He was the author of the *Privilèges, loix & coustumes de l'Isle de Jersey* (Law Society of Jersey 1953) and the *Manuscrits sur la Constitution, les Lois, et les Usages de Jersey* Vol. I–IV (The States of Jersey 1846).

17   *Doctrine* in the French sense of authoritative works explaining or interpreting the law. As was stated in *Cie Immobilière Viger v Lauréat Giguère Inc.* (1977) 2 R.C.S. 67 at

The absorption over the period of 500 years between 1204 and the beginning of the eighteenth century of legal rules modifying the *Grand coutumier* and of parts of the revised custom of Normandy did not constitute a threat to the integrity of Jersey law. The modified customary law, and even the rules absorbed from the Custom of Paris and the civil law, were not alien concepts. Just as any legal system can usefully draw influences from related systems of law on a comparative basis, Jersey law absorbed reforms and new approaches so as to accord with changing social and economic conditions. Even in 1861, the Royal Commissioners appointed to inquire into the civil, ecclesiastical and municipal laws of Jersey[18] were able to report:

> from a very early period ... [Jersey has] ... retained [its] ancient Norman law, except so far as it has in the course of time been modified or corrupted by subsequent enactments or usages. It was indeed contended before us that the common law of England has been introduced into Jersey. We do not see any proof of this ...[19]

The Commissioners referred to the practice of referring to commentators on the reformed custom of Normandy such as Basnage,[20] and added that Jersey lawyers had declared:

> that such works are not of authority on Jersey law; yet in point of fact they are frequently used as books of reference, and this has naturally, perhaps unavoidably, led to the gradual introduction of much foreign matter, so that what is now practically received as the common law of Jersey, may be described as consisting of the ancient Norman law, with subsequent accretions, some of which are mere developments of the earlier customs, and others interpolations of French law. It may be added that the circumstance of the Jersey lawyers receiving their legal education chiefly in France, helps to impart a modern French complexion to the jurisprudence of the Island.[21]

76, '*Le Code Civil ne contient pas tout le droit civil. Il est fondé sur des principes qui n'y sont pas tous exprimés et dont il appartient à la jurisprudence et à la doctrine d'assurer la fécondité.*' [The Civil Code does not contain the whole body of the civil law. The law is founded upon principles which are not all expressed and its fertility is assured by judicial decisions and the writing of scholars.]

18   *Report of the Commissioners appointed to inquire into the Civil, Municipal and Ecclesiastical Laws of the Island of Jersey, together with Minutes of Evidence* (Cm, First series, 2761 HMSO 1861).

19   ibid, iii.

20   Henri Basnage wrote his *Oeuvres contenant ses commentaires sur la coutume de Normandie* in 1678. His work has been much relied upon by the Royal Court ever since.

21   ibid, iii.

During the nineteenth century, even when substantial changes to elements of the customary law were being considered, as, for example, the need to change the tortuous system of guarantee which had become a serious threat to the unencumbered ownership of immoveable property, the lawyers looked to France. Significant parts of the *Loi (1880) sur la propriété foncière,* in particular the provisions relations to hypothecs, were drawn from the *Code Civil.*[22]

Yet the Commissioners also recorded that one of the sources of the law of Jersey at that time was Acts of the Imperial Parliament.[23] The Commissioners' assertion that 'The competency of Parliament to legislate for Jersey is unquestionable'[24] might now find fewer adherents,[25] but it is the case that Acts of the UK Parliament were occasionally expressed to apply to Jersey. In general, however, these were concerned with matters common to all British people, such as nationality, defence and so on. Rarely did an Act of the Imperial Parliament touch upon a matter of domestic law. Occasionally statutes were expressed to apply to Jersey with the consent, or at the request, of the Island Authorities, and were registered in the Royal Court.[26]

Nineteenth century – early twentieth century changes

The end of the Napoleonic wars in 1815 brought a significant surge in population. Many were retired army personnel who found the Island a comfortable place to live. The population rose from 30,000 in 1821 to nearly 60,000 in 1851, and nearly all that immigration was from England. The social consequences were considerable, not least in terms of the linguistic shift. Complaints were recorded by the Royal Commissioners in their 1861 report from English residents about court proceedings being conducted in French.[27] The English language was, however, gaining ground, and many of the immigrants who were engaged in business sought to persuade political leaders that English commercial statutes should be adopted. The *Loi (1861) sur les societes à responsabilité limitée* was based upon an earlier Companies Act of the UK. Although the position in relation to equity is not so clear,

---

22   See Rt P Marett, '*Lettre explicative du projet de loi amendé sur la propriété foncière*', reprinted at (1999) 3 Jersey Law Review 41.

23   ibid, iv.

24   ibid, vii. The view has been repeated in most official sources since then – see Royal Commission on the Constitution, *Relationships between the United Kingdom and the Channel Islands and the Isle of Man* (Part XI of Volume I of the Report, 1969–1973, HMSO 1973).

25   See, for example, J Jowell 'The Scope of Guernsey's Autonomy – a Brief Rejoinder' (2001) 5 Jersey Law Review 271: Miscellany, 'Terrorist Asset Freezing and the Evolving Constitutional Relationship' (2011) 15 Jersey and Guernsey Law Review 125.

26   For example, Sea Fisheries Act 1868.

27   ibid, xlviii. The Commissioners were not sympathetic to these complaints.

the Royal Court recognized in *Hawksford and Renouf v Giffard*[28] that the trustees were owners '*en droit*' whereas the beneficiaries were owners '*en équité*'. Much earlier, in 1789, there are references in Hemery and Dumaresq's report to the Privy Council[29] of the Royal Courts having an 'equity' jurisdiction. But that jurisdiction was thought in later decisions to be closer to the French concept of '*équité*' (a just tempering of statute law).[30] It was not until the latter part of the twentieth century that the law of trusts in an English sense obtained a firm foothold.[31]

Complaints from English immigrants in the middle of the nineteenth century were not confined to issues of language. For reasons beyond the remit of this chapter the period was not the Royal Court of Jersey's finest hour.[32] Justice was slow and incompetent. In 1846 Royal Commissioners were appointed to inquire into the state of the criminal law in the Channel Islands. They reported in 1847 for Jersey[33] and 1848 for Guernsey.[34] The report for Jersey was thorough and trenchant. It exposed many inadequacies in the criminal law. At the conclusion of their report it was stated:

> that some of the changes we propose will be displeasing to a numerous part of the inhabitants and that to another part it will appear that we have not gone far enough. So strong are the feelings of the extreme reforming party, that it was urged upon us to recommend measures which would stop little short of an absolute adoption of the English law, and the annexation of the island to an English circuit.[35]

Those recommendations were not made, but the Commissioners did controversially propose the removal of the Jurats from the Royal Court (which was not accepted), the creation of a Police Court and numerous modifications to the substantive criminal law (which were in time accepted). Following the general recommendations of the 1847 Commissioners, a number of Laws were

---

28　(1885) 210 Ex. 206 at 211.

29　Printed at the Jersey Press 1789.

30　See, for example, *Ex parte Viscount Wimborne* 1983 JJ 17 at 21–23, and *Lane v Lane* (1985–1986) JLR 48 at 57–60.

31　*Re Windeatt's Trusts* (1969) 2 All ER 324. Cf *Re Weston's Settlements* (1968) 3 All ER 338. For some, it was the Trusts (Jersey) Law 1984 that definitively implanted English-style trusts into Jersey law. See also P Bailhache, 'Introduction' in S Atkins (ed), *Insights into Trusts Law: The Channel Islands and Beyond* (Institute of Law 2013).

32　See G Le Quesne, *Jersey and Whitehall in the Mid-nineteenth Century*, 3rd Joan Stevens Memorial Lecture (*Société Jersiaise* 1992) for an erudite account of the constitutional struggles between the UK Government and the States of Jersey.

33　Royal Commissioners, *First report of the Commissioners – Jersey* (HMSO 1847).

34　Royal Commissioners, *Second report of the Commissioners – Guernsey* (HMSO 1848).

35　ibid, l.

passed by the States which amended the customary law by incorporating parts of English statutes. The *Loi (1895) modifiant le droit criminel* applied to Jersey certain provisions of the Criminal Law Amendment Act 1895 in relation to sexual offences. But the Royal Court itself and the Law Officers of the Crown were influenced increasingly by the common law of England. In *Foster v Att. Gen.*[36] the court considered in depth the customary law offence of fraud. The arguments all proceeded from a plea in bar by the defendant asserting that the offence did not exist in Jersey law. The Royal Court rejected that argument and was upheld by the Court of Appeal. The Court of Appeal analysed the case law of the preceding 200 years and found that Jersey lawyers had turned to France for help in developing the law of fraud in the first half of the nineteenth century and to England in the second half.[37] In the twentieth century, 'the use of English categories and English terms in prosecutions for fraud has increased very greatly, almost to the exclusion of any other mode of proceeding'.[38] Specific offences under the Larceny Act 1916 had been used as examples of fraud under Jersey law, and charged accordingly.

The importation of the English criminal law has not been confined to fraud. The law of homicide has imported concepts of diminished responsibility and provocation to reduce murder to manslaughter.[39] Infanticide and offences relating to the mistreatment of children have followed the English form. Perjury,[40] rape,[41] forgery, uttering, falsification of accounts, receiving stolen property,[42] conspiracy[43] and interferences with the process of justice[44] have largely followed English common law. Most statutory offences created since 1900, for example, in relation to customs and excise, misuse of drugs, and firearms, have been based upon corresponding English statutes. Yet the process of Anglicization of the criminal law is by no means complete. The Royal Court asserts a jurisdiction to declare the boundaries of established categories of crime, and to apply existing principles to new facts.[45] Some of the customary law offences, such as assault, are charged in English but are in fact *assaut*, which in Jersey law includes a battery. An *assaut grave et criminel* embraces all the different statutory offences of wounding, causing grievous bodily harm and so on, that are to be found in the English

---

36   1989 JLR 70 (Royal Court) and 1992 JLR 6 (CA).

37   From 1851 onwards there were numerous examples of prosecutions for '*avoir obtenu sous de faux pretextes*' [obtained by false pretences]. See *Att. Gen. v Rainey* (1851) 14 PC 447, unreported.

38   1992 JLR 6, at 21.

39   Homicide (Jersey) Law 1986.

40   *Att. Gen. v Venton* (CA) (1982) JJ 1; *Golder v Dodd* (CA) 1982 JJ 23.

41   *Att. Gen. v Makarios* (1979) JJ 85.

42   *Manning v Att. Gen.* (2000) JLR 32.

43   *Att. Gen. v Peacock* (2007) JLR *N* [57].

44   *United Capital Corp. Ltd. v Bender* (2007) JLR N [1]; *Shewan v Att. Gen.* (CA) 1999 JLR 192.

45   *Att. Gen. v Thwaites* (1978) JJ 179.

Offences against the Person Act, 1861.[46] Furthermore, not every modern English statute is followed. The reforms enacted by the Sexual Offences Act 2003 have not been replicated in Jersey.[47] In summary, the sources of Jersey's criminal law are thoroughly mixed, although there is little doubt that the customary law is gradually yielding to English influences.

The Surge of Danger Since 1945

Language and education

There is no doubt that the linguistic transition from French to English constitutes one of the principal threats and dangers for the integrity of Jersey law. Jersey was essentially a Francophone country until 1945. The influence of the English language had been felt from the middle of the nineteenth century but until the German occupation in 1940 the language of the law had been French. When English Acts, for example in relation to intellectual property law, were applied to the Island, they were applied by means of a Jersey Law written in French. For example, the Musical Copyright Act 1906 was applied to the Island by the *Loi (1908) au sujet des droits de compositeur,*[48] while the Copyright Act 1911 was applied to Jersey, with modifications, by the *Loi (1913) au sujet des droits d'auteur.*[49] The new Probation service was constituted by a law entitled the *Loi (1937) sur l'atténuation des peines et sur la mise en liberté surveillée,* even if the thinking behind the law was Anglocentric. From 1945 onwards, laws have been drafted in English unless they were amendments to a *Loi* drafted in French.[50] Until the early 1950s pleadings were drafted in French, and judgments of the Royal Court were issued in French, in the old *jugement motivé* style. From 1950 onwards judgments were (mainly) prepared and delivered in the English discursive mode, and in 1985 a professional series of Jersey Law Reports began to be published. From the early 1960s onwards, nearly all court proceedings have been recorded in

---

46   See C Pitchers, 'Grave and Criminal Assault: Another View' (2011) 15 Jersey and Guernsey Law Review 52.

47   See C Whelan, 'The Sexual Offences Act 2003 – is Jersey Falling Behind?' (2004) 8 Jersey Law Review 284.

48   <http://www.jerseylaw.je/Law/display.aspx?url=lawsinforce%5chtm%5cLawFil es%5c1900-1949%2fJersey_Law_04-1908.htm&print=y.> accessed 27 October 2013.

49   <http://www.jerseylaw.je/Law/display.aspx?url=lawsinforce%5chtm%5cLa wFiles%5c1900-1949%2fJersey_Law_01-1913.htm&print=y.> accessed 27 October 2013. Both the 1908 Law and the 1913 Law were repealed by the Intellectual Property (Unregistered Rights) (Jersey) Law 2011.

50   An exception might be said to be the *Loi* (1991) *sur la copropriété des immeubles bâtis* which enabled the sale of 'flying freeholds' – but that law was really an extension of principles embodied in the *Loi* (1880) *sur la propriété foncière.*

English. Conveyances of land, which remained in French until a change of rule in 2006, are now drafted in English.

The linguistic change was coupled with a change in the pattern of legal education. In the nineteenth century, Jersey lawyers had been educated in Caen, or in Paris. During the twentieth century it became the practice for lawyers to obtain a qualification at the English Bar before returning to study Jersey law, and the practice of studying at the *Université de Caen* was abandoned.[51] English technical terms began to be employed by lawyers in practice. After 1945 such technical terms began appearing in judgments of the court, and in statutes.

The linguistic shift caused by the education of the lawyers was compounded by the training and experience of the legislative draftsmen. Before 1945 law drafting was undertaken by the Law Officers of the Crown. In the 1950s an advocate was appointed as the first full-time draftsman, but on his appointment as Deputy Bailiff in 1963, he was replaced by an English barrister who never qualified in Jersey law. As the demands upon drafting time increased, more draftsmen were appointed but none of them has ever been a Jersey advocate or *écrivain* (solicitor). All have been recruited from Australia, New Zealand and other Commonwealth jurisdictions where the common law holds sway. The result has been that a number of statutes enacted since 1963 jar with the customary law. References to real and personal estate appear instead of references to immoveable and moveable property respectively.[52] Some of the thinking behind certain statutes reveals the mind of a common lawyer unschooled in the principles of the civil law.[53] Clearly, legislative draftsmen should have a working knowledge, at the least, of the principles of the customary and civil law. Until very recently, the means of achieving that end had not been obvious. With the foundation of a law school, the Institute of Law, it is to be hoped that legislative draftsmen will in future be required to attend at least part of the Jersey Law course.

The change of language in the law has reflected, albeit at a slower pace, the tipping of the linguistic balance amongst Islanders. In the political sphere, complaints are frequently voiced by Anglophone members of the legislature when

---

51   Studying at Caen University remains a requirement for admission to the Guernsey Bar.

52   The Probate (Jersey) Law 1949 is a surprising early example containing references to 'personal estate' rather than 'moveable estate'. The solecism was corrected in the Probate (Jersey) Law 1998. See also, for example, *Meaker v Picot* (1972) JJ 2161; *In re Greville Bathe Fund* (1973) JJ 2513; *In re Brown* (1997) JLR 137. For 'Real estate' see, eg Agricultural Land (Control of Sales and Leases (Jersey) Law 1974, art 5. Compulsory Purchase of Land (Procedure) (Jersey) Law 1961.

53   See, for example, Law Reform (Miscellaneous Provisions) (Jersey) Law 1960, where the draftsman has tried to transpose French legal words and phrases into an English context, even to the extent of introducing a defence of contributory negligence to an action in tort by the back door.

Projets de loi in the French language[54] are presented rather than draft laws written in English. Few advocates now speak French with any degree of competence. The ability to understand French texts is limited. Researching and deploying arguments based upon the commentators on the customary law texts is a serious challenge for many lawyers. Until 2008, when the Institute of Law was founded in Jersey, local lawyers were schooled almost exclusively in the common law. A few had qualified in Scotland, but most had their first qualifications from England, New Zealand, Australia and other common law jurisdictions. The Jersey Bar is now predominantly Anglophone.

The relative demise of the French language does not of course necessarily mean that the principles of law to be applied by the courts should be undermined. There are many mixed civilian/common law jurisdictions where the language of the law is (predominantly) English. When the Jersey Law Review was founded in 1997 the author's editorial foreword contained the following passage:

> We conclude with a word about language. The Bailiwick remains, in theory at least, a bilingual jurisdiction. Both English and French are the official languages of the Island. The reality on the ground is that Jersey is now primarily an Anglophone society, and that reality is reflected in this Review. Jersey law must be developed in a language which is understood by the majority of the Island's inhabitant ….
>
> The Editorial Board expresses the hope that the Jersey Law Review will stimulate its readers and, more importantly, will help to develop Jersey law to serve the changing needs of this small community. It will then have played its part, if we may respectfully adopt the words of the Jersey Judicial and Legal Services Committee, in ensuring 'the continuance of Jersey's legal heritage not as a mere memorial but as a living force'.[55]

Yet the consequences of the post-war changes undoubtedly had a marked effect on the development of the law, and led to a strong tendency, especially between 1960 and 1990, to draw upon English law sources. To these changes we will now turn.

Law of contract

In the light of these changes it was not surprising that in the latter part of the twentieth century advocates began to turn to common law authorities in making their submissions to the Royal Court. It was far easier to pick up *Chitty on Contracts* than to go to Pothier or Domat when researching a point of the law of obligations

---

54 A translation is of course always available, but that does not prevent the complaints because the authentic text is that in which the Law is originally drafted.

55 P Bailhache, 'Foreword' (1997) 1 Jersey Law Review 1, 3, referring to the Jersey Judicial and Legal Services Review Committee, *Final report* (RC12/1991) para 13.3.

or contract law, even though the court had on many occasions stated that Pothier was the authority to be preferred in determining the Jersey law of contract.[56] Some of the advocates were lazy, but regrettably the court too was indulgent. In *Colledge v Little Grove Hotel Ltd*, (a dispute involving the termination of a contract of employment) the court stated: 'The law to be applied in this case is not in dispute. It was agreed that the matters which justify the summary determination by an employer of a contract of employment are correctly set out in Halsbury's Laws of England.'[57]

In other cases the court recited without comment the principles of English law cited by counsel, and applied them.[58] Sometimes English, French and Jersey authorities were referred to in the same judgment.[59] Occasionally, however, principles of English contract law were specifically rejected as forming no part of the law of Jersey.[60]

In the last two decades the court has rediscovered the civilian roots of the law of contract.[61] Some shock waves were felt in the legal profession when the court stated in *Selby v Romeril* that:

> It is true that Pothier has often been treated by this court as the surest guide to the Jersey law of contract. It is also true, however, that Pothier was writing two centuries ago and that our law cannot be regarded a set in the aspic[62] of the 18th century. Pothier was one of those authors upon whom the draftsmen of the French Civil Code relied and it is therefore helpful to look at the relevant article of that Code. Article 1108 of the Code provides:
>
> '*Quatre conditions sont essentiels pour la validité d'une convention:*
>
> *Le consentement de la partie qui s'oblige*
>
> *Sa capacité de contracter*

---

56   *Wood v Wholesale Electrics (Jersey) Ltd* (1976) JJ 415; *Warner v Hendrick* (1985–1986) JLR 366, 371.

57   1970 JJ 1487, 1493. The Court went on to cite an English case where the Court of Appeal stated '…since a contract of service is but an example of contracts in general … '

58   For example, *United Dominions Corp. (CI) Ltd v Pinglaux* (1969) JJ 1123, 1137.

59   *MAB Investments Ltd v Vibert* 1972 JJ 2127; *McIlroy v Hustler* (1969) JJ 1181.

60   For example, *Channel Hotels and Properties Ltd v Rice* (1977) JJ 111.

61   *Selby v Romeril* (1996) JLR 210; *Macon v Querée* (2001) JLR 80; *Marett v Marett and O'Brien* (2008) JLR 384.

62   The judgment originally contained the rather more colourful phrase 'frozen in aspic'. See A Binnington 'Frozen in Aspic? The Approach of Jersey's Courts to the Law of Contract' (1997) 1 Jersey Law Review 21. The editor of the Jersey Law Reports, clearly a culinary purist, recast the phrase as 'set in aspic'.

Un objet certain qui forme la matière de l'engagement

Une cause licite dans l'obligation.[63]

In our judgment, it may now be asserted that by the law of Jersey, there are four requirements for the creation of a valid contract, namely (1) consent; (2)capacity; (3) an '*objet*'; and (4) a '*cause*'.[64]

The formation of a contract was thus firmly re-based on principles of the customary and civil law. No longer was *Chitty on Contracts* a sufficient companion for an advocate in the Royal Court. In the succeeding years the court has, more or less consistently, followed the path charted in *Selby*.[65] In *Mendonca v Le Boutillier*[66] construing a conditional sale agreement, the court referred to Pothier's *Traité du contrat de vente*,[67] but found that, on the point at issue, a conflicting provision in the *Code Civil* was a late eighteenth century invention. In *Steelux v Edmonstone*[68] counsel brought his *Chitty on Contracts* along with him but the court stated:

> Counsel referred us to passages from *Chitty on Contracts* … as to what constitutes a misrepresentation under English law. While English law and Jersey law may often arrive at the same conclusion in relation to the effect upon a contract of a false or fraudulent misrepresentation, the process of reasoning, and the route by which the journey is taken, are sometimes different. We find it necessary, therefore, to set out what we conceive to be the law in this area.[69]

In *Marett v Marett*,[70] a strong Court of Appeal[71] declined to deliver a detailed analysis of the Jersey law of contract, but applied unequivocally the principles set out in *Selby v Romeril*:

---

63   [Four requisites are essential for the validity of an agreement: the consent of the party who binds himself: his capacity to contract: a definite object which forms the subject-matter of the undertaking: a lawful cause in the obligation.]

64   1996 JLR 210, 218.

65   In *Cronin v Gordon Bennett* (2003) JLR Note 22, the Court held that the law of contract was underpinned by the theory of the autonomy of the will, expressed in the maxim *la convention fait la loi des parties*, which determined that a person could only be bound by contractual obligations expressive of his free will. In order to establish a contract of agency, there had to be a sufficient meeting of minds to constitute a *convention*.

66   (1997) JLR 142.

67   Paris 1830 edition.

68   2005 JLR 152.

69   ibid, 9.

70   2008 JLR 384.

71   Lord Sumption OBE, Sir John Nutting QC and Nigel Pleming QC.

There are four elements necessary to constitute a contract under Jersey law: (i) capacity; (ii) consent; (iii) *cause*; and (iv) *objet*. Ignoring capacity, which is not in issue, the Jersey law of contract determines consent by use of the subjective theory of contract (see Pothier, *Treatise on the Law of Obligations or Contracts*, trans. Evans, para 4, at 4; para 91, at 53; para 98, at 59 and Appendix V, at 35 (1806) and *Selby v Romeril*. And see *Mobil Sales & Supply Corp. v Transoil (Jersey) Ltd* and *La Motte Garages v Morgan* (which must now be considered *per incuriam* on this specific point in the light of *Selby v Romeril*).[72]

However, the occasional lapses by the court during the 30-year period up to 1990 have left conflicting authorities in some areas of the law, which remain to be resolved.[73] The legislature has also intervened to give a conflicting message as to whether the law of contract is really based on civil or common law. The Supply of Goods and Services (Jersey) Law 2009 appears to be largely based upon the Sale of Goods Act of the UK, and authors of an article in the Jersey and Guernsey Law Review even suggested that it would be permissible to consult *Chitty on Contracts* in certain respects.[74] It should be recalled, however, that the draftsmen of the Sale of Goods Act 1891 acknowledged their debt to Pothier.

Law of torts

In the law of torts,[75] the influence of English law came late. In 1953 the court stated:

> The word 'tort' is used here in the sense in which it is commonly used by English lawyers when they speak of the Law of Torts as opposed to the Law of Contracts. On grounds of convenience this may be permitted, provided that it is done without losing sight of the fact that this is a Jersey court administering Jersey law …[76]

As Nicolle stated in *The Origin and Development of Jersey Law*, when English influence came, 'it came in an overpowering wave'.[77] *Guernsey States Insurance*

---

72   ibid, 56–57.

73   See R Leeuwenberg, *'Une très grosse erreur*: Jersey's Mistake over Misrepresentation' (2013) 17 Jersey and Guernsey Law Review 5.

74   T Hanson and C Marr, 'An Introduction to the Supply of Goods and Services (Jersey) Law 2009' (2009) 13 Jersey and Guernsey Law Review 336.

75   In Jersey a *délit* is a criminal offence and not a civil wrong. See *Jersey FSC v A.P.Black (Jersey) Ltd and others* (2002) JLR 294, para.26.

76   *Guernsey States Insurance Authority v Ernest Farley and Son Ltd* (1953) JJ 47 at 48.

77   S Nicolle, *The Origin and Development of Jersey* Law (5th edn Jersey and Guernsey Law Review 2009) 66.

Authority v Farley was the last time for nearly 40 years that the court was to acknowledge the difference between a tort and a *tort*. In *Arya Holdings v Minories Finance Ltd*, after citing the above passage from *Farley*, the Royal Court stated:

> Having considered very carefully the later Jersey cases cited to me by counsel, I am drawn to the ineluctable conclusion that as time has moved on, we have moved ever closer to the English concept of tort. Advocate Dessain had no doubt that Winfield [on the Law of Tort] had supplanted anything on this subject that Dalloz might have to say.[78]

That perhaps overstates the case. In *Jersey Financial Services Commission v A.P. Black*[79] the court stated that it was clear that Jersey law had followed its own distinct path in developing the law of torts. It had retained a system of specific wrongs for which there was a cause of action, even if some of the wrongs were fairly general in character. The court referred to the many instances in the earlier cases where there was a reference to '*un tort*'. The court continued:

> It is the case, however, that in the modern period (mid-19th century onwards), Jersey lawyers and the courts have increasingly turned to English law both for labels to attach to particular torts and for assistance in defining the ambit of such torts. In *Curry v Horman* (1889, 213 Ex. 511) it was decided that *balayures amoncelées près d'une maison d'habitation constituent une nuisance.* [Sweepings that have been piled up near a dwelling-house may constitute a nuisance.] Many cases involving injury to reputation are recorded in the *Table des Décisions* towards the end of the 19th century under the rubric '*Diffamation*'. These references were made, however, against a background of knowledge of existing causes of action arising under the customary law. Jersey lawyers and the courts employed English terminology and, to an extent, legal principle to supplement but not to subvert the customary law.[80]

When *Arya Holdings* went to the Court of Appeal, Southwell JA stated:

> The Jersey law of torts derives primarily from the Jersey common law which has its origins in the Norman law of the ancienne coutume. In relation to the tort of negligence, Jersey follows the law of England (*T.A.Picot (C.I.) Ltd v Crills* ...) except as regards any point on which a different rule has been established in Jersey. In relation to other torts or other aspects of the law of tort, although careful attention is paid to decisions on English common law, the courts of Jersey have to found themselves on the common law of Jersey. Thus there may be causes of action in tort which are available in England but not in Jersey, and vice versa. A

---

78   (1995) JLR 208 at 215.

79   *Jersey FSC v A.P. Black (Jersey) Ltd and others* (2002) JLR 294.

80   ibid, 307 para 29.

D'Allain claim is a cause of action available in Jersey in accordance with Jersey common law, as a feature of the Jersey law relating to declarations en désastre but is naturally not also available in England.[81]

Law of property

The law of property has on the whole resisted any trend towards applying common law rather than civil law principles. The *Loi (1880) sur la propriété foncière*, a mini-code drafted by one of Jersey's most distinguished lawyers,[82] was based upon provisions of the *Code Civil*, and has been a bulwark against which most incursions have foundered. Maxims of the customary law, such as '*Promesse à heritage ne vaut*' have prevented the importation of English equitable remedies like specific performance.[83]

Yet in relation to the English remedy of proprietary estoppel, the court has vacillated. In *Felard Investments Ltd v Trustees of Church of Our Lady*, the church had built over land subject to a 'no-building' servitude. The plaintiff neighbour sought the demolition of the offending part of the building. The court was tempted. It stated: 'The argument that the court has the power, in an appropriate case, to legalise a breach of proprietary rights by ordering the payment of damages instead of requiring the breach to be remedied is attractive.' The court considered English authority but concluded 'that the doctrine of proprietary estoppel is not part of the law of Jersey, but nevertheless we have come to our view with some regret ...'.[84]

Six years later the court yielded to temptation. In *Pirouet v Pirouet* a son had occupied and worked a farm for 30 years on the basis that he would inherit the farm from his father. The son became a Jehovah's Witness and the father devised the property to his other two sons. The court distinguished *Felard Investments* by stating 'Although in [*Felard*] ... the Royal Court, in dealing with the extinction of a servitude, declared that the doctrine of proprietary estoppel was not part of the law of Jersey, we cannot avoid coming to the conclusion that the doctrine of

---

81   *Arya Holdings Ltd v Minories Finance Ltd* (CA) (1997) JLR 176 at 181. A '*D'Allain* claim' is a claim by a debtor that a declaration *en désastre* [of bankruptcy], which can be obtained *ex parte*, has been wrongly obtained by a creditor. The eponymous claim has its origin in the case of *D'Allain v De Gruchy* (1890) 214 Ex. 196.

82   Sir Robert Pipon Marett, 1820–1884, Solicitor General at the time when the Law was drafted, but Bailiff between 1880 and 1884. His son RR Marett was Rector of Exeter College, Oxford, and grandson Sir Robert Marett, a diplomat. See Robert Marett, *The Maretts of La Haule* (Société Jersiaise 1982).

83   *Gallichan v Gallichan* (1954) JJ 335; *Romeril v Davis* (1977) JJ 135; *Taylor v Fitzpatrick* (CA) (1979) JJ 1; *Basden Hotels Ltd v Dormy Hotels Ltd* (1968) JJ 911. In *Symes v Couch* (1978) JJ 119, the Court warned that the maxim would not be permitted to facilitate fraud. Part performance in reliance on a contract had taken place, and the Court ordered the defendant to complete the contract or pay damages.

84   (1979) JJ 19 at 27 per Ereaut, Bailiff.

equitable estoppel, and in particular the facet of it known as promissory estoppel, or estoppel by representation, is part of the law of Jersey and can be applied in appropriate cases.'[85]

In 2012, however, the pendulum swung back the other way. In *Flynn v Reid* the court stated:

> The central difficulty with applying the English doctrine of proprietary estoppel ... in Jersey is that it requires us to accept the principle that there is a theoretical division between the legal ownership of immoveable estate in Jersey and its beneficial ownership. ... we do not think that the doctrine of proprietary estoppel forms part of the law of Jersey if its effect is to create an equitable interest in land that exists in parallel with the legal interest.[86]

One day, perhaps, the issue will occupy the attention of the Court of Appeal. In general, however, it is possible to assert that the principles codified in the 1880 Law have enabled the law of property to remain true to its civilian roots.

Law of succession

For the last three decades argument has raged between those who would adopt the freedom of testation associated with common law countries and those who prefer the certainties of Continental systems.[87] At customary law a testator had very little freedom. The principle was '*La conservation du bien dans la famille*',[88] and the principal heir enjoyed considerable privileges. The law governed the devolution of moveable and immoveable property to a very large extent. Only in the matter of moveable property did a male testator have any right to make a will. Change came in the nineteenth century when the *Loi (1851) sur les testaments d'immeubles* enacted – '*Toute personne ayant capacité pour faire un testament de biens-meubles pourra disposer par testament de ses immeubles.*'[89] The *Loi (1926) sur les héritages propres* conferred unrestricted freedom of testation in

---

85   (1985–1986) JLR 151 at 160, per Dorey, Commissioner. *Pirouet* was followed by Page, Commissioner in *Maçon v Querée* (2001) JLR 80 in a case, ironically, involving a descendant of Mr Pirouet.

86   William Bailhache, Deputy Bailiff, in *Flynn v Reid* (2012) (1) JLR at paras 48–50.

87   See, for example, Legislation Committee, *Consultation Document*, (2 Jan 2001, RC3/2001); Keith Dixon, '*Légitime*: A Time for Reform?' (2002) 6 Jersey Law Review 247; Meryl Thomas, 'The Future of *légitime* – *vive la différence*' (2013) 17 Jersey and Guernsey Law Review 305.

88   The conservation of property in the family.

89   Art. 1. [Every person having the capacity to make a will of moveable property may dispose by will of his immoveable property.]

relation to immoveable property subject only to the widow's right of dower[90] and the widower's right of *viduité*.[91]

In post-war years there have been suggestions that the same freedom of testation should be extended to moveable property.[92] The Wills and Successions (Jersey) Law 1993 abolished a number of rules of customary law, and modified the rights of inheritance both in testate and intestate successions, but preserved the right of *légitime*.[93] Rights of *légitime* have been extended to illegitimate children and to civil partners. In an intestacy the surviving spouse or civil partner has been given a right of *usufruit* (or life enjoyment) of the matrimonial or civil partnership home.[94] In substance, however, the law of succession retains its identity with the customary law of Normandy.

The Court of Appeal

One of the constitutional reforms to which consideration was given in the aftermath of occupation and liberation was the process of appeal from decisions of the Royal Court. There are two divisions of the Royal Court, the *Nombre Inférieur* and the *Nombre Supérieur*. The Bailiff presided over both divisions and the only difference was the number of Jurats with whom the Bailiff sat. In the lower court there were two while in the upper there were seven or more. An appeal usually lay from the *Nombre Inférieur* to the *Nombre Supérieur*. Because Jurats were, until 1948,[95] judges of both law and fact, it was not unusual for an appeal to succeed notwithstanding that the presiding judge was the same person. A further appeal lay from the *Nombre Supérieur* to the Judicial Committee of the Privy Council. Their Lordships were conscious of their duty to apply the law of Jersey, and invariably did

---

90   The right to enjoy during her lifetime one third of the husband's immoveable property.

91   The right to enjoy during his lifetime the whole of the wife's immoveable property. Dower and *viduité* had different incidents.

92   In Guernsey those arguments have prevailed. The Inheritance (Guernsey) Law 2011 introduced a new system of freedom of testation very similar to that of England and Wales.

93   At customary law the legitimate children of a testator were entitled to one third of his moveable property as *légitime* if there was a widow, and to two thirds if there was not. A widow was entitled to one third of the testator's moveable property. The customary law rules have been modified by the Wills and Successions (Jersey) Law 1993.

94   Art. 5.

95   The Royal Court (Jersey) Law 1948, Art. 15(1) provided that 'In all causes and matters, civil, criminal and mixed, the Bailiff shall be the sole judge of law, and shall award the costs, if any'.

so.[96] However, a direct appeal from the Royal Court to the Privy Council was not regarded as satisfactory. In 1949, after lengthy consultation with the governments of the two Bailiwicks, the Court of Appeal (Channel Islands) Order was made by the Privy Council. For reasons that are still obscure, the Channel Islands Court of Appeal thereby constituted never sat.[97]

Over a decade was to pass before the Jersey Court of Appeal was constituted by the Court of Appeal (Jersey) Law 1961.[98] It is composed of the Bailiff and Deputy Bailiff of Jersey, who are *ex officio* the President and Vice-President of the Court, and a number of other judges or senior counsel appointed by Her Majesty as Ordinary Judges of the Court of Appeal. Most of the judges are English lawyers, but in recent years it has been the practice to appoint from the Scottish Bar as well. One might have thought that the presence of non-Jersey lawyers in the Appeal Court constituted a danger in that they might be inclined to apply legal principles with which they had most experience. That fear has proved, in most cases, to be misplaced. Admittedly the court was greatly influenced from the start by a distinguished Jerseyman, Sir Godfray Le Quesne QC,[99] who sat as a judge of the court for more than 30 years. But many other judges have made substantial contributions to the development of Jersey jurisprudence. The judgment of Southwell JA referred to above is an example of the court's care to apply the law of Jersey to cases before it.

Scottish judges, trained in another mixed jurisdiction, have made particularly valuable contributions. In *Haas v Duquemin*,[100] bad conveyancing practice had led to the creation of conflicting servitudes over a parking area held in co-ownership which the owners were unable to resolve themselves. On appeal to the Court of Appeal Hodge JA[101] held that the deadlock could if necessary be resolved by using a power of judicial regulation. He stated:

---

96   See *Godfray v Godfray* (1865) 3 Moo. PCCNS 316; 16 ER 120; for a more recent example, see *Snell v Beadle* (2001) JLR 118, where their Lordships considered the customary law doctrine of *déception d'outre moitié de juste prix* [a deceit involving more than half of the fair price]. Lord Hope of Craighead stated 'English law is of no assistance in this matter'. Unfortunately, nor was Scots law, which rejected the old Roman rule of *ultra dimidium justi pretii, ex re praesumitur dolus* [fraud is to be presumed from the fact of a price less than half of the fair value] many centuries ago. Perhaps that helped the Privy Council, by a majority of three to two, to limit the application of the doctrine in Jersey.

97   See T Sowden 'The Origin of the Jersey Court of Appeal' (2000) 4 Jersey Law Review 61.

98   A separate Guernsey Court of Appeal was constituted in the same year.

99   Sir Godfray Le Quesne QC (1923–2013) was a judge of the Jersey Court of Appeal between 1964 and 1997.

100   2000 JLR *N*-54; 8 August 2000, Jersey unreported.

101   P Hodge was a judge of the Jersey and Guernsey Courts of Appeal between 2000 and 2005 when he was appointed as a Senator of the College of Justice in Scotland. In October 2013 he succeeded Lord Hope of Craighead as a Justice of the Supreme Court of the UK.

Such a power exists in some jurisdictions with civilian traditions in their property law. In France, the courts have power to regulate on an interim basis the use by co-owners of property held in common. ... In Scotland, where we have drunk from the same fountain, judges have suggested that judicial regulation is available to resolve managerial deadlock. See, for example the cases cited by Professor Reid in Law of Property in Scotland, 3rd ed., para. 30 (1996) ... It seems to me that judicial regulation is available in the civilian tradition and that in principle it is available in Jersey.[102]

In *Gale v Rockhampton Apartments Ltd.*,[103] McNeill JA drew upon his Scottish experience when commenting on a reference in the Royal Court's judgment to Houard, *Dictionnaire du Droit Normand*,[104] and obligations arising from equity in quasi-contract, when he stated, 'I might pause to observe that this concept is well known to all students and practitioners of Scots law, as the obligation *negotiorum gestio* also held to arise under quasi-contract.'[105]

There is no evidence that Jersey law has been endangered by the presence on the Court of Appeal of members who are not qualified in the law of the Island. On the contrary, there are many examples of the appellate judges developing the law in accordance with its traditions.

Geographical Influences

Jersey is the largest of the Channel Islands with an area of 45 square miles (119.6 sq km) and lies 14 miles from the coast of Normandy and 85 miles from the closest point of England. The geographical position of the Island has not, however, proved to be a significant factor. The French mainland exercises no gravitational pull. The dominant commercial relationships in the twenty-first century are with the sovereign power, and it is from English law that the principal threats are coming.

Non-Legal, Local, Regional and International Influences

The constitutional relationship between Jersey and the UK is one that changed little over the centuries until the post-war years. Until 1940 the Island's autonomy in domestic matters had seldom clashed with the UK's responsibility for the conduct of Jersey's international affairs. In the aftermath of the German occupation, the Islanders had found a new sense of identity. They had been obliged for five years

---

102   *Haas v Duquemin* (2002) JLR 27, 39.

103   (2007) JLR 27 (Royal Court) and affirmed at 332 (CA).

104   D Houard, *Dictionnaire du droit Normand* (LeBoucher Le Jeune 1780) available at <http://www.jerseylaw.je/publications/Library> accessed 9 January 2014.

105   ibid, 350, para 39.

to look to their own interests as best they could. The relationship with the mother country had changed, even if those changes only gradually became apparent. The first manifestation came in 1950 when the Islanders asserted that they should not be bound by international agreements without their consent. The so-called Foreign Office Letters of 1951 made it clear that a treaty or international agreement was not to be taken as applying to the Channel Islands 'by reason only of the fact that it applies to the UK'.[106] Jersey became a member of international organizations in her own right.[107] In 1972 Jersey (with Guernsey and the Isle of Man) entered a separate relationship with the European Economic Community (as it then was) under Protocol 3 to the UK's Act of Accession.[108]

This gradual assumption of a separate international identity was statutorily acknowledged when the Crown sanctioned the States of Jersey Law 2005, the Preamble to which provides 'And whereas it is further recognized that there is an increasing need for Jersey to participate in matters of international affairs'. In 2007 the Lord Chancellor and the Chief Minister of Jersey signed a Framework Agreement, paragraph 2 of which provided 'Jersey has an international identity which is different from that of the UK'. In 2012 the Government of Jersey published for the first time its policy for conducting external relations.[109] In 2013 the office of Minister of External Relations was created.[110] Discussions have even taken place about the possibility of Jersey's becoming a sovereign State.[111]

These subtle changes in the constitutional relationship between Jersey and the UK over the last two or three decades have taken place at the same time as a resurgence of interest in Jersey's customary law, and a greater interest on the part of the courts to rediscover the roots of the Island's jurisprudence. It is difficult to avoid the conclusion that they are related, and that a greater political autonomy helps to support the independence of a country's legal system.

On the other hand, the influence of globalization cannot be ignored. The commercial expansion of the Island since 1945 and its emergence as an international finance centre have had a significant effect. Before the German occupation, commerce in the Island centred upon tourism and the agricultural industry. Lawyers were relatively few in number, and their work was principally concerned with the needs of a small agricultural community. The customary law was absorbed almost by osmosis. In the last 60 years the number of advocates has grown exponentially. Many new advocates have no family connection with

---

106   F de L Bois, *Constitutional History of Jersey*, (States of Jersey 1970) 270.

107   European Plant Protection Organization (in 1951) and International Social Security Association (in 1957).

108   European Communities (Jersey) Law 1972.

109   <www.statesassembly.gov.je/AssemblyReports/2012/R.140-2012.pdf> accessed 6 January 2014.

110   States of Jersey (Minister for External Relations) (Jersey) Regulations 2013.

111   *Dependency or Sovereignty? Time to Take Stock* (Jersey and Guernsey Law Review 2012).

the Island and little sense of Jersey's legal history. They practice commercial law of one sort or another, and have little need to consult Terrien,[112] Basnage,[113] or other writers upon the customary law. It is sometimes said that one of Jersey's attractions as a financial centre is that its law is based upon common law, and is therefore comprehensible to the (Anglophone) business community. That is of course, at least in part, a misconception. But it is true that there has been grafted on to the customary law a huge body of commercial law which is based upon English statutes and related concepts of the English common law.[114] Those influences of English law in matters of commerce spill over into other areas, like contract and the law of torts.

Strengths and Vulnerabilities

The size of the Island is of course a constant threat. A jurisdiction with a mere 100,000 inhabitants, even if some are litigious, and no more than four or five judges in the Royal Court is not going to have the capacity to create a body of judge-made law containing the solutions to all legal problems. It is true that the Jersey Law Reports expanded for the first time in 2012 to two volumes, but whole swathes of law need to be brought up to date. Neither the courts nor the legislature can undertake the whole task of law reform. The law of Jersey will continue to be vulnerable to incursions of foreign law because legislators, lawyers, and even judges, are indolent or careless. To develop the law in a manner consistent with its roots takes time and effort. It also costs money – which in the context of litigation will be the client's money.

On the other hand, the great strength of a system of customary law is that it is organic. It can change without legislative intervention. Given the will to develop the law to meet changing social and economic circumstances, the courts have the power to do so. In *Grove v Baker* the court stated:

> The Court is concerned only to apply the law of Jersey. If we can do so, we
> will apply the custom and the law laid down in previous decisions of this

---

112   Guillaume Terrien is the commentator most widely consulted upon *Le grand coutumier de Normandie*. The first edition appeared in 1574.

113   Henri Basnage wrote a commentary on the *Coutume reformée* that was first published in 1678 and was followed by a number of further editions. He is frequently cited by the Royal Court.

114   See, for example, Investors (Prevention of Fraud) (Jersey) Law 1967, Trusts (Jersey) Law 1984, Collective Investment Funds (Jersey) Law 1988, Companies (Jersey) Law 1991, Banking Business (Jersey) Law 1991, Limited Partnerships (Jersey) Law 1994, Insurance Business (Jersey) Law 1996, Limited Liability Partnerships (Jersey) Law 1997, Financial Services (Jersey) Law 1998, Separate Limited partnerships (Jersey) Law 2011, and Security Interests (Jersey) Law 2012.

court. If the law cannot be found in that way, we must adopt principles from elsewhere. ... Our customary law is organic and must absorb influences from other jurisdictions where a particular issue is not clear. It is the principles rather than the foreign law which are applied and, once applied, become the law of Jersey. The principles themselves will, in due time, need to be developed; in those circumstances the court may or may not develop the law in accordance with any changes which may have taken place in the jurisdiction from which the principles were originally imported.[115]

The court failed to add that such imported principles should be sympathetic to what has gone before.

The other strength of the customary law is the influence of what in France is called *doctrine* – the writings of learned commentators on the law. Indeed nearly all the writings upon the customary and civil law regarded as authoritative by the Royal Court (Terrien, Basnage, Routier, Domat, Pothier and others) fall under this heading. In the beginning legal scholarship played a major role in the development of Jersey law, even if it was also the law of the Duchy of Normandy. *Doctrine* embraces not only academic writings but also the comments of judges, practitioners and law teachers found in articles in legal journals and other places.

It is true that after the beginning of the eighteenth century there was very little academic writing on the law of Jersey. Le Geyt and Poingdestre, that distinguished duo of Lieutenant Bailiffs, wrote extensively between 1660 and 1710,[116] but after that – nothing, until Charles Le Gros wrote his *Droit coutumier de l'Ile de Jersey* in 1943.[117] However, more recently, there has been an increasing body of academic and professional writing, both in the Jersey and Guernsey Law Review[118] and in specialist publications such as works on insolvency and asset tracking (now in its 4th edition),[119] company law,[120] trusts,[121] and the drafting of trusts and will

---

115   2005 JLR 348 para 13.

116   Jean Poingdestre (1609–1691) wrote *Lois et coutumes de l'Ile de Jersey* (published by the Law Society of Jersey, 1928), *Commentaires sur l'ancienne coutume* (published by Law Society of Jersey 1907), *Remarques et animadversions sur la coutume reformée* (unpublished). Philippe Le Geyt (1635–1716) wrote *Constitution, loix et usages de Jersey*, sometimes described as *Manuscrits le Geyt*, (4 volumes published by States of Jersey 1846), and *Privilèges, loix et coutumes de l'Isle de Jersey* (Law Society of Jersey 1953).

117   Published by *Les chroniques de Jersey*, 1943; reprinted, with annotations, by Jersey and Guernsey Law Review 2007.

118   1997 – and published at www.jerseylaw.je.

119   A Dessain and M Wilkins, *Jersey Insolvency and Asset Tracking* (4th edn Key Haven Publications Ltd 2012).

120   M Dunlop, *Dunlop on Jersey Company Law* (Key Haven Publications Ltd 2010)

121   H Brown, *The Jersey Law of Trusts* (4th edn Key Haven Publications Ltd 2013)

trusts,[122] which help to fill some of the gaps. In addition, study guides produced by the Institute of Law provide a useful resource.[123] Such publications may fall short of the major works by, for example, Scottish institutional writers, but they nevertheless provide important material for judges and practitioners.

Conclusion

Is Jersey's legal system an endangered species, and, if so, what can be done to prevent its disappearance like the Mauritian dodo? There certainly are threats. The change of language, the inability of lawyers and legislative drafters to understand customary law texts, and the insidious influence of alien legal terms of art have already been mentioned. The overpowering weight from the sovereign State can be crushing. The legal systems of many small jurisdictions are dependent upon the interest and enthusiasm of a tiny number of lawyers and scholars for their survival. Jersey is no different. Without that continuing interest, a tide of inertia would drag the law of Jersey closer and closer to the law of England.

In the Durrell Wildlife Conservation Trust, education is seen as the key to the survival of endangered species. It is probably no different in the context of Jersey's jurisprudence. Unless aspiring advocates are taught the differences between the law of Jersey and the law of those countries where their initial training took place, and imbued with some sense of enthusiasm for those differences, the future would indeed be bleak. However, the foundation of a law school, the Institute of Law, gives some hope that the tide is turning.

It is now a legal requirement for aspiring Jersey lawyers to study the Jersey Law course at the Institute and to pass the examinations set by Visiting Academics.[124] The course is delivered by a team of Visiting Academics from the UK and France working with adjunct professors who are local advocates specializing in each area of law. The availability of the course, and the level playing field that it represents for the first time for those studying Jersey law, has led to a notable increase in the number of students. Within five years, there will be more qualified Jersey advocates who have been immersed in the customary law through studying at the Institute than those who have not.

An English law degree is now offered in association with the External Programme of the University of London. Links with other academic institutions in France and Spain have also been created with a view to encouraging research,

---

122   J Kessler QC and P Matthams, *Drafting Trusts and Will Trusts in the Channel Islands*, (Sweet and Maxwell 2007).

123   Published at www.lawinstitute.ac.je.

124   Advocates and Solicitors (Qualifying Examination) Rules 1997. A candidate applying to sit the final examination must have enrolled upon an approved course of instruction (art.1). The Institute of Law is at present the only institution approved to offer a course of instruction.

both into the law of Jersey and into areas of comparative law. A bold programme of expansion is under way. It remains to be seen whether the Institute of Law will remove all the dangers threatening the integrity of Jersey law, but the expectation is that at least the rot will have been stopped.

Chapter 5
Mauritius

The legal system of Mauritius has been marked by defining moments, or 'accidents of history', which have influenced the mix of laws, for example, the signing of the Capitulation of the French to the British troops in Mauritius in December 1810 under which the British undertook to allow the inhabitants to preserve their laws which included, in particular, the pre-Napoleonic criminal law of France, the Code Napoléon, the Code de Commerce, and the Code de Procedure Civile. Tony Angelo shows that it was around this core that the British colonial administration and the common law of England operated from 1810. Following the Treaty of Paris in 1814, this undertaking in the Capitulation was confirmed by Proclamation in Mauritius.

Mauritius is also a country where the important events, people and geography have had a profound effect of the subsequent legal system. Notably, the liberation of the slaves in 1834 was a precursor to significant changes in the employment law of Mauritius because the influx of indentured labourers from India meant that a significant local employment law developed outside of the Civil Code regime. In the years that followed independence in 1968, this Indo-Mauritian community influenced the direction of the law. Yet despite the waning of the power of the French culturally oriented community, an ambitious law reform programme not only resulted in the updating of the Code Napoléon but also the retention of the core elements of the French legal heritage via the French language.

As Angelo demonstrates, perhaps unexpectedly and in the face of globalization and the adoption of the common law in specific areas, Mauritius retains a strong mixed legal system and even today is taking steps to ensure that the unique legal culture of these islands is retained. An interesting example of a mixed legal system with codes in French but now with English as the official language, an intriguing mixture of population and languages, Mauritius may also be moving towards blending the elements in this mixed legal system. The core elements of the legal heritage still remain in French, but laws related to economy and globalization reflect common law thinking with everything operating within the 'droit commune' of Mauritius.

Mauritius: 'Capitulation, Consolidation, Creation'

Tony Angelo

Introduction

Mauritius is an archipelagic State which extends over a large area of the southern Indian Ocean.[1] The main island is the Island of Mauritius and it is there that the bulk of the 1.3 million inhabitants of Mauritius live. Ethnically they are 68 per cent Indo-Mauritian, that is to say persons of Indian ethnic background and predominantly Hindu or Muslim. The Creole community represents 25 per cent of the population and together with the Franco-Mauritians they represent the bulk of the Christian and predominantly Roman Catholic community. There are no indigenous inhabitants. At the time of European colonization the island was uninhabited.

Mauritius has civil law which is firmly based in the French legal tradition and founded on the *Code Napoléon* of 1804. This chapter will address the question of whether the legal system of Mauritius is, because of its mixed French and common law legal heritage, endangered or at risk of becoming endangered.[2]

To address this question the chapter will first consider the relevant history of the Mauritius legal system and those historical events which have served to give to Mauritius law its defining features. Also considered will be the languages of Mauritius, the pattern of legal education, the available reference texts and the role

---

1   A good introductory text to Mauritius and its colonial history is D Hollingworth, *They Came to Mauritius* (OUP 1965). There is also the more personal text of de Burgh Edwardes, *L'histoire de l'Ile Maurice 1705–1914* (Issoudun 1924). For a legal history the best text is the *Etudes de droit privé français et Mauricien* (Presses Universitaires de France 1969). Seven of the 16 chapters in that text deal specifically with the law of Mauritius and its evolution to 1 July 1965. Specifically on the civil law is R D'Unienville, *L'Evolution du Droit Civil à L'Ile Maurice 1721–1968* (Best Graphics 1994).

2   Most obviously by the common law. On the persistence of civil law principles in Vanuatu, Seychelles and Mauritius, see T Angelo, 'A Tale of Three Codes' in *Private Law Festschrift für Ingeborg Schwenzer* (Stämpfli Verlag AG 2011) 51–67; T Angelo, 'Variations on a Theme: When is an Attorney-General not an Attorney-General?' (2011) 23 Bond LR 1–10; AH Angelo, 'Nagol Jumping Should Return to Pentecost: A Conspectus of the French, English and Custom Law of Vanuatu' in Comparative Law Centre, *Toward Comparative Law in the 21st Century* (Chuo University Press 1998) 1011–1033.

of the final court of appeal. Following a consideration of these background factors the chapter will conclude with an assessment of the current state of the Mauritius legal system, the continuing role of French civil law culture in the system and the likely directions of the system in the future.

History

The key dates for the legal history of Mauritius are 1810, 1834, 1968 and 1983. The following historical commentary uses those dates as reference points.

The first European contact[3] with Mauritius was by the Portuguese[4] who used it as a waypoint to India. The Dutch had a settlement (1638–1710), but the first territorial claim was that of the French in 1715.[5] From this date until 1810, Mauritius was a French colony. The French brought slaves from Africa to Mauritius to work the sugar plantations.

1810 The French Capitulation

The defining moment for the law of Mauritius came in December 1810 with the signing of the Capitulation of the French to the British troops in Mauritius. The significant clause in the Capitulation was that the British undertook to allow the inhabitants to preserve their laws.[6] Following the Treaty of Paris in 1814, the undertaking in the Capitulation of 1810 was confirmed by Proclamation in Mauritius in 1815.[7] The laws that were preserved were in particular the pre-Napoleonic criminal law of France, the *Code Napoléon*, the *Code de Commerce* and the *Code de Procédure Civile*. The British colonial administration with the common law operated around this core of civil and criminal law.[8] Had Mauritius been settled in the same way as, for instance, Australia and New Zealand were settled, Mauritius would have had a purely English law system.

---

3   There were earlier contacts by Malay sailors, and Arabs (they called Mauritius *Dinarobin*).

4   Pedro Mascarenhas in 1505. He called the island *Ilha do Cirne*.

5   The population of Mauritius in 1767 was 15,000 slaves, 4,000 whites and 600 free blacks.

6   The *Acte de Capitulation de l'Ile de France* made between the British and French commanding officers recorded agreement in Art. 8th '*Que les habitants conserveront leurs réligion, loix, et coutumes*'.[The inhabitants shall preserve their Religion, Laws, and Customs'].

7   Promulgated by Governor Farquhar in the name of George III on 29 April 1815.

8   Writing in 1988, Professor Daudet assessed the mixed system by origin as approximately two thirds English and one third French. Y Daudet, '*L'Enseignement du droit* à Maurice' (1988) I Mauritius Law Review (2nd Ser) 131–154, 132.

1834 Liberation of the slaves

In 1834, the slaves were liberated[9] and that liberation was a precursor to significant changes in the employment law of Mauritius. With the influx of indentured labourers from India,[10] a local employment law developed outside of the *Code Napoléon* regime. From then till the twenty-first century the industrial law has developed significantly in a manner specific to the situation in Mauritius and to its changing economic face from an exclusively sugar-producing economy to the labour-intensive light industrial activities, manufacturing of garments and tourism of the post-independence period.

1968 Independence

Mauritius became a sovereign State within the Commonwealth on 12 March 1968.[11] The existing laws were preserved.[12] Independence represented, in communal terms, a shift in political power from the Francophone and Creole community to the majority group of ethnic Indians. Almost immediately the Government embarked on a project to 'decolonize' the law of Mauritius to remove the colonial imprints from it.

The community was excited by independence and immensely proud of the mixed legal heritage. The mixed legal system was celebrated too by the barristers who were typically all trained in one of the Inns of Court in London and who, until they returned to work in Mauritius, had no French law experience. They were all fluent in French and English, and had the support of the *avoués* and the notaries who were the gatekeepers for the French legal traditions.

1983 Patriation of the Civil Code

The excitement about independence, the inadequacies of the existing law for a new State and perhaps some slight rancour about the British colonial period led to an ambitious law reform programme which included the updating and promulgation of the *Code Napoléon* as a Mauritius Civil Code.[13] The *Code Napoléon* had never

---

9   The total population in 1834 was approximately 100,000 of whom at least 70 per cent were slaves.

10   There were 200,000 workers brought from India to Mauritius in the period 1835–1865 alone.

11   Mauritius became a republic on 12 March 1992.

12   Mauritius Independence Order 1968 s5.

13   Parliament enacted in 1981 that the *Code Napoléon* would be published in a revised and complete form under the name the *Code Civil Mauricien* - Revision of the Laws Act s7. The *paen* of the Burgh Edwardes in his *L'histoire de L'Ile Maurice* (n1) 51, does not seem out of place in this context: '*L'Ile Maurice demeure la perle de l'Océan Indien. Elle restera, nous en sommes certains, chère au Gouvernement Impérial autant qu'à sa patrie*

been published as a text in Mauritius and practitioners used annotated copies of old editions of the Dalloz *Code Civil*. The result of these endeavours was that by 1983, with significant input from French scholars, there was a Mauritius Civil Code, totally reformed to suit local needs. The Code was promulgated as a whole as the *Code Civil Mauricien* in 2001 and thus its status as the *droit commun* was confirmed.

The Code revision programme, which was inspired by developments in the French law particularly in France, took account of the local specificities (Muslim and Hindu religious law) and also reintegrated into the Code those elements of the Code which had been repealed and replaced by English language statutes. As part of the modernization process, a number of new topics were added to the Code.[14]

The Inherited Law

The Capitulation of 1810 guaranteed to the inhabitants of Mauritius that they could keep their laws. The particular laws which were guaranteed in this way are considered in the following paragraphs.

Civil Code

The *Code Napoléon* served to retain the French *droit commun* in Mauritius. It was however subjected to significant English language amendments over time. Early changes were made by the British Government to the *Code Napoléon* in respect of family matters. Much relating to civil status,[15] marriage and matrimonial causes[16] in

---

d'origine, la France, aujourd'hui amie et alliée de l'Angleterre pour toujours' [Mauritius is the pearl of the Indian Ocean. It will remain, we are sure, dear to the Imperial Government as it is to its country of origin, France, today the friend and ally of England for always.]

14   For instance arts 2202–2203-7 (64 articles in all) incorporate into the Code the principles relating to fixed and floating charges [*des sûretés fixes et flottantes*], which were originally introduced into Mauritius by the Loans, Charges and Privileges (Authorised Bodies) Act. For commentary on this development, see '*Les sûretés fixes et flottantes en droit Mauricien'* (1988) 1 Mauritius Law Review (2nd Ser) 1–75, and R Hein and A Robert 'Analysis of the Loans, Charges and Privileges (Authorised Bodies) Act No 45 of 1969' (1977) Mauritius Law Review 13–27; 'The Loans, Charges and Privileges Act of 1969' (1980) Mauritius Law Review 21–38.

15   Substantial amendments to the civil status laws were made by Ordinance 17 of 1871. That Ordinance and arts 34–101, 144–170 and 192 of the Civil Code were all repealed and replaced by the Civil Status Ordinance 1890. The prime motivation for this and similar reforms was to have the laws in English for the English administrators.

16   The laws of divorce underwent major changes between 1872 and 1899. The Ordinance of 1872 repealed and replaced arts 229–265, 276–294 and 297 of the *Code Napoléon*. By 1899 arts 295, 298, 308 and 309 had also been repealed. The Divorce and Judicial Separation Ordinance 1882 became the governing law.

the Code was repealed and replaced by English language statutes. The matrimonial causes law was modelled on that of England. These and similar amendments had a major effect on the coherence of Book I of the Code. Additionally specific legislation took account of the religious and cultural specificities of the various social groups in the community.[17] However, because the law of persons tends to be more local and more specific changes to it are likely to impact less on the structure of the system as a whole. Conversely, property and obligations, which are core elements of any legal system, were little affected by the British colonial regime or the post-Independence regime.

Commercial Code

The *Code de Commerce* was affected in a substantial way by specific commercial legislation following English models. The French commercial law was not as well suited to the needs of the colonial traders as the common law. The developments were seen as being both necessary and inevitable given the establishment of English banks and other commercial enterprises in Mauritius and the considerable increase in commercial activity with the UK.

The result was that at an early date commercial law statutes were developed in English. The English law had greater flexibility in respect of chattel securities, for instance chattel mortgages and pledges without dispossession. Statutes included the Privilege of the Treasury Ordinance 1846, the Commercial Pledges Ordinance 1871, the Pawnbrokers Ordinance 1872. the Civil Pledges Ordinance 1894, the Lien on Motor Vehicles Ordinance 1939, the Hire-Purchase (Credit Sales) Act 1964 and the Loans Charges and Privileges (Authorised Bodies) Act 1969. Mauritius did not, however, adopt the trust.[18]

Significant among these pieces of legislation which either repealed provisions in the *Code de Commerce* or simply overrode them and rendered them ineffective was the law on bankruptcy.[19] The amendments began in 1838 with a substantial shift in 1853 with an Ordinance based on the then current English bankruptcy statute. After that, the law of Mauritius continued to follow the legislative

---

17   For instance, the Indian Marriage Act and the Muhammadan *Waqf* Act (now the *Waqf* Act).

18   There was a major debate about trusts in the National Assembly in 1989. The current Trusts Act 2001 provides for off-shore trusts in the international context and added a Title on '*Fiducie*' to the *Code Civil Mauricien* (new arts 1100–1 to 1100–6). See further A Angelo, 'The Trust and Mauritius' in *De tous horizons* (Société de Legislation Comparée 2005) 681–706.

19   The first bankruptcy law of Mauritius was in the Code of Commerce Book III. From 1853 the law changed to follow the English laws of bankruptcy. The Bankruptcy Ordinance 1887 reflected the English Bankruptcy Act 1883. The Mauritius statute applied only to traders. See G Newton *The Bankruptcy Law of Mauritius* (2nd edn Central Printing Establishment 1892).

developments in England till the Ordinance of 1887 which was almost an exact copy of the English Act of 1883. That law remained in force until 2009.[20]

Another main replacement of the material in the *Code de Commerce* was the extension to Mauritius of the English Merchant Shipping Act of 1854 (later 1894). The English merchant shipping law continued in force until repealed by the Mauritius Merchant Shipping Act 1986.The civil aviation legislation was similar but had more extensive subsidiary legislation. It was finally replaced by local legislation[21] with the establishment of the local air carrier Air Mauritius and the internationalizing of its services.

A Companies Ordinance of 1912 replaced the law in the Code relating to *sociétés anonymes* and the *sociétés en commandite par actions*.[22] There was also the Bills of Exchange Ordinance of 1914 and the Matrimonial Property Ordinance of 1949. The latter Ordinance introduced to Mauritius an additional matrimonial property regime, that of the separation of property – the primary consequence of which was that a woman who was married under this regime maintained her individual capacity as if she were single.

More resistant to change was the *Arrêté du XVI Frimaire An XII* (relating to the tax on the registration of documents) because of its revenue significance. It was in French, but was amended regularly in English. Wholesale reform was rejected because of the potential for inadvertent loss of revenue. The law was finally reproduced as an English language statute, the Registration Duty Act, in the 1981 *Revised Laws of Mauritius*.

Civil procedure and evidence

Mauritius has remnants of the original *Code de Procédure Civile*, and also a Civil Procedure Act which is heavily influenced by the common law.

With British rule came the British system of administration of justice and the jury system. By the 1840s it had been noted[23] that the English word 'evidence' had come into common use in Mauritius. The Evidence Ordinance 1881 provided that, unless otherwise provided in a special law, the English law of evidence would be applied in all the courts of the colony.

---

20   The Insolvency Act 2009 repealed the longstanding Bankruptcy Act and the Insolvency Act.

21   Civil Aviation Act 1974. The British Orders were phased out gradually over a number of years.

22   The key Ordinance and shift from the *Code de Commerce* was the Companies Ordinance 1912. Post-Independence reforms have been influenced by common law reforms in other parts of the Commonwealth. Mauritius has in this area followed international best practice. The current legislation is the Companies Act 2001.

23   By Bruzaud in the *Revue Judiciaire* 1843. See RM D'Unienville, '*L'Evolution du droit civil Mauricien*' in *Etudes de droit privé français et Mauricien* (Presses Universitaires de France 1969) 89 at 106.

Criminal Code

The French Penal Code of 1791 was adopted by the Mauritius Colonial Assembly in 1793. It continued in force until 1838 when it was repealed and replaced by a local code which drew its inspiration principally from the French Penal Code of 1810.[24] A curiosity of the Criminal Code is that it is in French, but has been subject to a number of amendments in English. The statute[25] is therefore a mixture of French and English provisions. The application of the Code is subject to criminal procedural rules[26] and evidential rules of English origin while the substantive provisions have a French law background.

Constitutional and administrative law

As a consequence of London's taking over the administration of the country, the constitutional law and administrative law are almost exclusively based on the common law of England. There are few if any concessions to French legal thinking in these areas.[27] Equally the law relating to the courts evolved rapidly

---

24   The history of the Code is an interesting one. In the early years of the British colonization the English judges had difficulty in applying the French Penal Code. The tendency and wish was to apply the English criminal law, which they knew. This tendency was not acceptable to the authorities in England and via despatch of 16 April 1831 the Secretary of State for the colonies told the Governor of Mauritius that there was no need for a substantial Penal Code reform exercise in Mauritius because 'in almost every part of the continent of Europe, but more especially in France, the revision of the Criminal Code has, of late years, occupied the attention of the most eminent Jurists and Statesmen ... their labours have removed the greater part of the difficulties in which the subject was formally involved and it would be in the highest degree irrational if any feelings of national rivalry were permitted to obstruct the adoption of any of these improvements in the Criminal Code for which Europe is indebted to the profound wisdom and research of the authors of the French Digest ... however desirable the gradual assimilation of the Colonial to the English Code may be as a firm bond of union between the two countries, His Majesty will not sacrifice to this uniformity of system, the more important object of treating with respect either the habits and the inclinations of this faithful subjects in the Colony, or even those honest prejudices, which the Colonists of French origin may cherish in favour of the institutions of the country under the dominion of which they formerly lived'.
A Penal Code of Mauritius of 1832 was disallowed by the Colonial authorities in London and it was only in 1838 that a revised dual language Penal Code was approved for Mauritius and the *Code Pénal* of 1791 finally repealed. As recounted in LE Venchard, *Codes annotés de l'Ile Maurice - Code Pénal* volume 1 (Best Graphics 1994) XI–XIII.

25   'Statute' refers to all forms of primary legislation other than the Constitution. In colonial times, the main form of statute was the Ordinance. The principal forms of statute inherited from the French were codes.

26   See primarily the Criminal Procedure Act.

27   Despite the constitutional changes the role of the *Ministère Public* remains as does the *Curatelle*.

from 1810 and its French-style court system to the current English-style system which is a three tier, single hierarchy system with the Judicial Committee of the Privy Council at its apex.

The Crown Law Office, now the State Law Office, is a product of substantial changes in 1957 at which time the members of the Office of the *Procureur General* were given English titles. There was an Attorney-General, whose deputy became the Solicitor-General; all other offices of the *Procureur*'s department became Crown Law officers.[28] By the time of independence in 1968, the Mauritius Constitution had an Attorney-General in the English mould, a Crown Law Office headed by a Solicitor-General, and an independent Director of Public Prosecutions who was responsible for criminal prosecutions.

International law

In public international law matters, Mauritius follows very closely the principles and procedures of the UK.[29] The entering into an international obligation by the Executive binds the State at international law but produces no direct effect at the domestic level until the legislature has passed implementing legislation relating to the international obligations.

Private international law[30] is somewhat less clear in that for a considerable time the thinking was dominated by French legal principle and the *Code Napoléon*. During the twentieth century there was a perceptible shift to English Conflict of Law principles and that was supplemented by several pieces of legislation based on English Conflict of Law precedents.[31]

Conclusion

Through all this there are some common threads. In the field of public law, generally speaking, the persuasive default system of principle is the English common law. In the field of private law (including commercial law[32]) the default system is the *Code Civil Mauricien*. Therefore the *droit commun* for Mauritius can fairly be said to be the French based principles of the French Civil Code as developed in Mauritius by specific legislation and the Mauritian case law.

---

28   Angelo (n2) (2011) 23 Bond Law Review 1–10.

29   See for instance, Convention abolishing the Requirements of Legislation for Foreign Public Documents Act; Convention on the Civil Aspects of International Child Abduction Act.

30   AH Angelo and V Glover, *Private International Law – Mauritius* (Kluwer 2010).

31   See, for example, the Bills of Exchange Act, and the standard colonial legislation such as the Maintenance Orders Enforcement Act and the Reciprocal Enforcement of Judgment Act.

32   Though there are English law influenced Acts in all major fields of commercial activity, the rules of, for instance, contract remain those of French origin.

Geographical and Political Relationships

France, in the guise of the island of Réunion,[33] is 220 kilometres from Mauritius. It is the closest foreign country. Next closest geographically to the west is Madagascar and southern Africa. To the north is Seychelles. From a law perspective none of these countries is influential. All have Romanist systems but beyond the collaborative influence of SADC[34] there is no impact on Mauritius. Links with Réunion are primarily social and touristic. The links with southern Africa, and South Africa especially, are for trade and tourism.

Politically and economically the relationships with the EU, India and China are very important. The key EU partners are the UK and France with which the historical links are maintained at many levels. They are the primary sources of persuasive legal precedent. In the case of Mauritius, geographical proximity and regional linkages count for less than history.

Mauritius, as a small, unusual and isolated country, could have survived in the past because of its isolation and insignificance in economic terms. Those very factors may, in the twenty-first century, work against an exotic legal system. Such a system is unable to link with others in a similar situation and the current trends to globalize trade and finance have internationalized and made uniform a number of areas of law which had less importance in the past.

Language[35]

The Constitution of Mauritius, in article 49 under the heading 'Official language', states, 'The official language of the Assembly shall be English but any member may address the chair in French.' The other major legislative provision on language is found in the Interpretation and General Clauses Act 1974 section 10 under the heading 'French expressions in enactments'. That section states, 'Where in an enactment a French term or an expression is used, or an English term or expression is explained by reference to a French term or expression, the interpretation of the enactment shall be in accordance with that of the French term or expression.'

The *Code Civil Mauricien* is all in French as is the *Code de Commerce* and the *Code de Procédure Civile*. The Criminal Code is a curious amalgam of French and English: approximately half of the provisions are provided in parallel columns in a dual language text; the other and newer provisions are only in English. There

---

33   Réunion is an overseas department of France.

34   The Southern African Development Community was formally established by treaty in 17 August 1992.

35   For a comparative consideration of the role of language and the legal profession in the continuation of the French civil tradition in countries with a British colonial experience see T Angelo, 'A Tale of Three Codes' in *Private Law Festschrift für Ingeborg Schwenzer* (Stämpfli Verlag AG 2011) 51–67.

are some instances where, within even the same provision, there is a mixture of English and French.

A particular feature of the legal system of Mauritius is that it is a country without an indigenous people. Further, the most recent colonizers, the British, were never a large group of people in Mauritius. There was, however, from the nineteenth century, a substantial group with a British rather than a French colonial experience – the Indian indentured labourers. As a language for public affairs, English was their preference. This was different from the preference for French of the small French community and the descendants of the slaves from the French colonial era. Nevertheless, the Indo-Mauritians were not and are not a homogeneous ethnic group; they are a group with a great range of languages, religions and customary practices.

The language of the legislature and judiciary is English.[36] This is interesting because official statistics would indicate that there are fewer than 1 per cent native English speakers in Mauritius and approximately 3 per cent native speakers of French. The lingua franca is Creole. For some people Creole will be the first language but for most it will be a second language. The first language will probably be Hindi, Tamil or Cantonese. It can safely be said that for most people the language of the law will be a second or third language and one learned at school.

Legal Profession

Mauritius has a history of a strong legal profession.[37] At the time of the Capitulation the profession was organized along French lines with *notaires*, *avocats* and *avoués*. There was local legislation covering the *notaires*.[38] The first statutory provision for *avocats* and *avoués* was made in 1833 but lapsed in 1836. The next major statute was Ordinance 9 of 1855. By rules of court of 6 February 1852 the professions of *avoué* and *avocat* had thenceforth to be exercised by separate persons, and *avocats* had to have been admitted as barrister or advocate in a superior court of UK or Ireland.

---

36   French as the language of the Courts was suppressed by Order in Council of 13 September 1845. When Parliament amended the Civil Code, it did so under the rubric of a Civil Code Amendment Act and thus met the requirement of legislating in English – though the substance of that amendment were in French.

37   A delightful history is presented in *Bicentenary Mauritius Bar 1787-1987* (Best Graphics 1987).

38   For instance, Edict of June 1766; *Arrêtés 27 Fructidor An XII, 14 Pluviose An XII, 22 Floréal An XII, 16 Prairial An XII*; Proclamation 4 March 1811.

With the advent of the University of Mauritius, the possibility of local training for lawyers and even of a merging of the legal professions was considered.[39] In the twenty-first century, though the professions have a similar university grounding, they remain distinct with separate practical requirements for each branch.

Legal Education

At the same time as the major 'decolonizing' of the legislation of Mauritius was being undertaken. steps were being taken for the localizing of legal professional training. The University of Mauritius was established in 1971 and the Law Faculty and an LLB in 1985.[40] As a result, there are now many members of the profession who have been trained locally and in the law of Mauritius. This is in contrast to those who preceded them. Previously barristers were trained almost exclusively in England in the common law, and the attorneys and notaries were trained by way of local apprenticeships and had extensive knowledge of the French civil law system.

The purpose of the establishment of the local law degree was to make access to the law professions both more accessible (because there was no need to travel abroad to study) and the educational background of all law practitioners more uniform. The goal was to make the three branches of the profession all 'learned' in the sense of their requiring a law degree for admission to practice.

The University of Mauritius LLB programme was taught initially by collaboration between English and French universities with many courses taught by short term visitors. That pattern was followed in the twenty-first century by a more clearly local based professoriat. The undergraduate law programme at the University of Mauritius reflects the mixed law heritage of Mauritius. Courses are taught in both English and French and relate directly to the law of Mauritius. From 2013 the University of Mauritius has offered a Law Practitioners Vocational Course for candidates who want to practise law in Mauritius. It is taught in both English and French.[41]

---

39   There has been occasional discussion of the merger question. See, for instance, the papers from the first Mauritius Judicial Conference in (1989) 2 Bar Chronicle 42–47.

40   Y Daudet, '*L'enseignement du droit à Maurice*' (1988) 1 Mauritius Law Review (2nd Series) 131–154. Before the establishment of the law degree at the University of Mauritius, delivery of legal education at tertiary level in Mauritius had been done from the Réunion base of the University of Aix-en-Provence. A *maîtrise* was offered by that university to students in Mauritius.

41   The topics covered are set out in the Second Schedule to the Law Practitioners (Amendment) Act 2011. The current Law Practitioners Act was enacted in 1984.

Under the Law Practitioners Act,[42] citizens of Mauritius who have obtained a professional qualification[43] which entitles that person to practise as a barrister in England and Wales, Australia, New Zealand, Canada or France may apply for admission to practise in Mauritius as a barrister. The Mauritius lawyer will typically do the three-year LLB, pass a vocational course,[44] and undertake a period of pupillage under a senior practitioner.[45]

The Courts

The hierarchy of courts follows the English pattern. There is a single system with three tiers of superior courts: the Supreme Court, the Courts of Appeal[46] and the Privy Council. The main inferior courts are the Districts Courts, the Intermediate Criminal Court and the Industrial Court. Mauritius has long had the Judicial Committee of the Privy Council in London as its final court of appeal. That was retained at Independence in 1968 and again when Mauritius became a republic in 1992.[47]

There has been a small but regular flow of appeals to the Privy Council. Some have been on commercial matters but most are on criminal and constitutional issues. The heartland, the *droit commun* of the system, has rarely been addressed. In the nineteenth century the situation was somewhat different in that there were a number of Privy Council decisions on appeal from Mauritius which dealt with private law matters. A survey of those cases indicates that the fact that a court sitting in London was deciding matters on the French Civil Code created no problems.[48] The Privy Council handled the French language Civil Code with ease

---

42   The Act in force in November 2012 was promulgated as Act 55 of 1984. It was most recently amended by the Law Practitioners (Amendment) Act 2011. For a recent (though not always accurate) commentary, see RJ Gunputh, 'The Professional and Vocational Training of Lawyers according to the Anglo-Saxon Model in a Mixed Legal System – The case of the Republic of Mauritius' in I Krasnicka and M Perkowska (eds) *How to Become a Lawyer* (Peter Lang 2013).

43   Which means a law degree from the University of Mauritius or the UK, or an approved institution in the US, a Commonwealth country or a civil law State.

44   A candidate is allowed no more than six attempts at the vocational exams, and those six attempts must be made within six years from the date of the first attempt.

45   The period depends on the academic qualification of the pupil and whether the pupillage is as a barrister, attorney or notary. The periods range from 12 to 24 months.

46   The Court of Civil Appeal is a division of the Supreme Court (Court of Civil Appeal Act); the judges of the Supreme Court are the judges of the Capital Court of Criminal Appeal (Criminal Appeal Act).

47   Section 81 of the Constitution.

48   The Privy Council also heard appeals from other parts of the Empire where the law was French, for example Quebec.

and gave advice well within the cultural expectations of the French law. Indeed, in some cases French law issues were decided in the Privy Council before there were recorded decisions on the same points of law in France.[49]

There were law reports from a very early date.[50] This was perhaps the British influence but it served also to imbed civil law principles by recording their operation for posterity. Mauritius had, for instance, its own body of case law on article 1384 of the *Code Napoléon*[51] and ultimately followed the French interpretation when the Code was reformed in the 1980s.

A random sample of judgments from 2012 and 2013 of the Supreme Court of Mauritius on a range of subjects showed that the Court infrequently referred to judgments from foreign jurisdictions. Approximately 75 per cent of the judgments did not mention any foreign judgments. The majority of the precedents referred to were Mauritian. When judgments did refer to precedents from foreign jurisdictions, most were from the UK. A few decisions of the Privy Council on appeal from Mauritius were cited. In the sample there was only one reference to a French case and a few references to the French Civil Code or a Dalloz Encyclopaedia.[52]

The Chief Justice and the Senior Puisne Judge are appointed by the President as provided in s77 of the Constitution. The Puisne judges and the judges in the inferior courts are appointed by the Judicial and Legal Service Commission established under s85 of the Constitution. The minimum qualification for appointment for judges of the Supreme Court is entitlement to practise as a barrister before the Supreme Court for not less than five years. The established pattern has been for newly admitted barristers who enter the State service, to do so as a junior officer in the Attorney-General's Chambers and, in the course of their careers, to progress through the hierarchy of courts and the hierarchy of state counsel to, ideally, become a judge of the Supreme Court.

---

49   *HM Procureur v Bruneau* (1865–1867) LR Priv C App 169. See also LM Bérenger and CR Pérombelon, *Guide pratique en matière de successions* (Imprimerie Minerva 1911).

50   Law reporting in Mauritius began in 1843 with *La revue judiciaire de l'Ile Maurice* by R Bruzaud (E Baker 1845). That publication was short lived. It was followed in 1861 by the Mauritius Law Reports which have continued to be published on an annual basis since then. Additionally W Greene in 1884 produced a *Digest of the Reported Criminal Jurisprudence of the Supreme Court of Mauritius from 1842 to 1883* (Mercantile Record Company's Printing Establishment 1884).

51   See *Mangroo v Dahal* (1937) MR 43, and comment by AH Angelo in (1971) 4 Comparative and International Law Journal of South Africa 57–71.

52   This is very different to the statistics from a similar survey for Seychelles – a smaller but historically related jurisdiction. The Seychelles Court of Appeal frequently refers to cases from the UK.

Distinctive Features

Looking back from the early twenty-first century, two factors stand out in relation to the development of the legal system of Mauritius. They are:

1. the distinctive nature of the population and its relationship to the development of the employment law of Mauritius; and
2. the dedicated programme for the patriation of the legal system in the decades immediately following independence in 1968.

Individually or together these are identifying features of the Mauritius legal system.

Population and employment law

The population is relatively large and it is diverse in terms of language, religion, race, culture and material wealth. In the pre-independence social economic texts prepared by Burton Benedict and by Titmuss and Meade,[53] the picture presented was a depressing one of an overpopulated country dependent on a single agricultural product for its economic survival.[54] Despite that, in a country otherwise lacking in

---

53   Three seminal texts on the state of Mauritius were published in the period immediately preceding independence in 1968. They all describe a small country with a population of 600,000 which was more than 99 per cent dependent on its sugar production. Burton Benedict wrote *Indians in a Plural Society* (HMSO 1961). The other two books were reports to the Governor of Mauritius: JE Meade, *The Economic and Social Structure of Mauritius* (Methuen 1961), and R Titmuss, *Social Policies and Population Growth in Mauritius* (Methuen 1961). These books, and the latter two in particular, describe the future of Mauritius with foreboding eg Meade at paragraph 2: 89 'The economic future of Mauritius is dominated by its population problem. The review which we have made of this problem has convinced us that unless resolute measures are taken to solve it Mauritius will be faced with a catastrophic situation', and at paragraph 10: 1 '...time is now very short; and disaster will ensue unless the Government of Mauritius can on this occasion promptly take the necessary, though in some cases unpopular, measures to bring into effect in all its aspects the necessary economic and social revolution'. In similar vein Titmuss projected that without change Mauritius was likely to have a population of 3 million by the year 2002. It was stated that the projections were realistic and well based in statistical data. The conclusion on the prospects for Mauritius from the projections – 'Frankly, they amount to economic, social and political disaster' (237).

54   This view of things was unhappily reinforced by VS Naipaul in his essay on Mauritius entitled 'The Overcrowded Barracoon' (*Sunday Times Magazine*, 16 July 1972, reprinted in the 'Overcrowded Barracoon' (Andre Deutsch 1972)), an essay in a collection of that name of 1972. The Mauritius Government reaction to the essay was that all books by VS Naipaul were banned.

natural resources, a large labour force has always proved to be a major economic asset of Mauritius, and that resource has been fully exploited.

In 1810 the main source of labour in Mauritius was slaves. After several failed attempts at abolition, slavery finally ended in 1834. This social change did not come without difficulty, and a consequence was that, very quickly and for several decades, slave labour was replaced by indentured labourers from India. The labourers were initially male and contracted for periods of up to five years to particular sugar estate employers; they lived on the estates. Early labour and immigration laws were enacted to provide for this labour force. [55] The labour legislation dealt with recruitment, transport and repatriation. It also had minimum standards for healthcare on the estates and minimum standards of food rations.[56]

The early labour legislation was consolidated in a major enactment in 1852. That was reviewed and further consolidated by the Labour Ordinance which was enacted in 1922. This was in turn replaced by the Employment and Labour Ordinance 1938 which remained in force as the basic labour law until independence. The 1938 law no longer focused on the Indian indentured labourers, but did reflect those origins. The Labour Act 1975 that followed was not revolutionary but it no longer displayed the historical origins of the employment rules.[57]

In 1938, following industrial unrest among the workers in the sugar industry, the Industrial Associations Ordinance was passed.[58] This was the forerunner of the Industrial Relations Act 1973, which provided for trade unions, industrial arbitration and remuneration orders.

The laws reflect the high dependence of Mauritius on the sugar industry until the 1970s. Other legislation, such as the Cane Planters and Millers Arbitration

---

55   The industrial success of this scheme led to its being replicated in the Colony of Fiji.

56   Labour Ordinance of 1878, art 42. The allowances for male Indian immigrants over 18 'shall in no case be less than the following: Rice: 750 grammes per diem. Dholl: 250 grammes per week. Salt fish: 250 grammes per week. Ghee or oil: 125 grammes per week. Salt: 125 grammes per week'.

57   Until 1834 Mauritius had the *Code Noir* (Louis Sala-Molins, *Le code noir* (PUF 1987)). Mauritius then progressed to labour legislation to deal primarily with migrant labour from India; and finally moved to a modern system of employment laws in the 1970s.

58   On matters of employment law there is useful comparative comment in BC Roberts *Labour in the Tropical Territories of the Commonwealth* (LSE University of London, Bell and Sons 1964). In particular, pages 19, 114, 122, 182, 207, 224 and 264.

In the Debates of the Council of Government session 1938–1939 (Government Printer, Mauritius 1940) there is substantial discussion and historical information relating to the employment situation in Mauritius in the debates on the Bill 'to make provision for the formation, registration and regulation of employers and employees industrial associations'. The Governor speaking to the Bill at its first reading stated that the Bill was 'the most important measure before the Legislature this Session' at pages 6–10, 22–62 and 67–75. 1938 was also the year for a consolidating Labour Ordinance, the debates on which are found in the same volume of the Debates of the Council of Government session 1938–1939.

and Control Board 1973, complements the labour legislation and provides, and has provided since independence, a comprehensive modern and responsive body of legislation for the employment sector.[59] The legislation deals with industry control, with employers and employees, and with trade unions. Throughout the economic development period since 1968[60] the labour market was controlled in several ways, but primarily by industrial awards (Remuneration Orders) made under the Industrial Relations Act 1973. Those Orders covered almost all wage paid labour employment from domestic servants through to dock workers.

In order to exploit fully the opportunities provided by the Yaounde and Lome conventions,[61] Mauritius became an offshore processing zone with extensive legislation to meet that need. The Export Processing Zones Act 1970 was introduced to take full advantage of the abundance of labour in Mauritius and the export opportunities provided by the ACP Treaty. This Act has its own employment provisions and operates largely independently of the Labour Act and of the Industrial Relations Act 1973.

The late twentieth century economic strength of Mauritius was built on the success of these processing zones. Following closely on those developments was the success of the tourist industry which in turn relies heavily on labour legislation.

The indentured labour system affected the *Code Napoléon* and the employment provisions within it. The employment law in Mauritius was initially developed in English specifically for the sugar industry and then, more than a century later, the employment law was again significantly developed with East African influences. These developments took place alongside the existing provisions of the *Code Napoléon* but it was only in 1975 that the provisions of the latter were expressly superseded in favour of the English language Labour Act 1975.[62]

---

59   LE Venchard's, *Labour Laws of Mauritius* went through several editions. The First in 1983 provided a consolidated collection of Acts and subsidiary legislation and a Digest of Supreme Court decisions on major aspects of the labour law.

60   At independence, there was an extensive body of labour law: A Workmen's Compensation Act, an Industrial Courts Act, an Apprenticeship Act, an Employment and Labour Act, a Termination of Contracts of Service Act, a Boilers Act, a Safety of Dockers Act and a Security of Employment (Sugar Industry) Act. Most of these statutes were repealed and replaced by the reforming Labour Act of 1975.

Consistent with the importance of the sugar industry, there was also a substantial body of legislation relating to that industry: the Mauritius Sugar Industry Research Institute Act and the Sale of Canes (Control) Act 1964 (which took on renewed strength as the Cane Planters and Millers and Control Board Act 1973).

61   The Yaounde (1964) and Lome (1975) Conventions were the predecessors of the 2000 Cotonou EU–ACP Agreement.

62   Arts 1780 and 1781 of the Civil Code were repealed in 1975. Art. 1780 now reads: '*Les contrats de louage des gens, de travail qui s'engagement au service de quelqu'un seront régis par le Labour Act*'. [Contracts for the hire of workers who are engaged in the service of another are governed by the Labour Act.] Art. 1781: '*Le louage de service fait sans determination de durée peut toujours cesser par la volonté d'une des parties contractantes.*

In 1968 Mauritius began life as an independent nation, seriously divided on communal and political lines. By the 1990s, however, Mauritius was being paraded in the ACP Treaty context as a success and as a model to emulate. From a situation of substantial unemployment, Mauritius had moved to being a State which was importing labour from East Africa. It had also become a State with a diversified economy in which the main colonial export, sugar, had, in earning capacity, been overtaken by tourism, the production of textiles and light industry.

This change was achieved by a dedicated government programme. It benefitted from political stability (often maintained by periods of emergency) and a multilingual population.[63] Education standards were high and educational achievement was a national goal. There was an abundance of medical doctors, lawyers and others with tertiary qualifications. The development of the independent nation was built on this.

Patriation of the system

In 1810 Mauritius had a strong legal culture and the colony had considerable self-confidence. That self-confidence and the strength of the legal profession continued through the nineteenth century and were reflected in an early pattern of law reporting.[64]

The Solicitor-General, LE Venchard, writing in 1981,[65] said that until 1948, the laws of Mauritius were clearly either French or English. The system was a mixed one in which certain areas of law were dependent entirely on the law of England and other areas were dependent on the law of France. The year 1948 was chosen

---

Néanmoins, la résiliation du contrat par la volonté d'un seul des contractants ne peut être admise que dans les conditions et formes requises par le Labour Act.' [The hire of services for a non-fixed period can be terminated by the wish of one of the contracting parties. Nevertheless, the termination of the contract by the will of only one of the contracting parties is subject to the conditions and other requirements set out in the Labour Act.]

63   Most speak, in addition to a maternal language, Mauritius Creole and some French and English.

64   In 1961 the official Mauritius Law Reports celebrated a century of publication. Mauritius has had several eminent law chroniclers and collections of legislation and well-referenced Digests: FA Herchenroder and E Koenig, *The Laws of Mauritius* (Government Printer 1922); Greene's, *Digest of the Reported Criminal Jurisprudence of the Supreme Court of Mauritius 1842–1883* ((Mercantile Record Company's Printing Establishment 1884); Hugues', *Digest (1861–1901)*; Nairac's, *Digest* (PG Burnstead 1927); Lalouette's *Mauritius Digest (1926–1943)* (Government Printer 1947 with supplements to 1960); V Glover, *Abstract of Decisions of the Supreme Court of Mauritius (1966–1981) (1982–1986)* (Precisgraph 1982 and 1993); R D'Unienville, *Nomenclature (1964–1973)* (Quickprint 1988); LE Venchard (with Glover and Angelo), *New Mauritius Digest* (Best Graphics 1999): and LE Venchard, *Codes annotés* (7 vols) (Best Graphics 1995–1998).

65   LE Venchard, *'L'application du droit mixte'* (1982) Mauritius Law Review 29–44 at 34.

by Venchard because that was the year from which elected representatives of the people participated in the legislative process. With their participation came the legislative expression of local interests. This was the start of the development of a set of laws specific to Mauritius, which responded to the local circumstances and needs. That development was pursued and saw significant acceleration in the period immediately following independence in 1968 through until the mid-1980s in which the main legal event was the completion of the reform of the *Code Civil.*

A consequence of the strength of the legal culture and the local pride in it was that when Mauritius gained independence it committed itself with vigour to a sustained effort to patriate its laws. That meant that the French laws should be reviewed and promulgated as Mauritius laws, and that all British colonial laws should be reviewed against the independence constitution to see that they were compatible with the supreme law.

The laws of the British colonial era were also to be updated to reflect contemporary Mauritius conditions and rewritten as necessary to reflect the fact that they were laws for Mauritius, not laws drafted for England. A Law Revision Unit[66] was set up in the Attorney-General's office (the *parquet*). Through until 1990 that Unit had a staff ranging in number from about eight to 40 persons at one period of intense activity. The first product of this particular endeavour was the publication, in bound cyclostyled form, of a full consolidated text of the primary and subsidiary legislation of Mauritius as at 31 December 1971.[67] There were approximately 9,000 foolscap pages of text. This was the first such text since 1920. The Lane edition[68] of 1948 was the major collection in use. It was, however, incomplete and its use was impeded by the fact that, though it was edited to 1945, it was not in force until 1951. This time gap meant that much legislative activity had occurred since the collection was edited and that legislative activity had necessarily related to the pre-Lane version of the laws. When the Lane version became law there were therefore contradictions, often irresolvable, between the legislation in force and the Lane text.

In the 1970s project on the decolonizing of the law, one matter was the compatibility of the existing legislation with the Independence Constitution. At several points the provisions of the *Code Napoléon* were either different from the entrenched constitutional rights or duplicative of them. In order to avoid confusion and possible litigation about the relative meanings of the Code and Constitution, some provisions of the Code were repealed.

Having identified the law in force, the second step was a stocktake and a major tidying of the law book. Legislation contradictory to the Constitution was repealed. Legislation which was outdated and no longer being used was repealed, and many

---

66   The Unit existed de facto from 1970. Its role was formalized by the Revision of Laws Act 1974.

67   Published in 1972.

68   C Lane, *The Laws of Mauritius in Force on the 31ˢᵗ day of July, 1945* (Waterlow and Sons Ltd 1946) 5 volumes.

minor amendments were made to legislation in order to align the legislation with the Constitution (for example, the names of constitutional officers), and to remove contradictions between various pieces of legislation. There were several statutes enacted for this purpose. The first was the Laws of Mauritius (Correction of Errors and Minor Amendments) Act 1973,[69] and the Revision of Laws Act 1974 under which 400 pieces of legislation were repealed as redundant.

The third step was to review the tidied law book and, over an extended period, to reform each Act and its supporting regulations one by one. This was supported by legislation, the Revision of Laws Act 1974, and by a modern interpretation statute.[70] The first formal product of this law reform exercise was the *Revised Laws of Mauritius 1981* which had official force. It dealt with the Acts and appeared in six volumes.[71]

Running parallel to these legislative endeavours relating to the general legislation was a French Government supported programme to reform the *Code Napoléon* and the *Code de Commerce*.[72] This endeavour produced the *Code Civil Mauricien*. Significantly it was a substantial reinforcement of the French legal culture in the private law field. The Code is in French, was informed by the

---

69   Which occupied 105 pages of legislation.

70   Interpretation and General Clauses Act 1974.

71   Subsidiary legislation was dealt with separately. Statutes carried forward from the colonial period were from Independence designated as Acts. The collection therefore contained all the statutes in force at the given date.

72   The programme for reform of the Civil Code was indicated by a commission convened in 1958 in the lead up to independence. The conclusions of that body were picked up in 1971 by the Attorney-General, and Mauritius committed itself to a substantial reform of the *Code Napoléon*. There were several objectives. One was to update the civil law, the second was to fully adapt it to the circumstances of Mauritius, and thirdly those involved in the reform project were instructed to consider also the reforms to the code that had occurred in France so that Mauritius would have a civil law well adapted to its future needs. A progress report on the revision of the Mauritius Civil Code was published in October 1975 under the title *Livre blanc sur la révision du Code Civil Mauricien*. That White Paper of 30 pages gave a stocktake of progress with the revision to that date and also addressed the question whether the Code should be totally rewritten or whether it should be revised little by little. It also commented on the issue of the piecemeal or step by step reform. The conclusion was that the Code should be reformed by a step by step process and in general but not exclusively the appropriate pattern was to follow the order of the articles in the Code. The product was seen in a number of Civil Code amendment statutes from 1978 to 1984. The reform work was completed with the major legislation of 1983 Acts 7, 8, and 9.

The history and pattern of this Civil Code reform is fully covered in LE Venchard, *Code Civil* in *Codes Annotés de l'Ile Maurice* (2nd edn Best Graphics 1995). See also R Garron, '*La Reforme du Code Napoléon*' (1980) Mauritius Law Review 39 ; and by the same author, '*La réforme du Code Napoléon relative au statut d'époux et à l'autorité parentale*' (1982) Mauritius Law Review 83 and '*La réforme du Code Napoléon relative aux mariages civils et religieux*' (1982) Mauritius Law Review 153.

contemporary French law, and had its integrity restored by most of the English language stand-alone statutes, which had superseded the Codes being repealed and re-enacted in French in the appropriate position in the Code.[73] To assist in this project there were several French specialists and *missionaires* engaged in the revision of the *Code Napoléon* in Mauritius. The person responsible for the final product was Professor Garron. His task was one of reform and of reintegration.

    Another feature of this patriation endeavour was that the law should bring together and take account of the religious or cultural norms of the main social groups in the country. Before independence there had been specific rules, for example for Indian marriages and the Islamic *waqf*. New efforts were made after 1968 and specifically in the field of Muslim personal law. A Pakistani jurist, Ansari produced a report for the introduction of Muslim personal law into Mauritius.[74] Eventually discussion of this report produced legislation for the operation of Muslim personal law.[75] That legislation remained in force for a number of years but then was amended in 1990[76] following an adverse report from the United Nations Human Rights Committee. The new provisions provided a more limited recognition of Muslim personal law.

Conclusion

In terms of a legal status being endangered, there are external and internal factors. Externally, the obvious threat for a country like Mauritius is the Anglo-American style globalization and its impact on legislation.[77] Primarily, although not exclusively, in the field of finance and commerce there is a substantial drive to uniformity which is supported by, for instance, the conditionalities of international loans. These areas are, however, not the heartland of the system. Though, there is much recent legislation reflecting that globalization pattern, that legislation tends to be specific and there is not a great deal of litigation on it.

---

    73   In the preparation for the *Code Civil Mauricien* the marriage and divorce law was reinserted into the Civil Code and the Loans, Charges, and Privileges (Authorised Bodies) Act, the Civil Pledges Act, the Commercial Pledges Act, the Lien on Motor Vehicles Act, and the Privilege of Treasury Act were all repealed. The labour law remains outside the Code – see (n65).

    74   MA Ansari, *Muslim Personal Law* (Government Print, 1981).

    75   The *Code Napoléon* (Amendment No 2) Act 1981, Civil Status Act 1981 s25–36.

    76   Civil Status (Amendment No 2) Act 1990.

    77   International codes such as the United Nations Convention for the International Sale of Goods, would, in fact, favour French based systems because of the greater influence in their development of Roman law principles than those of the common law. For instance, many statutes that reflect an Anglo-American commercial model assume that consideration is an element essential to the validity of a contract. The *Code Civil Mauricien* follows the French *Code Civil*; consideration is not an element of contract.

From an internal source the change from the present system would come if the French legal culture fell out of favour and particularly if, as was mooted in the recent reference of the *Code Civil Mauricien* to the Law Reform Commission, the French legislation were promulgated in English.

Against this background it is difficult to conceive of the Mauritius legal system as being an endangered one. The core elements of the French legal heritage remain and remain in the French language. Statutes relating to the economy and globalization reflect in a significant way common law legal thinking but they operate in specific areas and do not derogate from the *droit commun* of Mauritius. The risk, if any, is of an internationalized legal system, or of a legal system so dominated by common law thinking that the French cultural aspect is lost. On current evidence the likelihood is that that will not happen. Rather, the law of Mauritius will continue to be something unique in itself[78] and less clearly the mixed common law/French law system that it earlier was.

---

78 '...*[O]n constate que ce pays a su realiser un sycrétisme entre ces deux grandes familles juridiques. Il n'y a pas seulement mixité mais, plutot, métissage juridique ... avec la creation d'un droit veritablement national et qui a donc, en definitive, sa personnalité propre.*' [This country has been able to establish a union between the two great families of laws. There is here not just a mixing of the systems but rather a legal blending of them ... with the resultant creation of a law which is truly national and which has therefore, in the final analysis its own specific personality] Y Daudet, '*L'Enseignement du Droit à Maurice*' (1988) 1 Mauritius Law Review (2nd Series) 131 at 133.

Chapter 6
Seychelles

While Seychelles experienced some of the same historic events as Mauritius, later events have meant that it has been much more difficult for Seychelles to maintain an equilibrium between the civil law elements introduced by the French once they had landed on the islands in 1742 and made their first settlement with slaves in 1770, and the common law elements introduced after 1814 when France handed over the islands to the British.

Lacking any indigenous population, the islands were vulnerable to the imposition of the laws of others from the start. Seychelles had the further ignominy of being a colony of a colony as it was not administered by the métropole but by the French colony of Mauritius. It was not until 1903 that Seychelles became a colony in its own right. This fact led us to decide that in our spectrum, the Seychelles chapter should follow the Mauritius one. Although potentially a classic mixed legal system with clear cut divisions between the common law in public law and French civil law in private law, the health of that mix was undermined from the outset by the gradual eradication of French as the medium of education in schools and the role of commonwealth judges in the courts of Seychelles triggered the decline of the supremacy of French civil law and culminated in the translation and promulgation of the Civil Code of Seychelles in the English language in 1975. The change of language, so that civil law operates in a common law context, started to erode the civil law tradition.

As Mathilda Twomey points out, efforts to recuperate and re-establish a balance were made following independence in 1976, with attempts to forge its own identity and stamp a distinct Creole character on its laws, and continued with the one party socialist republic which followed the coup d'état of 1977. Political change and a new constitution in 1993 creating a multi-party and democratic Seychelles has, however, had a corresponding impact on earlier attempts to create a distinct national legal system. Similarly models of governance imposed by hegemonic globalization and by the pressures of regionalization of Southern Africa and the Indian Ocean Rim have threatened to erode a distinctly mixed legal system.

Twomey claims that the struggle is not over. The role of the School of Law at the new University of Seychelles and the recruitment of Seychellois judges and judges from other mixed jurisdictions in its Court of Appeal are evidence of continuing attempts to address the overwhelming ambiguities and inconsistencies of the two cohabiting and constituent elements of its legal system and the external pressures of macroeconomic forces and to develop the authenticity and integrity of the Seychellois legal system. As a micro-jurisdiction far from its civil law parent source the Seychellois legal system remains mixed but at risk and the crucial contemporary question is how the mixed legal system can best be maintained?

Seychelles: 'Things Fall Apart? – The Mixing of Fate, Free Will and Imposition in the Laws of Seychelles'

Mathilda Twomey

Introduction

It is sometimes useful to set aside some of the theoretical explanations for legal transfers and for the formation of legal systems such as the functionalist analysis[1] or the autopoeitic theory of law[2] in order to examine and perhaps better understand the context and future development of national legal systems.[3] It is equally useful to acknowledge that the creation and development of legal traditions is a long and slow process and reflects 'historically conditioned attitudes about the nature of law'.[4] This deeply ingrained approach to law reflects to some extent the heritage, culture, language and national identity of the people who provide the context in which the law exists. Law's embeddedness in culture and community has long been maintained.[5] A positive view of legal culture[6] is to demonstrate that legal

---

1   R Michaels, 'The Functional Method of Comparative Law' in M Reimann and R Zimmermann (eds) *The Oxford Handbook of Comparative Law* (Oxford University Press 2006). Chapter 10.

2   See G Teubner (ed), *Autopoietic Law: A New Approach to Law and Society* (de Gruyter 1987).

3   See E Örücü and D Nelken *Comparative Law: A Handbook* (Hart 2007); B Fekete, 'Cultural Comparative Law?' in P Cserne and M Könczöl (eds), *Legal and Political Theory in the Post National Age* (Peter Lang 2011) 40.

4   JH Merryman and R Pérez-Perdomo, *The Civil Law Tradition* (3rd edn Stanford University Press 2007) 2.

5   See C de Secondat Montesquieu, *De l'esprit des lois*, (Garnier 1784). See also R Cotterrell, *Living Law: Studies in Legal and Social Theory* (Dartmouth 2008). For a critique of legal culture and legal tradition, see R Michaels, 'Legal Culture' in J Basedow, K Hopt and R Zimmermann (eds), *Max Planck Encyclopedia of European Private Law* (Oxford University Press 2012) 1060.

6   See P Legrand, 'Comparative Legal Studies and Commitment to Theory' (1995) 58(2) Modern Law Review 262; D Nelken, 'Understanding/Invoking Legal Culture' (1995) 4 Social and Legal Studies 435–452; and C Varga, 'Law as Culture' in C Varga (ed), *Comparative Legal Cultures* (Dartmouth 1992) 9.

society develops 'to make, find, interpret, and confirm law'[7] in a way somewhat similar to and reminiscent of the function of Rodolfo Sacco's legal formants.[8] Hence while imperialism and globalization, in the past and today, have had pervasive consequences, the changes and alterations dictated by the domestication of their legal instruments in local cultures and communities must also be put in perspective.[9] Although the two concepts of legal tradition and legal culture are not synonymous,[10] they both contextualize and provide an understanding of the development and sustainability of law in national jurisdictions. Lawrence Friedman states that law 'is not a collection of doctrines, rules, terms and phrases. It is not a dictionary, but a culture; and it has to be approached as such'.[11]

This chapter briefly explores the historical and political birth of Seychelles and the transfer of the French civil law system into the young colony, followed by its formal Capitulation to the British in 1814 and the resulting consequences for the legal system; specifically the initial introduction of common law to its public law and later the mixing of laws of the two legal systems within Seychelles. It reviews the legal changes brought by independence, the 16-year socialist one-party rule, the restoration of multi-party democracy in 1993, the collapse of the Seychellois economy in 2008 and the recent *IMFization* of its public and private law. The chapter argues that much of this development was the result of a mixture of fate, free choice on the part of Seychelles but also the imposition of laws through colonialism and contemporarily the new *rule of law*[12] as dictated by the World Bank and the International Monetary Fund (IMF).

It also considers the status of the Seychellois legal system and queries whether its mixed legal system is endangered; whether the forces of history and the present economic relations dictate that *things fall apart*; it explores the *acculturation* or

---

7   A Afilalo, D Patterson and K Purnhagen, 'Statecraft, The Market State and the Development of European Legal Culture' in G Helleringer and K Purnhagen (eds), *Towards a European Legal Culture* (Beck/Hart, Munich-Oxford, Forthcoming) Available at SSRN: <http://ssrn.com/abstract=2044096> accessed 20 January 2014.

8   R Sacco, 'Legal Formants: A Dynamic Approach to Comparative Law (Instalment I of II)' (1991) 39(1) The American Journal of Comparative Law 1; 'Legal Formants: A Dynamic Approach to Comparative Law (Instalment II of II)' (1991) 39(2) The American Journal of Comparative Law 343.

9   See I Hussin, 'Circulations of Law: Colonial Precedents, Contemporary Questions' (2012) 2(7) Oñati Socio-Legal Series 18.

10   See the debate between P Glenn, *Legal Traditions of the World: Sustainable Diversity in Law* (2nd edn Oxford University Press 2004) and Varga (n6).

11   L Friedman, 'Some Thoughts on Comparative Legal Culture' in DS Clark (ed), *Comparative and Private International Law: Essays in Honor of John Henry Merryman on his Seventieth Birthday* (Duncker and Humblot 1990) 52.

12   Hussin (n9). She describes the changing meaning of 'rule of law' including the World Bank view of rule of law as legal institutions for a market economy.

creolizing[13] of all the acquired legal traditions within Seychelles and enquires whether the apparent national legal implosion is normative.

The Influence of History and Language on the Legal System of Seychelles

French rule

There were no indigenous peoples in Seychelles and therefore no indigenous laws. The legal tradition that operates is the fateful result of the legal systems of two colonial empires that owned and administered the islands in the eighteenth, nineteenth and twentieth centuries. The archipelago of 115 islands in the West Indian Ocean today have a population of 89,700,[14] a mix of European, African and Asian peoples, the descendants of the early French settlers and African slaves brought to the islands in the eighteenth century, of the English colonizers of the nineteenth century, and of Chinese and Indians who arrived as traders in the nineteenth century and early twentieth century.

Seychelles' history is closely associated with that of Mauritius (known as *Isle de France* until 1810). The French took possession of the latter in 1715 and it was administered by the *Compagnie des Indes* (French East India Company) from 1722. In 1742 after it was ceded back to France, the Governor General of Mauritius, Mahé de Labourdonnais, concerned about English ambitions in the Indian Ocean and determined to see the island remain as a support base from which French interests in India would flourish,[15] despatched Captain Lazare Picault on a voyage of discovery in the surrounding seas. On 22 November 1742, he sighted and landed on Mahé, the main island of Seychelles.[16]

The composition of the population of Seychelles as well as the first laws imposed by the colonial administration would have consequences both on the language and the law of Seychelles today. Until 1770, no settlement was made on the islands by the French.[17] The first settlers comprised 15 whites, 7 slaves, 5 Indians and 1 *negress*.[18] By 1774 there were 775 slaves and a further 200 slave

---

13   Creole in Seychelles also known as Kreol, is the lingua franca as well as being an official language together with English and French. The word Creole in Seychelles may also denote its people, customs, traditions or cuisine.

14   2011 Statistics, Seychelles National Bureau of Statistics <http://www.nbs.gov.sc/> accessed 20 January 2014.

15   R Allen, *Slaves Freedmen and Indentured Labourers in Colonial Mauritius* (Cambridge University Press 1999).

16   J Bradley, *The History of Seychelles* (Clarion Press 1940) 10.

17   D Scarr, *Seychelles since 1770: History of a Slave and Post-Slavery Society* (Hurst and Company 2000) 2.

18   G Lionnet, *The Seychelles* (David and Charles 1972) 70.

children born in the colony. There were still fewer than 50 white families.[19] White settlers were to come from Mauritius and also the French métropole including 70 Jacobin deportees.[20] At the time of Capitulation to Britain in 1814, the composition of the population would have been more or less the same as recorded by a census taken in 1804: 215 whites, 86 coloured and 1,820 blacks making a total population of 2,121.[21]

During the era of French rule *à travers* Mauritius, the laws of Seychelles had four distinct periods: first, the laws of the *Compagnie des Indes* from 1722 to 1766,[22] second, the royal decrees promulgated by the King of France from 1766 to 1790 including the *Code Noir*,[23] third, the edicts published by the Colonial Assembly of Mauritius from 1790 to 1803, and fourth, the laws of *Decaen*[24] from 1803 to 1815.[25] It is important to distinguish in these laws those that applied to the whites, those to the free blacks and those to the slaves: civil law for the white population consisted of the *Coutume de Paris* and the *Code Louis*,[26] for civil procedure and the *Code Noir* for the population of slaves. The coloured and freed slaves (*les affranchis*) existed in an uncertain in-between legal regime, the rules of which were sometimes those applicable to the white citizens while at other times those applicable to the slaves despite the fact that an edict of 1723 had provided that they were to enjoy the same rights and privileges as those persons born free.[27]

A *Code Pénal* was published on 15 October 1791 and adopted by the Colonial Assembly of Mauritius in 1793. The *Code Civil* was promulgated in Mauritius on the 25 September 1805 as was the Law of 3 September 1807 which was in effect a new edition of the Civil Code under the title of *Code Napoléon*. Decaen published the French *Code de Procédure Civile* on 20 July 1807 and after several modifications the *Code de Commerce* on 1 October 1809 and the new *Code Pénal* in 1810. During Decaen's administration, litigants in Seychelles had the right of

---

19   Bradley (n16) 24.

20   Lionnet (n18) 87.

21   Bradley (n16) 124.

22   There was little legislation apart from those relating to slavery. These in any case ceased to have effect after 1788. See V Glover, 'Legislative Drafting in Mauritius: A Developing Discipline' <http://www.opc.gov.au/calc/docs/Loophole_papers/Glover_Aug2011.pdf> accessed 20 January 2014.

23   The *Code Noir* formed part of Louis XIV's edict of 1685 providing for the policing of slavery.

24   Charles Decaen was Captain-General of all French settlements north of the Cape of Good Hope including Seychelles.

25   Glover (n22).

26   The *Code Louis XIII* also known as '*Grande Ordonnance de Procédure Civile* of 1667', was a comprehensive legal code attempting a uniform regulation of civil procedure throughout France.

27   R d'Unienville, *L'evolution du droit civil* à L'Ile Maurice *(1721–1968)* (Best Graphics 1994) 37–40.

appeal to the Supreme Court in Mauritius. That court was composed of a president, vice-president, three judges, four clerks, and a government commissioner with his clerk and the clerk to the court. There was no jury. Seychelles was allowed a Justice of the Peace, a clerk to the Justice and to the court. Criminal affairs were judged by French laws of 1670 until these were repealed in the revolution of 1793.[28]

In this first period, if we are to avoid a Eurocentric perspective, it is impossible to treat the laws exclusively as either transfers or impositions. Seychelles as a national entity was only in its nascent stage and since it had no indigenous people, Seychelles did not fit within the definition of either *settler colony* or *colony of occupation*.[29] The settler colony invariably involved the invading Europeans annihilating, displacing and/or marginalizing the indigenes.[30] An example would be early settlement in South Africa. Colonies of occupation denoted a different type of colonization whereby the Europeans settled temporarily in small numbers and were concerned mainly with the exploitation of resources while promoting and safeguarding the geopolitical interests of the metropolitan State.[31] An example would be India.

Neither concept was applicable to Seychelles. The white settlers and the slaves became the *indigenes*, simultaneously colonizing and colonized. For the white settlers (the colonizers) in Seychelles, the laws were certainly an extension of metropolitan law albeit through the agency of another quasi-colonial power (Mauritius). For the slaves (the colonized) who had neither a common cultural or racial whole, since they did not emanate from one distinct region of Africa but from the disparate reaches of the Horn of Africa, East Africa, Madagascar, Burundi, Malawi, Zaire, South Africa, Zambia and Zimbabwe,[32] the laws were certainly an imposition in every sense of the word.[33]

British rule

In the nineteenth century, Mauritius and Seychelles were fought over by the French and the British because they commanded the important trade route between India and the Cape. Piracy by the French corsairs was a menace to the British East India

---

28   Bradley (n16) 122–123.

29   See A Johnston and A Lawson, 'Settler Colonies' in H Schwarz and S Ray (eds), *A Companion to Postcolonial Studies* (Blackwell 2005) 360.

30   See B Ashcroft, G Griffin and H Tiffin, *Post-Colonial Studies: The Key Concepts* (2nd edn, Routledge 1995) 193.

31   See D Kenneth Fieldhouse, *The Colonial Empires: A Comparative Survey from the Eighteenth Century* (Weidenfeld and Nicolson 1966).

32   JE Harris Evanston, *The African Presence in Asia: Consequences of the East African Slave Trade* (Northwestern University Press 1971).

33   See J Houbert, 'The Indian Ocean Creole Islands: Geo-Politics and Decolonisation' (1992) 30(3) The Journal of Modern African Studies 465.

Company ships sailing from India.[34] Seven capitulations in total of Seychelles to the British took place during French rule and by July 1810, de Quincy, the French administrator in Seychelles, had received a copy of the proclamation of Sir Robert Farquhar, the first Governor of the nearby *Isle de Bourbon* (Réunion), captured from the French, inviting Mauritius to surrender to British rule. On 3 December of the same year, after a short battle, Mauritius finally fell to the British and because of its dependency on its mother colony, so did Seychelles. The terms of the Mauritian Capitulation ensured the continuation of existing laws, specifically Article VIII which stated: '*que les habitants conserveront leur religion, leurs lois et coutumes.*'[35]

For the most part of the French and English administrations, the link with Mauritius would remain and essentially Seychelles was 'a colony of a colony' until 1903, when it became a fully-fledged colony in its own right, severing its dependency status from Mauritius.[36] The abolition of slavery in 1835 led to the repeal of the *Code Noir* and made the *Code Napoléon* the common law of all Seychellois irrespective of descent or status.[37] The British administered Seychelles but unlike the French, did not settle English people on Seychelles soil. As Seychelles entered the twentieth century its population was about 20,000, composed:

> of French and Anglo-Saxon elements, with blacks of different sorts from India, Madagascar, and every part of Africa; a few Chinese shopkeepers ... In the 'society' of the islands [in 1907, were found those] as have continued to keep their families untarnished – there are remarkably few that have done so – together with the pure-blooded descendants of such English officials and planters as have settled on the islands since their annexation.[38]

In the eyes of Stanley Gardiner, Seychelles society then was quite racially distinctive. The blacks had evolved into four classes: 'those who own land, separated further into those who have and those who have not Western blood, and those who have no land, *enfants des iles*, and foreigners.'[39] The foreigners were recently freed slaves, still with their tribal markings.[40] Those with land had mostly acquired this because of the *Code Napoléon* which entitled illegitimate children to

---

34   M Franda, *The Seychelles, Unquiet Islands* (Gower Publishing Company 1982) 13.

35   Art.VIII, Capitulation of Mauritius, 1810. (The inhabitants will retain their religion, their laws and customs ...)

36   Letters Patent, August 31, 1903.

37   d'Unienville (n27) 26, 46.

38   J Stanley Gardiner, 'The Seychelles Archipelago' (1907) 29(2) The Geographical Journal 148. See also M Twomey 'Legal Salmon: Comparative Law and its Role in Africa', in Salvatore Mancuso (ed) *Comparative Law in Africa* (Juta forthcoming).

39   Gardiner (n38) 156.

40   ibid.

succeed to shares in their white landowner parent's property if their illegitimacy had been recognized by him before his death.[41]

During the first 80 years of British rule, Seychelles continued to be administered by Civil Agents and Commissioners under the direct orders of the Governor of Mauritius and by implication under Mauritian law. Although an Order in Council in 1888 created both a Legislative Council and a Supreme Court in Seychelles, in the case of the former it reserved legislative power to Mauritius and in the case of the latter it was subordinate to the Supreme Court of Mauritius.

The laws enacted from 1810 to 1840 are collectively referred to as the Code Farquhar. This contained local ordinances, the Governor's Proclamations and other Public Acts or Notices of the Executive Government either in the English or the French language or in both languages, in which case both versions were deemed authoritative. In effect that period saw the operation of French law in an English context but this included some tampering with the *Code Napoléon*; for example, in order to facilitate their work the British administrators repealed the provisions relating to civil status but re-enacted most of them in the English language. In this context, the Supreme Court of Mauritius on many occasions, including in an appeal from Seychelles, ruled that the provisions of the Civil Status Ordinance were a mere translation of the articles of the Code and that, in interpreting these provisions, the court would be guided by French doctrine and jurisprudence.[42] After 1841, all laws, including those that amended the French Codes, were to be written in English.

By 1900, there was still only one court in Seychelles which had jurisdiction over both civil and criminal matters not necessitating a jury. In cases of appeal and serious criminal offences, recourse was had to the Supreme Court of Mauritius.[43] The digest of decisions of the Court of Appeal[44] from 1870 to 1902 shows that the judicial style of decision writing had already changed from the French style to that of English reasoned judgments.

Once Seychelles became a fully-fledged British colony, the erosion of French law became much more evident. Section 21 of the 1903 Order in Council applied the English law of evidence *except where otherwise provided.*[45] The mixing of laws from the common law and civil law traditions was also vigorous, for example,

---

41 Arts 756 and 760 of the *Code Civil*.

42 See Law Reform Commission of Mauritius Background Paper Reform of Codes [October 2010] <http://lrc.gov.mu/English/Documents/Reports%20and%20Papers/34%20 reform-codes.pdf > accessed 20 January 2014.

43 M Murat, *Gordon's Eden or, The Seychelles Archipelago* (Foreign and Commonwealth Office Collection 1900) 14.

44 P Bourke, *A Digest of the Ruling Decisions of the Supreme Court of Seychelles from 1903 to 1933 and the Reported Cases on Appeal Therefrom to His Majesty's Privy Council from 1870 to 1902* (Government Press 1934).

45 This wording has been preserved to this day in s12 of the Evidence Act, Cap 74, Laws of Seychelles.

the 1904 Penal Code was a patchwork of the previous French Code with some importations from the British Indian Penal Code. It was to remain in force until 1955 when it was replaced by a new Penal Code, this time based on the Penal Code of East Africa which was itself derived from English law.[46] The Seychelles Code of Criminal Procedure and the Seychelles Code of Civil Procedure were promulgated respectively in 1919 and 1920. In the case of the latter, again because of the retention of the *Code Napoléon*, several provisions of the original French Civil Procedure Code were also saved. Some Napoleonic Code provisions, notably in relation to the law on domicile[47] and the law of defamation[48] were also amended with the introduction of English law concepts.

At the same time the Seychellois population itself was hybridizing. MT Reid, the Financial Commissioner from Britain who visited Seychelles in 1933, records that the population had risen to 27,444 but, by then, the *métissage* of race was already well underway. He stated that the composition of the population could no longer be recorded because 'it would be difficult to do so where there are many of mixed blood making no claim to be pure white'.[49] Of their identity, he stated '[t]hey are French in outlook, politically Seychellois first though British subjects as well. They resemble French people in many ways, but a tropical environment has done its work ... [producing] a disposition to a feckless hedonism ...'[50]

In this second period of legal history, the style of colonial administration and legal transfer is starkly different. British colonial policy was one of *association* and indirect rule compared to that of the French policy of *assimilation* into a greater France.[51] The French viewed their national patrimony as worthy of export and they intimated to the colonized that if they adopted French language and culture they would ultimately become French and even French citizens.[52] This was never replicated by the British either because they considered themselves superior or recognized their subjects were culturally different, and were quite happy to rule at arm's length.[53] Hence, the British legal transfer was not wholesale, as for example

---

46   Scarr (n17) 149.

47   Domicile Act, Cap. 66, Laws of Seychelles.

48   Defamation Ordinance, 1948, repealed and replaced by Art.1383-3 of the Civil Code of Seychelles.

49   Bradley (n16) 346.

50   ibid.

51   See RF Betts, *Assimilation and Association in French Colonial Theory, 1890–1914* (University of Nebraska Press 2005) and JR Horne 'In Pursuit of Greater France: Visions of Empire among Musée Social Reformers, 1894–1931' in J Clancy-Smith and F Gouda (eds), *Domesticating the Empire: Race, Gender, and Family Life in French and Dutch Colonialism* (University of Virginia Press 1998).

52   Betts (n51).

53   See D McCarthy, *International Economic Integration in Historical Perspective* (Routledge 2006).

in the case of the Civil Code, but was more subtle, measured and apparently consensual; one step at a time over a longer period of time.

Independence

Although time was to act as melting pot to blend Seychellois identity into what it is today, contained in Reid's summary above is an intimation of a crisis that was to manifest itself in terms of a paradoxical sense of alienation and a reflective identity in the national psyche, language and even law. A close parallel can be drawn between the development of Seychellois Creole and identity and Seychellois law. This is mapped out in Fernando Ortiz's[54] concept of *transculturation* where there is a progression from hostility (against the black), to compromise (by the slyly subversive slave), to adaptation (on the part of the imitative mulatto), to vindication (of the blacks and mulatto) and finally to integration.[55]

By the time of its independence in 1976, the Seychelles population had melded into a distinct nationality but with some underlying identity problems persisting. The three languages of English, French and Creole were still widely used by different sectors of the population. Despite what can be largely regarded as a successful hybridization in both nationhood and legal structure, there remained a lack of a holistic cultural identity perpetuated by inequality in terms of land distribution, wealth, education and language. Creolization offered a way out of the identity crisis but to this day remnants of colonialism remain. Traits from the French settlers, though considerably weakened, persisted. During British rule the interests of the French *'plantocracy'* were so well served that the British administration did nothing but 'strengthen the allegiance of the élites to French culture, thereby making the British feel alien in their own crown colony'[56] and in so doing created a third layer in Seychellois society. The Creoles for their part, when it suited them, resented both *les colonisateurs anglais* (the English colonizers) and the *grands blancs* (the old landed families descended from the first French settlers).[57] However, class struggle did not initially lead to much politicization partly because the *grands blancs* and the British exiles concentrated their efforts on attacking the Government and subduing the Creoles.[58] It was only *métissage*[59] and the astute decision by the socialist Government in 1981 to make Creole an

---

54   F Ortiz, *Etnia y Sociedad* (Editorial de Ciencas Sociales 1993).

55   S Nair, 'Creolization, Orality and Nation Language in Carribbean' in H Schwarz and S Ray (eds), *A Companion to Postcolonial Studies* (Blackwell 2005) 238.

56   J Houbert, 'The Indian Ocean Creole Islands: Geo-Politics and Decolonisation' (1992) 30(3) The Journal of Modern African Studies 465, 468.

57   Scarr (n17) 178.

58   ibid, 130.

59   *Métissage* seems to be the only politically correct word for interracial breeding as miscegenation is viewed by some contemporary scholars as being offensive. See R Newman, 'Miscegenation' in Kwame Appiah and Henry Louis Gates, Jr. (eds) *Africana:*

official language[60] which completed the creolization of the Seychellois, mended the schism and in many ways unified its people.

However, vestiges of colonialism remain not only in the Creole psyche but also, substantially, in the legal and political infrastructure of Seychelles. Civil administration continues to mirror the British system. The 1993 Constitution now provides that the national languages of Seychelles are Creole, English and French but laws may provide for the use of any one or more of these languages for any specific purpose.[61] Court language, laws and official documents are all in English. Interpreters are used in court to translate Creole testimony into English, both for the advantage of non-Seychellois judges but also for the court record. More and more judges and legal practitioners are from a common law background and speak little French. The loss of French to Creole and the increasing use of English in the past 30 years have undeniably contributed to the erosion of the civil law tradition.

By far the biggest assault on French law was the translation and recodification of the Napoleonic Code. While the Seychelles Civil Code remains faithful to the French *Code Civil* in form and structure and retains the same numbering for the articles,[62] there are many innovations; for example, the rules relating to guardianship[63] and the partial introduction of the concept of trusts in cases of co-ownership of property.[64] It is difficult to ascertain the real reason behind the translation and recodification apart from making it easier to assimilate Seychelles into the Commonwealth. Many express the view that it was because aspects of the Code had to be amended to meet the challenges of nationhood.[65] Professor Alexander Chloros who drafted the new Code even stated that:

> [w]ithout a new Code, the attachment of Seychelles to the original French Civil Code would have become little more than a fiction. For hardly any part of that Code could for long remain relevant to modern conditions [as] modern legislation on British models would have completely superseded the Code.[66]

The Encyclopedia of the African and African American Experience (Basic Civitas Books 1999) 1320.

60   L Campling, H Confiance and M-T Purvis, *Social Policies in Seychelles* (Commonwealth Secretariat 2011).

61   Art.4, Constitution of the Republic of Seychelles, 1993.

62   See AG Chloros, *Codification in a Mixed Jurisdiction: The Civil and Commercial law of Seychelles* (North Holland Publishing 1977) 7.

63   Art.402–422, 429–437 Civil Code of Seychelles.

64   Art.818 of the Civil Code of Seychelles.

65   See A Sauzier 'The Influence of the French Judicial Model on the Seychelles' (Nicole Tirant-Gherardi tr.) <http://www.bas.sc/law-journal-1/theinfluenceofthefrenchjudicialmodelontheseychelles> accessed 20 January 2014.

66   See Chloros (n62).

This argument is not entirely convincing as comparisons with Mauritius prove otherwise. Their Civil Code remained with some exceptions much the same after their independence and until today remains in the French language assuring a more pronounced bijuralism; yet it cannot be said that either their economy or nationhood suffered because of it – the tweaking that happened in Mauritius were mainly in terms of economic not legal policies.[67]

It must also be pointed out that other aspects of the civil law system have been eroded. For example, while article 5 of the French Civil Code states that a judicial determination on an issue of law has no declaratory force in subsequent cases and Chloros had intended the new Code to say much the same, the new article 5 of the Seychelles Civil Code in stating that 'judicial decisions shall not be absolutely binding ... but shall enjoy a high persuasive authority' has more or less introduced the doctrine of precedent in civil cases much along the same lines as is presently applicable in criminal cases.

While French had been the medium of education in schools up to 1945, its replacement by English and the gradual loss of spoken French to both English and Creole – a bitter battle fought in the War Years between the *grand blancs*, the Marist Brothers and the Catholic Church against the British administration[68] – was another nail in the coffin of civil law as fewer legal practitioners and judges turned to the French jurisprudence in civil cases.

The three republics of Seychelles

Since independence Seychelles has known three republics. The first, inaugurated on Independence Day in 1976, lasted less than a year and was replaced by a socialist one-party State which saw Seychelles initially ruled by presidential decree. The achievements of the Albert René Government in the area of social development, and particularly housing, health and education, are undeniable but the list of human rights contained in the second constitution was unenforceable as they were only contained in the Preamble of the Constitution and their enjoyment stated as an 'intention' only.[69] This accounted in many respects for numerous human right abuses during the period.

67　See for example L Yeung Lam Ko, 'The Economic Development of Mauritius Since Independence' Research Working Paper No. 6, School of Economics, University of New South Wales, Australia <http://wwwdocs.fce.unsw.edu.au/economics/Research/WorkingPapers/1998_6.pdf accessed 20 January 2014.

68　Scarr (n17) 128–163.

69　The Preamble, Constitution of Seychelles Decree 1979 (abrogated 1993) states: 'We the people of Seychelles hereby declare our intention ... to secure the enjoyment by every person of certain fundamental rights and freedoms...' See on this point B Baker, 'Seychelles: Democratising in the Shadows of the Past' (2008) 26(3) Journal of Contemporary African Studies 279, 280.

The era also saw the passing of some interesting socialist laws, sometimes potentially in conflict with provisions of the Civil Code. One of these was the Tenant's Rights Act 1981, the purpose of which is described in section 4 as being:

> ... to assist in enabling every Seychellois family to own its own home by giving security of tenure to Seychellois who own and occupy a home on another person's land or who are residential tenants, and by enabling those Seychellois to purchase the land or premises and, in the administration of this Act, regard shall be had to that object.[70]

Other laws in the same vein include the People's Housing Mortgages Act 1981 and the Lands Acquisition Act 1978. The Civil Code survived completely unscathed from the socialist era and many of the socialist laws were repealed or substantially amended after the 1993 Constitution.

Excesses of the Government and hostility to an open economy resulted in US$ 32,000,000 'outstanding in advances to politically-advantaged individuals as well as state-owned enterprises'[71] by the financial year 1988–1989. The socialist dream was starting to unravel and by the end of 1991 foreign currency reserves were down further. Seychelles was increasingly under pressure for a return to democracy from London, Paris, Washington and Bonn.[72] Finally it was President Albert René's attendance at the Commonwealth Heads of Government conference in Harare, Zimbabwe on 20 October 1991 which led him to initiate the move from a single-party government to a multi-party democracy.

The third constitution in 1993 provided for a democratic multi-party sovereign republic with the President as head of the Executive. Legislative power was vested in a unicameral assembly consisting of 25 members. A judiciary comprising a Court of Appeal, a Supreme Court, a Constitutional Court, subordinate courts and tribunals were provided for.

The period post-independence was an era of great legal upheaval in Seychelles. This continues in some respects to this day. It cannot be said that any stability has been reached in terms of the law making enterprise or the bedding down of a coherent legal system. In this respect, post-colonial theory assists in understanding Seychellois legal hybridity.[73] Using the language of Homi

---

70   Tenant's Rights Act 1981, Cap. 235 Laws of Seychelles, repealed 1992.

71   Scarr (n17) 197.

72   ibid, 199.

73   Hybridity as a legal concept can focus on mixes of Western positive law cf V Palmer, *The Third Legal Family* (2nd edn, Cambridge University Press 2012) or mixes with non-Western elements of positive law cf E Örücü, 'Family Trees for Legal Systems: Towards a Contemporary Approach' in M van Hoecke (ed), *Epistemology and Methodology of Comparative Law* (Hart 2004) 359 or deep legal pluralism in which positive law is mixed with other law-like normativities cf SP Donlan, 'To Hybridity and Beyond: Reflections

Bhabha,[74] a study of the Seychellois legal system at present depicts a tortured identity, a 'double inscription of cultures' that are both of the colonizing and the colonized producing 'two kinds of authority and two kinds of authenticity'.[75] The concepts developed by Bhabha, central to post-colonial theory have resonance in Seychelles: hybridity, mimicry, difference, ambivalence. What is queried is whether in enacting legislation and deciding cases, especially in view of the current influences of globalization, Seychelles can use her own authoritative voice or just that of her former colonial masters given the enduring complexity of her identity which has only been partially cured by creolization. Post-colonial traits persist as is evident in the practice of law today, for example, despite the enactment of the Civil Code nearly 40 years ago plaints[76] are still filed in the Supreme Court alleging *faute* when the Civil Code of Seychelles clearly introduces 'delict' and 'fault'.[77] The second revision of the Civil Code of Seychelles launched in May 2013 may provide the opportunity to provide both Seychellois authority and authenticity in its laws but it is unclear how *mixité* will endure into the future.

Practising Law in Seychelles

It is clear that given the complexity of the layers of imposed and transferred law and the emerging chosen law that Seychellois law is unique. The question arises as to the legal education of its practitioners in such an environment.

Previously, under the Barristers and Attorneys Act, the Law Officers Act and the Queen's Counsel Act 1971, those admitted to the Bar of England and Wales and who had obtained a law degree were entitled to practise in Seychelles. These Acts have been repealed and replaced by the Legal Practitioners Act of 1996. There are now five main routes to qualify as an attorney in Seychelles: firstly through the UK by obtaining a qualifying law degree[78] and then successfully completing the Bar Vocational Course or the Legal Practitioner's Course and a two-year pupillage at an approved chambers in Seychelles; secondly through the Mauritian route – obtaining a law degree at the University of Mauritius, successfully completing the Mauritian Bar Exams and a two-year pupillage in Seychelles; thirdly through

---

on Legal and Normative Complexity' in V Palmer (ed), *Mixed Legal Systems, East and West: Newest Trends and Developments* (Ashgate forthcoming), <http://ssrn.com/abstract=2151899> accessed 20 January 2014.

74   H Bhabha, *The Location of Culture* (Routledge 1994)136.

75   Johnston and Lawson (n29) 369.

76   In Seychellois procedural law a plaint is a statement of claim initiating civil action before the courts.

77   Paper presented by Bernard Georges at the launch of the Second Revision of the Civil Code of Seychelles on 6 May 2013 (copy with author).

78   s5 (1) (a) (iv) of the Legal Practitioners Act 1996 provides that these are degrees at institutions and of a level approved by the Minister in consultation with the Chief Justice.

France by completing the education phase of qualifying as a lawyer in France and then sitting the Seychelles Bar Exams followed by a two-year pupillage in Seychelles; fourthly though the new University of Seychelles law degree which is in effect a degree of the University of London, following which the candidate has to sit the Seychelles Bar exams and complete pupillage for two years; fifthly as an articled clerk which involves a long and laborious period of local study, consisting initially of an Articleship Entrance Exam followed by six years of study at an approved chambers after which one sits the local Bar exams followed by another two years of pupillage. Degrees from any other country are not acceptable.

The 'lego-global' degree offered by the University of London through the University of Seychelles has only components of English common law (including English contract and tort law, land law and equity and trusts which are all totally inapplicable in Seychelles) which apart from providing a homogeneous, ill-suited and inappropriate programme is in many ways a missed opportunity to give a solid training and understanding of mixed jurisdictions. The University of Seychelles has this year introduced a fourth year of Seychellois law components after the degree course.

Legal practitioners operate within a fused system. There are no distinct professions of solicitors and barristers as operated during French colonial rule where the three distinct professions of *avoués, avocats* and *notaires* existed.[79] There is also no separation in terms of audience before the courts as far as solicitors and barristers are concerned. There are a handful of law firms, but the majority of lawyers are sole practitioners. The main other legal practitioner in Seychelles is the notary who draws up authentic documents and performs conveyances.[80]

The latest addition to legal practitioners in Seychelles has been firms specializing in the new offshore business industry. The agents for incorporating and maintaining international business corporations, international trusts and foundations are called corporate service providers or trustee service providers. These are corporate entities licensed and regulated by the Seychelles International Business Authority Act (SIBA) 2005. Cases emanating from these entities are governed by a parallel set of laws[81] only applicable to them which are beginning

---

79   The three distinct professions continue to operate in Mauritius. In France the Law n° 2011-331 of 28 March 2011 on the modernization of French legal professions has merged representation by the *avoués* with the *avocats* before the Courts of Appeal. Rights of audience before the *Cour de Cassation* are still restricted to specialist advocates who are accredited to argue cases before the *Cour de Cassation* and the *Conseil d'Etat*, referred to as *avocats au Conseil d'Etat et à la Cour de Cassation*.

80   s3, Notaries Act, Cap. 149, Laws of Seychelles.

81   See, for example, the International Business Companies Act 1996 and the International Trusts Act 2000.

to cause ripples of conflict where they interface with local laws, most noticeably in terms of trust provisions.[82]

As a small jurisdiction with a limited number of legal practitioners, judges in Seychelles are drawn from practitioners locally and from the Bench of other Commonwealth countries.[83] Traditionally they have come from as far away as the UK and the Caribbean to closer jurisdictions such as those of East Africa, Sri Lanka and Mauritius. The biggest challenge to the mixed and unique jurisdiction of Seychelles has been the appointment of non-Seychellois judges with little knowledge of the political, economic and cultural traditions or the intricacies of the mixed legal system of Seychelles. The difficulty in *perception* by jurists dealing with a system that is not their own, is generally acknowledged.[84] Undoubtedly this lack of perception does influence the decisions of the practitioners and ultimately the character of law. Although there is no empirical evidence that the background of judges influence judge-made law, it is evident when reading decisions of the Seychellois courts that judges with common law backgrounds often superimpose common law notions and concepts onto and in opposition and contradiction to the Seychelles Civil Code provisions in civil cases. The criticism is less applicable in cases of judges from other types of mixed jurisdictions such as the judges from Sri Lanka; in their case it is perhaps their lack of French that may ultimately undermine the mixity of the Seychelles legal system. The same general criticism may apply to the majority of Seychellois legal practitioners and judges who qualified through universities in the UK.

If the University of Seychelles was to maintain its present programme of teaching modules on Seychellois law there is a real and substantial possibility that the existing mixed jurisdiction might be maintained.

The Role of the Court of Appeal

Although judicial decisions are only one of the many legal formants of a legal system, their role cannot be underestimated.[85] The judicial power of Seychelles is vested in the Judiciary,[86] consisting of the Court of Appeal, the Supreme Court, the Magistrates' Courts and tribunals. The Supreme Court has both original jurisdiction and supervisory jurisdiction over subordinate courts, tribunals and adjudicating authorities. The word 'supreme' is now an anomaly; it is not supreme in the sense of being a court of final resort (the Court of Appeal is). Historically it was

---

82   See recently *Zalazina & ors. v Zoobert Ltd & Ors* (unreported) (2013) SCA 28/11 [17].

83   The first Seychellois Chief Justice, Sir Nicholas France Bonnetard was only appointed in 1959.

84   Sacco (n8) I of II, 33.

85   ibid. See also Sacco (n8) II of II.

86   Art.119(1) Constitution of the Republic of Seychelles.

supreme in Seychelles, as appeals from it in civil matters were heard in Mauritius until independence in 1976, and in criminal matters in East Africa until 1954 and ultimately to the Privy Council until 1976 (independence). The jurisdiction of the Supreme Court is exercised in practice by a single judge, although Article 125(4) of the Constitution does provide that a Bench of more than one judge can exercise the jurisdiction of the court. When it sits as a Constitutional Court its jurisdiction and powers have to be exercised by at least two judges. It has all the powers, privileges and jurisdiction of the High Court of Justice of England and is also a court of equity having power to do justice when there is no remedy at law.

Decisions of the Supreme Court in civil and criminal matters given at first instance or on appeal are subject to appeal to the Court of Appeal as are the decisions of the Constitutional Court. The Court of Appeal consists of a President, two or more Justices of Appeal and other judges who are ex-officio members of the Court (drawn from the Supreme Court in certain circumstances). Until 2004, the Court of Appeal was not resident in Seychelles. The Court endeavours to deliver a unanimous decision but it is not uncommon to have more than one judgment including dissenting judgments. It still continues to sit trimestrally. The first Seychellois Court of Appeal judge was only appointed in 2005 and the first Seychellois President of the Court of Appeal in 2007.

As a court of last resort it has the opportunity and duty to correct mistakes and resolve conflicting decisions made by judges in previous cases. The authors Louis Edwin Venchard, Sir Victor Glover and Professor Anthony Angelo writing in 1997 summarize the reasons for conflicting judgments as being:

a. the failure to recognize that the law applicable in Seychelles is neither English or French law but that of a mixed jurisdiction where a hybrid prevails;
b. the unsatisfactory harmonization of the English principles on to laws of French inspiration;
c. inadequate transitional provisions at the time of the promulgation of the Civil Code of Seychelles Act 1975;
d. the enactment, on certain topics, of parallel legislation which did not always take account of the existing provisions of the Code;
e. the uncertainty caused by providing that in certain cases, 'the principles of English law shall apply', without specifying whether the reference was to the principles applicable when Seychelles severed its ties with the UK or those principles which apply when a case is before the court.[87]

Unfortunately this continues to be the case today. It was the wish of the authors above that the court would use its 'judicial ingenuity' to resolve the conflicts by reversing or distinguishing the relevant judgments.[88] As a member of the Court

---

87 See LB Venchard, VJF Gosk and AH Angelo, *The Law of Seychelles through the Cases* (Best Graphics 1997) x–xi.

88 ibid, x.

of Appeal the author acknowledges the will of the court to correct such mistakes while being mindful of the danger of being overly forceful or imperious in relation to the decisions of previous or lower courts or engaging into too much judicial activism.

Regional and International Influence

Before its independence Seychelles was very much an insular society. It had no airport until 1972 and depended on infrequent shipping for contact with the outside world. Its legal system was much less porous than it is today given its remote geographical location. The advent of technology and the involuntary rapprochement resulting from the World Wide Web has left its legal system 'cognitively open'[89] to regional and international influences. Although, it is not clear what effects these influences will have, they may yet be the most important meta-legal formants[90] of the Seychellois legal system.

Similarly, the geographic position of Seychelles at the intersection of major shipping routes has given it a strategic importance. This point was brought home recently in the incidents of Somali piracy and the concerted efforts by the international community to make Seychelles the focal point of their coordination programme to combat the crime. Hence Seychelles quickly amended its Penal Code to update the medieval piracy laws it had inherited from England.[91]

International influences on domestic law include those of international and regional organizations, for example the Commonwealth, the *Organisation Internationale de la Francophonie* and the African Union. However, more influential are those organizations engaged in promoting cooperation with other African States with the primary focus of economic development or integration, for example the Common Market for Eastern and Southern Africa (COMESA) and the Southern African Development Community (SADC).[92] Their stated principles and motivations include the promotion of sovereign equality; solidarity, peace and security; human rights, democracy and the rule of law. The SADC's vision includes inter alia economic well-being, freedom and social justice; peace and security for the peoples

---

89   See N Luhmann, ' Closure and Openness: On Reality in the World of Law" in G Teubner (ed), *Autopoeitic Law: A New Approach to Law and Society* (de Gruyter 1988) 335.

90   Sacco (n8).

91   See, for example, P Lehr, 'Piracy and Maritime Governance' (2013) 9(1) Journal of the Indian Ocean Region 104.

92   See Declaration and Treaty of SADC <http://www.sadc.int/index/browse/page/119> accessed 20 January 2014. Its Member States are Angola, Botswana, DRC, Lesotho, Madagascar, Malawi, Mauritius, Mozambique, Namibia, Seychelles, South Africa, Swaziland, Tanzania, Zambia and Zimbabwe. See S. Mancuso, 'Creating Mixed Jurisdictions: Legal Integration in the SADC region (2012) 5(2) Journal of Comparative Law 146.

of Southern Africa. It also aspires to emulate the *Organisation pour l'Harmonisation en Afrique du Droit des Affaires* (OHADA)[93] operating in the French speaking west and central African States with harmonized business law enabling economic integration of its Member States. Those harmonized laws trump domestic laws and to date nine uniform Acts have been promulgated across OHADA's 16 Member States.[94] Although some recent reports have indicated a rise in the activity by the informal sectors in these countries resisting the uniformizing forces of OHADA and others have documented its shortcomings, including the limitation of using only the French language on a Continent where other important languages including English, Spanish and Portuguese are utilized, together with the World Bank's initial dismissal of the use of French-business influenced law, the overall economic success of the organization is now being increasingly recognized even by the World Bank[95] and has put paid to the legal origins theory.[96] OHADA however operates in African countries which have inherited the French civil law system.

SADC proposes to go even further than OHADA to codify both common principles and non-State practices of its Member States.[97] Whether that will be possible given that its members have neither a common source of legal tradition nor a common European language is questionable. In any case even the suggestion that the harmonization of African laws is possible by passing through the lens of African legal pluralism[98] may be misconceived. The maintenance of legal diversity is not clearly spelt out and many of the legal constructs used are Eurocentric and inappropriate. In any case the recent decisions in *Campbell v Republic of Zimbabwe*[99] and *Louis Karel Fick & Others v Republic of Zimbabwe*[100] display the

---

93   Organisation for the Harmonisation of Business Law in Africa.

94   For a list of the Uniform Acts see <http://www.ohadalegis.com/anglais/regltionohadagb.htm> accessed 20 January 2014.

95   See C Dickerson, 'Harmonizing Business Laws in Africa: Ohada Calls the Tune' (2005) 44 Columbia Journal of Transnational Law 17. See also R Beauchard and MJV Kodo, 'Can OHADA Increase Legal Certainty in Africa?' (2011) The World Bank, Justice and Development Working Paper Series, 45.

96   For the legal origins theory see R La Porta, F Lopez-de-Silanes and A Shleifer, 'The Economic Consequences of Legal Origins' (2008) 46(2) Journal of Economic Literature 285. The authors argue that countries with common law traditions generally have better economic outcomes than those with civilist traditions as they are more market orientated. This led to the imposition of many common law instruments initially by the World Bank even in countries with civilist traditions or mixed jurisdictions like Seychelles. An example would be the International Trust Act 1994.

97   Mancuso (n92).

98   See S Mancuso, 'Harmonisation of Laws and Convergence between Common Law and Civil Law Legal Families: Lessons from the OHADA Experience' <http://www.tipmoz.com/library/resources/Oldsite1/Harmonization_of_Laws_in_SADC_Mancuso.pdf> accessed 20 January 2014.

99   SADC (T) 2/2007.

100   SADC (T) 01/2010.

'toothlessness' of both the Tribunal and SADC itself which leaves undecided the sustainability of the legal integration process.[101]

Adherence to imposed legal frameworks where the ground work has not been laid out adequately also leads to domestic noncompliance. COMESA, for example, provided Seychelles with the technical assistance to prepare the legal structure necessary for public procurement and the training of government officials and private bodies for best buying practices. It must be borne in mind that such initiatives were introduced in the midst of a persistent Seychellois mind-set and culture following the 16-year one-party rule. Hence, despite its enactment in 2008, the Public Procurement Act is still not applicable to certain public bodies such as government owned companies and other statutory institutions, and this coupled with the lack of enforcement to ensure adherence with the provisions of the Act leads to a general lack of transparency and incoherence in many sectors.[102] Yet according to the UN, Seychelles leads Africa in its infrastructure consolidation, improved efficiency in the delivery of government services and e-government.[103] Similarly, the same criticism can be applied to the policies of the IMF and the World Bank in their imposition of legal instruments that have little appreciation of the existing domestic legal system. Although the laws concern the operational framework of public finance, these international organizations often underestimate tenacious domestic and informal practices. This largely echoes Roger Cotterell, law's community;[104] the concept of law's embeddedness in culture and his emphasis on the 'localized as against the centralized, and on diversity as against uniformity'.[105] It is a recognition of the fact that law as a global concept must embrace a healthy pluralism. Similarly John Gillespie in his analysis of legal transfers in East Asia shows how underestimated interpretative communities are and how they constrain the globalization of law.[106]

The socialist policies inculcated in the Seychellois mentality for nearly two decades are generally difficult to shift – privatization is slow; the enhancement of transparency and the improvement in the governance of state owned enterprises seems to be repelled as Seychelles continues to resist the full blown market

---

101   In both of these cases the Tribunal found that the Zimbabwean Government had acted unconstitutionally in seizing the land of white farmers and ordered that the plaintiffs be compensated. The decisions were ignored by the Zimbabwean Government.

102   See Annual Report 2011, Report on the Activities of the National Tender Board <http://www.ntb.sc/images/tenders/annrep2011.pdf> accessed 20 January 2014.

103   See UN Public Administration Programme <http://www.comesa.int/ index.php?option=com_content&view=article&id=100:seychelles-leads-africa-in-e-government-development&catid=5:latest-news&Itemid=41> accessed 20 January 2014.

104   R Cotterrell, *Law's Community: Legal Theory in Sociological Perspective* (Clarendon Press 1995).

105   ibid 322.

106   J Gillespie, 'Towards a Discursive Analysis of Legal Transfers into Developing East Asia' (2008) 41(2) New York University Journal of International Law and Politics 101.

policies advocated by both the IMF and the World Bank. Yet there is persistence in this respect by the IMF and willingness by the Seychellois Government to ensure Seychelles adheres to these policies in order to benefit from the tranches of loans promised.[107] While one can hardly bite the hand that feeds it there are concerns in relation to some of the legislation adopted, notably in the anti-money laundering legal structure and in the legislative framework governing offshore activities especially trusts. Anti-money laundering legislation is complicated as it is generally accepted that while it deals with the proceeds of criminal conduct, its provisions are essentially civil in nature.[108] The concept is even more problematic especially in terms of rules of procedure and evidence when trying to graft such legislation onto civil law or mixed jurisdictions.[109] Similarly, the proposed Trusts Bill 2011 failed to take into consideration existing property provisions in the Civil Code of Seychelles and ignored the fact that the common law trust concept does not exist in Seychelles and that such a proposal could only allow a statutory trust regime in the offshore structure.[110]

Perhaps, the major concern to the Seychelles mixed jurisdiction does not lie in globalization itself but rather on the derivation of these globalized policies from common law doctrines and norms exclusively. Hence, since France ceded Seychelles to Britain in the early nineteenth century the only new influence of French civil law has been in decisions of the Seychelles courts where the *arrêts* (decisions) of the *Cour de Cassation* or *Cour d'Appel* have been applied or in the use of *la doctrine* (legal doctrine or jurisprudence) especially in reference to the *Encyclopédie Dalloz*, Sirey, Ripert, Planiol, Mazeaud, Carbonnier and Capitant[111] in judicial decisions.

---

107   See 'International Monetary Fund: Seychelles: Letter of Intent, Memorandum of Economic and Financial Policies, and Technical Memorandum of Understanding November 30, 2012 and Attachment 1: Memorandum of Economic and Financial Policies for 2013' <http://www.imf.org/external/np/loi/2012/syc/113012.pdf> accessed 20 January 2014.

108   See, for example, the Seychelles Court of Appeal cases *Financial Intelligence Unit v Mares Corp* (unreported) SCA 48/2011; *Hackl v Financial Intelligence Unit and anor* (unreported) SCA 10/2011 and *Financial Intelligence Unit v Cyber Space Ltd* (unreported) (2012) SCA 27(a)/2012, the Irish cases of *Gilligan v Criminal Assets Bureau and others* and *Murphy v GM. PB and Ors* (2001) IESC 82 and the South African case of *Simon Prophet v The National Director of Public Prosecutions* CCT 56/05.

109   ibid, Seychelles Court of Appeal cases.

110   See the reaction of Bar Association of Seychelles at <http://robingroom. blogspot.ie/search?updated-min=2011-01-01T00:00:00%2B04:00&updated-max=2012-01-1T00:00:00%2B04:00&max-results=24> accessed 1 August 2013.

111   These are French legal theorists and treatise writers.

Conclusion

Iza Hussin concludes that 'law as a travelling phenomenon is an inescapable reality' but that 'the route it takes, and the people, ideas, institutions and interests with whom it travels, are crucial for what law might become'.[112] Her views echo those of other authors on the undervaluation of context and culture in the development of legal traditions.[113] The resistance of Seychellois domestic law to international and regional influences must therefore not be underestimated.

In surveying the historic and current status of Seychellois law it is undeniable that just as aspects of civil law, common law and globalized legal constructs were transferred or imposed on Seychelles, an element of choice fashioned by the unique Seychellois culture and tradition will continue to determine and shape the legal system. It is this reality which provides hope for those who esteem the values of legal pluralism and hybridity. The coherence of laws can be developed at a domestic level despite the influences of external norms. Equally, the circularity of law[114] in terms of the influence of the domestic laws of national States and transnational law and vice versa must also not be underestimated. The danger to Seychellois legal *mixité* is that most of the transnational law is from the common law tradition. The emergence of Seychellois nationhood and its creolization is a further challenge to the continued *mixité* of its law but since legal systems are not static, the Seychellois legal system may well be on the course of what may be perceived as a Seychellois finality, although paradoxically such a concept is itself perhaps not achievable in terms of legal traditions. Finally, the progressive fracturing of what may have been a somewhat seamless but mixed legal tradition may yet yield a distinctive and unique legal system.

---

112   Hussin (n9) 18–19.

113   See for example Cotterell (n104) and Gillespie (n106).

114   G Teubner, 'Global Bukowina: Legal Pluralism in the World Society' in G Teubner (ed), *Global law without a state* (Dartmouth 1997) 3.

Chapter 7
Quebec

Often cited as a classical mixed jurisdiction system, to include Quebec in a collection of our title might seem like an affront to many. Certainly compared to Seychelles the civil law elements which contribute to the Quebec legal system seem well entrenched and it may well be the case that few jurists in the province would consider that the status of Quebec as a mixed legal system is at risk.

As shown by Sophie Morin, historically this has not always been the case and things might have turned out differently. However, the 1994 adoption of the new Civil Code of Québec marked an apparently definitive and symbolic turning point entrenching the influence of civilian law in the civil or private law of Quebec, and contributing thereby to the overall mixity of the system. Indeed today the status quo of a mixed legal system is so generally accepted as to be unquestioned. Morin asks whether this leads to complacency. Are there potential risks which demonstrate echoes of the past and which today may have more serious consequences, such as the loss of French language competence among Supreme Court judges, lack of professional private law experience (and therefore exposure to civilian legal traditions) prior to appointment to the bench, and lack of vigilance among jurists to ensure that the civil law component of private law is not swamped by common law elements, thereby putting at risk the mixity of the whole system?

Indeed Morin suggests that it might be asked whether the unquestioning acceptance of the civil law tradition in private law in Quebec has resulted in a purée so that the distinct elements are no longer identifiable and the private law can no longer be regarded as mixed but as simply Quebec private law shorn of its distinct civil and common law parts. If this is so how does that affect the whole system? Is Quebec in fact no longer a mixed system in which one can distinguish the different component parts but a hybrid one in which these distinctions have become blurred and a new creation has arisen? Or is it the case that the Quebec system is recognizably distinct within the broader Canadian legal system and among world systems but no longer attached to its civilian roots? Is it the case that in Quebec, where identity is no longer linked to nationalism, confidence and autonomy indicate that the mixity itself may be in danger?

In this chapter Morin considers whether by conducting a sort of temporal découpage, what emerges could be called 'threats of the past' resurfacing in the future precisely because civil law jurists, armed with a freshly asserted identity, no longer feel that the mixed system is fragile and at risk. To the contrary, perceiving the system as a reliable strength, they may have let their guard down.

Quebec: 'First Impressions Can be Misleading'

Sophie Morin

The Danger in Question

'Where is the danger?' That question has been on my mind for weeks, because at first glance, I did not perceive any imminent threat lurking around Quebec's mixed system of law. In fact, it seemed to me that Quebec's mixity had nothing to worry about. It was not in danger of disappearing and it did not seem at all nervous about its future. This initial impression left me puzzled for a few weeks. But I could not stop there: I had to find any evidence of possible threat – even potential risk, however minimal that risk might be.

Somehow it seemed to me that the very lack of apparent danger was itself a clue that I needed to pay attention to and think about. The assessment of risk is ultimately a matter of perception and of factors such as the intellectual position and perspective of the observer. In the eyes of a Quebec jurist, then, what might represent a threat or danger to the mixed legal system she works in?

It should be mentioned at the outset that, although it is a fine idea to be on the lookout for any potential threats, the vast expanse under scrutiny – the Quebec legal system – is a real jungle as result of its mixed origins. Under Canadian federalism,[1] Quebec – a province in political terms – is subject to public law based on common law and is also subject to federal laws, also based on common law, governing certain aspects of private law, such as bankruptcy and divorce. However, federal private law sometimes has gaps and may be supplemented by the private law of the province where the issue arises, which means that Quebec's system of private law – which is based on civil law – sometimes completes the federal private law, which is based on common law.[2] Adding further complexity to the jigsaw puzzle is the fact that, in addition to being bijural, Canada is a bilingual country: common law in Canada is made in English but also in French, and civil law is made in French but also in English. Canada's organization and its history result in many points of intersection between rules derived from the civil law and

---

1   Constitution Act, 1867, 30 & 31 Victoria, c. 3 (UK).

2   Federal Law–Civil Law Harmonization Act, No. 1, S.C. 2001, c. 4; Federal Law–Civil Law Harmonization Act, No. 2, S.C. 2004, c. 25.

others from the common law. There is a word to describe all this: bijuralism. And in that, we are in the thick of mixity.

As Quebec's legal system is complex,[3] there is also diversity within the province's system of private law.[4] I chose to limit my remarks here to Quebec private law this approach being consistent with the traditional (and first) concept of Quebec's mixity.

So, starting from the premise that the mixed nature of Quebec private law is *not* threatened, I began to wonder about the basis of this perception. I came to the conclusion that one explanation may reside in our history: compared to a certain period in our past, any threats that persist today (assuming there are any) would necessarily be less menacing or even non-existent. Quebec jurists undoubtedly perceived such threats more clearly in the past: those threats were denounced and put in the spotlight for scrutiny. They were also widely discussed in the *doctrine* (that is, legal scholarship). It would seem that those threats of the past no longer exist today.

From this observation, another explanation begins to take form. Maybe there is indeed a threat today, but because it is nothing at all similar to the threats of the past, it remains unnoticeable or is simply not recognized as a threat. So, what of my perception that the mixed nature of Quebec civil law is not at risk? Is it simply a conditioned reflex? What could be more normal, in fact, than to look for danger where it always seems to have been and, moreover, in the form it has always taken? This led to the result that since I did not see a threat in its usual form, I concluded that it simply does not exist because the mixed nature of Quebec private law was not endangered nor was the mixed nature of its legal system.

Because you have to start somewhere before delving into the potential or real threats likely to affect the mixed nature of Quebec civil law, it will be useful to review a few key elements of a context that is probably already well known.

A Selected Piece of History: The Place of Civil Private Law in the Mixed Legal System of Quebec

When looking for warning signs of threats to the mixed nature of civil law, one cannot be overly parsimonious with the central historical and sociological themes. Certainly the history of Quebec, at least in broad outline, is probably too familiar to jurists interested in mixed jurisdictions to justify dwelling on it at length here. But the fundamental and founding element of the unique nature of the Quebec legal system arises from that history: the clash of cultures. It all began in 1534 with the beginning of French colonization. In 1760, the 'Conquest' marked the transfer

---

3   HP Glenn, 'Quebec: Mixité and Monism' in E Örücü, E Attwooll and S Coyle (eds) *Studies in Legal Systems: Mixed and Mixing* (Kluwer Law 1996) 1.

4   For an example relating to civil procedure, see D Jutras, '*Culture et droit processuel: le cas du Québec*' (2009) 54 McGill Law Journal 273, 290 *et seq.*

of New France into British hands. Within the territory of New France – which became Lower Canada in 1791 and eventually Quebec in 1867 – the population has always been predominantly Francophone. However, from the moment of the 'Conquest', the voice of authority was no longer French, but English. This is a very basic historical structure, but it will suffice as the backdrop for the remainder of this discussion.

Within this structure, various dualities developed and continue to exist even today. A non-exclusive list that immediately comes to mind would include: French/ English, Francophone/Anglophone, federal/provincial, and from a legal point of view, civil law/common law.[5] These dualities have very often been the source of perceived danger. It would probably be too easy to say that 'the other' is a source of fear and mistrust … and yet.

These dualities – those I have mentioned and others – generally evoke a variety of reactions that are ultimately expressed either as resistance (and preservation of something pure), or as assimilation (and the loss of that same pure something). Between these extremes there are, of course, many nuances: mixity (*mixité*), intermixing (*métissage*), hybridization, and so on.[6] Again, this is familiar to students and researchers of mixed legal systems.[7] For the moment, I am not too interested in the nuances; instead, I propose to focus on the extremes of the spectrum by examining a specific period of Quebec's legal history.

These two reactions – resistance and assimilation – can easily be tracked in Quebec's legal history. The authorities of the territory, first French and later English, dictated the law. From the colony's beginning, various forms of French customary law applied until, in 1664, the King of France decreed the implementation of the Custom of Paris. After the 'Conquest', the British tried to introduce their legal system, but were forced to backtrack. To start off, in 1764, the Royal Proclamation abolished the existing legal system – that is, French law – and replaced it with English law. The new British subjects then signed a petition demanding to be ruled and judged according to the same system of laws, customs and ordinances into

---

5   A Popovici, '*Libres propos sur la culture juridique québécoise dans un monde qui rétrécit*' (2009) 54 McGill Law Journal 223, 230–231.

6   M Morin, '*Dualisme, mixité et métissage juridique: Québec, Hong Kong, Macao, Afrique du Sud et Israël*' (2012) 57 McGill Law Journal 645.

7   For example: 'Racial and cultural dualism lead to legal dualism, whether as a mixed system or legal pluralism […] The preservation of a legal tradition has been shown to be related to the growth of national and cultural consciousness, a feeling of "otherness" and power. However, when two systems co-exist, the stronger one, demographic or otherwise, may take over, over-shadow or overthrow the other. The conclusion may seem simple, that is, if one hopes to preserve fidelity to a legal culture or heritage, one must rescue it from suffocation by the other law, in most cases by common law procedural methodology. The factors in maintaining a legal tradition generally referred to are: shared language and terminology, legal education and legal literature; closeness to the mother of the component to be preserved and the value attributed to the distinct cultural background.' E Örücü, 'Mixed and Mixing Systems: A Conceptual Search', in E Örücü, et al. (n3) 335, 349–350.

which they were born. Professor André Morel, in an article entitled '*La langue et l'acculturation juridique au Québec depuis 1760*',[8] stated that the petitioners did not show hostility towards the conqueror's legal system. Rather, they affirmed their readiness to submit to that system providing that is was well understood,[9] 'And it is this language barrier that constitutes, during that period, the central focus of their grievances, because English had become the language of the law and of lawyers and judges.'[10]

The graft of a new system onto the old did not take, despite the power of the English. Their new subjects simply chose to abstain from bringing cases to court when needed – completely avoiding the courts when dealing with family issues and only bringing suit in certain business and contract cases. Ten years later, in 1774, the *Acte de Québec* ordered the restoration of the old legal system, in a context in which there had been less British immigration than had been anticipated and in which French-speakers remained in the majority.[11] Although French law was restored, the Governor of the province had received instructions from London to reintroduce English law in the form of ordinances, an effort that met with little success. But public perception was the exact opposite: English law was thought to be widespread and far-reaching.[12] André Morel argues that this impression, which was out of step with the reality, shows that legal acculturation is not reserved to lawmakers: 'It can also result from the actions of the judicial power, when that power is almost entirely in the hands of judges from Great   Britain or its other North American colonies, as was the case of the judiciary in Lower Canada for several decades.'[13]

Not speaking French, unfamiliar with civil law and seeing no advantage for the colony in doing otherwise, these judges applied English law, prompting André Morel to conclude that, 'Once again, but in a reverse process, the language of law was – for the people of Quebec – a distinctive factor of contact and acculturation.'[14]

I have chosen to present this particular view of history from among many possible views, precisely because it is an appropriate lead-in for what follows. When one examines the mixed nature of Quebec civil law, language is obviously a key factor, but not in isolation. Dualities, resistance and assimilation are recurring themes in Quebec history and they are important in understanding the mixity of its legal system, and in particular for understanding the mixity of its private law.

---

8   A Morel, '*La langue et l'acculturation juridique au Québec depuis 1760*' (1990) 24 *Revue Juridique Thémis* 99.

9   ibid, 102.

10   ibid.

11   ibid, 105.

12   ibid, 105–106.

13   ibid, 106.

14   ibid, 106.

Mixity is the Danger

Quebec private law has been considered as mixed ever since, dare I say, the concept has been entrenched. We need look no further than the Civil Code of Lower Canada (CCLC) adopted in 1866, which contained laws originating from the Custom of Paris, the Napoleonic Code, common law and the *lex mercatoria*. Quebec private law was thus mixed in substance and it then evolved – and is still evolving – in a procedural environment and judicial structure modelled, to a large extent, on the institutions of common law. The form of judgments handed down in Quebec has long favoured the English style rather than the French. The final court of appeal, which is the Supreme Court, is the same for Quebec as for other Canadian provinces – for both private law and public law cases (and thus laws derived from civil law and common law traditions). The Supreme Court has had general jurisdiction since 1875.

The Supreme Court of Canada was the subject of much criticism during the first half of the twentieth century, likewise the Privy Council, which acted as a court of last instance in civil matters until 1949. In the eyes of many, the Supreme Court and the Privy Council embodied a threat to Quebec civil law – not to its mixed nature, but rather to the purity and integrity of its French origins. The mixing and intermixing of legal systems were seen as the threat at that time. The words of Pierre-Basile Mignault, written in 1922 when he was a justice of the Supreme Court of Canada, capture this perception of the threat perfectly:

> For the people of Quebec, our civil law is our most precious asset after our religion and language. It is a legacy we have received from our fathers, to be maintained and passed on to future generations. It is our duty and responsibility to honour and preserve our civil law, to ensure the purity of its *doctrine* and keep it safe from any influence that would prevent it from being what it should be.[15]

In connection with the events of history outlined above, language and identity were intertwined with a strong legal nationalism. Quebec jurists kept their eyes on the Supreme Court and the Privy Council, fearing assimilation of civil law into common law and denouncing the Court's (and the Privy Council's[16]) standardizing

---

15   P-B Mignault (1922) 1 *Revue de Droit* 56, 116. On this point see also two fundamental texts: S Normand, '*Un thème dominant de la pensée juridique traditionnelle au Québec: la sauvegarde de l'intégrité du droit civil*' (1987) 32 McGill Law Journal 559; M Morin, '*Des juristes sédentaires ? L'influence du droit anglais et du droit français sur l'interprétation du Code civil du Bas Canada*' (2000) 60 *Revue du Barreau* 247.

16   S Normand, '*Un thème dominant de la pensée juridique traditionnelle au Québec: la sauvegarde de l'intégrité du droit civil*' (1987) 32 McGill Law Journal 559, 581.

efforts. So many articles were published on this issue that it was practically a favourite topic within Quebec *doctrine*.[17]

I will not dwell on all the fine details of interpretation, legal reversals and other machinations of the time. A quick examination of the complaints made by Quebec jurists will suffice to demonstrate that during a certain period – now generally considered to be over – civil law had quite a hard time in the Supreme Court: its largely civil law character was seen as threatened and the standardizing efforts of the court always tended in the direction of common law, leading towards intermixing of common law with civil law. This was due in part to the method used to interpret the CCLC. The court considered the Code to be a statute and therefore interpreted it according to the canons of the common law; that is strictly and literally, thus flouting the notion that a Civil Code, by its very nature, must be interpreted liberally. At that time the court also interpreted the civil law as if it were a foreign law, and if there were similarities with common law, it was interpreted as if it were common law.

Another determining factor in the attitude of the court towards the civil law was the application of stare decisis, which was alien to the civil law, of course, but taken for granted in a judicial system organized according to the rules of common law. The authority of legal precedent was not in itself a threat to civil law as such authority was largely accepted, with certain nuances, in Quebec, where legal judgments were also beginning to take on some stylistic features of common law judgments.[18] What posed a threat to civil law was the imposition of a precedent from the common law – a precedent thus alien to the civil law – to justify a decision, without making sure that the reasoning was consistent with the general philosophy of civil law.[19]

Such efforts to standardize the law eased towards the end of the 1960s and the beginning of the 1970s,[20] as the Supreme Court became aware of the unjustified mixing of civil law caused by its decisions. Although legal *doctrine* and even

---

17   On that subject see: J-L Baudouin, '*La Cour suprême et le droit civil québécois: Un bilan, un constat, une prospective*', in G-A Beaudoin (ed), *The Supreme Court of Canada – La Cour suprême du Canada* (Éditions Yvon Blais 1985) 125; J-L Baudouin, '*L'interprétation du code civil québécois par la Cour suprême du Canada*' (1975) 53 *Revue du Barreau Canadien* 715; E Caparros, '*La Cour suprême et le Code civil*' in Beaudoin ibid, 107; L LeBel and P-L Le Saunier, '*L'interaction du droit civil et de la common law à la Cour suprême du Canada*' (2006) 47 *Cahiers de Droit* 179; A Popovici, '*Le rôle de la Cour suprême en droit civil*' (2000) 34 *Revue Juridique Thémis* 611.

18   For an analysis see PJ Dalphond, '*Le style civiliste et le juge: le juge québécois ne serait-il pas le prototype du juge civiliste de l'avenir?*' in N Kasirer (ed.), *Le droit civil, avant tout un style?* (Éditions Thémis 2003) 81.

19   J-L Baudouin, '*L'interprétation du code civil québécois par la Cour suprême du Canada*' (1975) 53 *Revue de Barreau Canadien* 715, 724 *et seq*; E Caparros, '*La Cour Suprême et le Code civil*' in Beaudoin (ed) (n17) 107, 110.

20   Baudouin (n17) 125, 129

some Quebec judges who have sat on the Supreme Court have condemned, sometimes scathingly, the ways of the court and the Privy Council, in its time, a simple explanation for this state of affairs can be put forward, having to do with knowledge: knowledge of civil law and knowledge of the French language. It is possible that the interpretive reflexes that led judges to fall back on common law were not so much driven by a single standardizing ideology, but rather by the near impossibility of gaining a thorough grasp of civil law. Under the circumstances, Quebec civil law/private law became a foreign law for many judges. Either they knew little or no civil law and, for lack of a better solution, necessarily referred to what they did know, namely common law, or they had little or no knowledge of the French language, which had the effect of almost completely (but, in fact, not totally) preventing them from becoming familiar with legal *doctrine* (of Quebec, and also of France) and with the body of case law.[21]

The Civil Code of Québec and the Crystallization of a State of Mind

When the new Civil Code of Québec (CCQ) came into effect in 1994 it was a major event in Quebec legal history. This codification was necessitated by the obsolescence of the CCLC and the loss of overall coherence due to multiple legislative interventions around the edges of the Code.[22] The CCQ is not simply an updating of the CCLC, but a veritable recodification. One author has suggested that, had it not been written, Quebec 'was at risk of gradually losing its civil law tradition and being submerged under the common law', adding that 'the Civil Code would have become one law among many others and the body of case law would have become increasingly important'.[23] In some ways, the CCQ has given a new impetus to Quebec civil law.

Should the impact of this codification be considered a rupture with the past or a continuation? Although the content of the CCQ differs from that of the CCLC, it can only be called a continuation. A continuation because, first of all, the majority of the articles of the CCQ have been carried over from past law, sometimes updating the substance of the law, but most often changing only the form.[24] As for style, the Code remains civil law, as Adrian Popovici observed: 'The tradition is

---

21   Baudouin (n19) 725; L LeBel and P-L Le Saunier, '*L'interaction du droit civil et de la common law à la Cour suprême du Canada*' (2006) 47 *Cahiers de Droit* 179, 185.

22   M Cantin Cumyn, '*Les innovations du Code civil du Québec, un premier bilan*' (2005) 46 *Cahiers de Droit* 463, 465–466.

23   A Grenon, '*Codes et codifications: dialogue avec la common law?*' (2005) 46 *Cahiers de Droit* 53, 70–71.

24   A Popovici, '*Libres propos sur la culture juridique québécoise dans un monde qui rétrécit*' (2009) 54 McGill Law Journal 223, 23–232; P-G Jobin, '*Le droit comparé dans la réforme du Code civil du Québec et sa première interprétation*' (1997) 38 *Cahiers de Droit* 477, 480 and 481.

carried on particularly in the form: the civil law style of the lawmakers supports the commitment of the majority of the judiciary to the civil law tradition.'[25] A continuation then, even though the Code contains some innovations by adopting new laws and new institutions (including the law of trusts, which is certainly the most well-known innovation). The Code also innovated by inserting a preliminary provision,[26] described by many as the most important new element of the CCQ and the interpretation of which leads to a variety of views on the mixed nature of Quebec law. Thus it has been argued that, based on the preliminary provision, Quebec common law is expressed *intra muros* of the CCQ but also *extra muros*, which in a way legitimizes the place of common law throughout private law.[27] In contrast, the preliminary provision was also seen as ending the duality of the *ius commune* (public law being tied to common law and private law being tied to civil law); the *ius commune* was now unified and the fact that a particular case concerned public law was no longer sufficient cause to exclude application of the civil law for the sole benefit of the common law.[28]

Based on this quick overview of the contributions of the CCQ to substantive law, it is clear that the CCQ is no exception to the general rule that the adoption of a code often marks a turning point in legal history. This is especially so since this codification was a success, as can be easily seen almost 20 years later. But beyond this type of technical analysis, the CCQ may also be considered an affirmation of a legal identity and a manifestation of confidence, particularly noticeable in the relationship that contemporary Quebec jurists have with the civil law.

These jurists work in a legal environment which has undergone profound changes since the 1950s: the development of an academic community and, subsequently, varied legal writings and *doctrine*[29] – writings that gradually broke away from French *doctrine* and dared to stand on their own merits.[30] A distinct

---

25   ibid.

26   The preliminary provision reads as follows: 'The Civil Code of Québec, in harmony with the Charter of human rights and freedoms (chapter C-12) and the general principles of law, governs persons, relations between persons, and property. The Civil Code comprises a body of rules which, in all matters within the letter, spirit or object of its provisions, lays down the *jus commune*, expressly or by implication. In these matters, the Code is the foundation of all other laws, although other laws may complement the Code or make exceptions to it.'

27   D Jutras, ' *Regard sur la common law au Québec: perspective et cadrage*' (2008) 10 *Revue de la Common Law en Français* 311, 311–312.

28   Cantin Cumyn (n22) 463, 469.

29   S Normand, '*La littérature du droit comme* élément *structurant du champ juridique québécois: une perspective historique*', in Y Gendreau (ed.), *La doctrine et le développement du droit – Developing Law with Doctrine* (Éditions Thémis 2005) 1; S Gaudet, *'La doctrine et le Code civil du Québec'* in *Le nouveau Code Civil: interprétation et application Journées Maximillien-Caron 1992* (Éditions Thémis 1992) 223.

30   P-G Jobin, '*L'influence de la doctrine française sur le droit civil québécois: le rapprochement et l'éloignement de deux continents'* (1992) 44 *Revue Internationale de*

legal identity and a sense of confidence began to develop. As one scholar who has examined the issue of civil law identity rightly points out:

> The recognition of the Civil Code as a special element of cultural identity no longer gives rise to the passionate reactions it used to provoke. Occasionally there are authors who defend civil law, but their writings are intended to ensure the cohesion of a legal system tied to the civil law tradition rather than to hold on to an intrinsic element of a community.[31]

The CCQ no longer retains the facet of identity linked to nationalism that the CCLC had.[32] Within the broader legal community – beyond the circle of private law experts – the Code no longer has the same symbolic meaning or untouchable status, a position now reserved for the Charter of Rights and Freedoms.[33] In spite all this, I still believe that the adoption of the CCQ represents, for Quebec private law, an affirmation of identity, the gateway to an era of confidence, and an expression of autonomy. In it we find indications of overflowing optimism, foreseeing a possible influential role for the CCQ in the territory of Canadian common law influenced private law, both in terms of influencing federal legislation, now harmonized with provincial rights, and in terms of inspiring future codifying laws.[34] However, such enthusiasm is tempered, once again, by the language barriers and the lack of familiarity with the civil law background to the Code and with Quebec law as a whole, that still prevail among the vast majority of Canadian jurists.[35] Nevertheless, the threats of the past – related to the preservation of the purity of the civil law (both because national identity was at stake in the eyes of some and, more prosaically at the legal level, because the conduct of the Supreme Court progressively intermixed common and civil law) – appear to indeed be in the past and the CCQ may mark the beginning of a new era.

Droit Comparé 377; P-G. Jobin, 'La *circulation de modèles juridiques français au Québec: quand ? comment ? pourquoi ?*' in G Bras Miranda and B Moore (eds), *Mélanges Adrian Popovici – Les couleurs du droit* (Éditions Thémis 2010) 599.

31   S Normand, '*Le Code civil et l'identité*' in S Lortie, N Kasirer and J-G. Belley (eds) *Du Code civil du Québec: contribution à l'histoire immédiate d'une recodification réussie* (Éditions Thémis 2005) 619, 651.

32   ibid. See also: J-L Baudouin, '*Réflexions sur le processus de recodification du Code civil*' (1989) 30 *Cahiers de Droit* 817; Normand (n16) 559.

33   S Morin, '*Pourquoi j'emmènerais le législateur au musée s'il voulait discuter de l'avenir du Code civil du Québec*' in J Andino Dorato, J-F Ménard and L Smith (eds), *Le droit civil et ses codes: parcours à travers les Amériques* (Éditions Thémis 2011) 87.

34   Grenon (n23) 72–74.

35   J-F Gaudreault-Desbiens, *Les solitudes du bijuridisme au Canada* (Éditions Thémis 2006).

Mixity in Danger

If the adoption of the CCQ marked a turning point in Quebec legal history, might it also have marked the moment when the mixed nature of civil law entered a fragile phase, potentially putting it at risk? The answer might well be yes, which would transform my first impression – that there was no threat hanging over the mixed nature of Quebec law – into a false impression.

I would like to emphasize at the outset that currently, in Quebec private law or even in Quebec law as a whole, there is no uniform and organized discourse concerning the threat or threats that the mixed legal system may be facing. This is of course in sharp contrast with the past when attention focused on the actions of the Supreme Court and the Privy Council. This absence of apparent concern undoubtedly influenced my initial perception that the mixed nature of Quebec private law is not and would not be in danger and that therefore the mixed nature of the system as a whole would not be at risk.

As there is no apparent danger, it was necessary to look for any indications, however slight, that could be harbingers of a trend. To do this, I dissected (without attempting a comprehensive review) the writings of Quebec jurists – for the most part scholars and experts on civil law – that dealt with or even touched on the mixed nature of our legal system. In my search for threats in the current context, my attention was naturally turned to texts written at the time the CCQ was adopted. So, if you will, follow along with me as I examine the trends in the writings of authors who do not necessarily share the same opinions with regard to the existence of a threat. Their comments sometimes overlap and certain broader currents may emerge, revealing a veiled glimpse of the threat … perhaps just a vague outline, but enough to keep us vigilant.

As I have already pointed out, any current threat to the mixed legal system, brought about by a predominantly civil law influenced private law and a common law influenced public law, no longer resembles that of the past. This view is widely held and there is no clear evidence to suggest otherwise. Even before the CCQ was adopted, during what I would call the transitional phase, many expressed this opinion. For example, in 1989, a time when the attitude of the Supreme Court was sharply criticized, Jean-Louis Baudouin wrote:

> Moreover, in my opinion, the threats to the so-called mixed nature of Quebec civil law, or rather its intermixing with common law, so often denounced by legal *doctrine* and the body of case law since 1866, are much less worrisome today than they were a century ago. Quebec law has become, in my opinion, quite independent and strong enough to incorporate certain useful or advantageous elements of common law easily enough without being dependent on, or even a slave to, the common law for precedents and interpretation, as was the case in the past. It seems, in fact, very healthy that a system should evolve with the times and borrow rules from another system if they are deemed valid and useful. On the other hand, borrowing a rule does not mean borrowing the methods of

interpretation nor the indiscriminate imputation of the interpretation of the text made by foreign courts. In the history of Quebec civil law, there have been many examples of this unfortunate habit, but that phenomenon is, I believe, a thing of the past.[36]

Eleven years later, in 2000, Adrian Popovici also noted the absence of danger, at least as it had been manifested in the past, while adding a new reason for concern that was a sign of the times:

> However, today the Supreme Court is generally no longer considered a serious threat to the future of civil law. Are we right in taking this view? In part. But in part we are also mistaken. … But I believe that the threat to civil law now comes from elsewhere: not from outright contamination by common law in private law, but from more insidious and pernicious contamination by constitutional law.[37]

Today, the Supreme Court hears extremely few private law cases across Canada.[38] When the CCQ was adopted, some experts anticipated that the court would take on an increasing number of such cases, but this did not occur. At the Supreme Court, appeals are usually heard by permission and the majority of cases currently heard fall under public law, and therefore under common law.

The fact that only a tiny number of private law cases are heard by the Supreme Court changes nothing, because the authority of the judgments handed down by the court even in the few that are heard remains important. That is why I must highlight a fairly recent event, which nonetheless holds echoes of the past. In 2006 and in the fall of 2012, two judges were appointed to the Supreme Court; at the time of their appointments, both were unilingual Anglophones – and they still are. These two judges do not make up part of the mandatory three judges who must come from Quebec.[39] These appointments, of course, provoked criticism – to which the Government has turned a deaf ear. Some argued that these appointments are unconstitutional because they are contrary to Article 16 of the Canadian Charter of Rights and Freedoms, which provides that English and French are equal.[40] This is a sensitive issue and these nominations, which are made by the federal government, could have given rise to political opposition, which obviously occurred, but which I will not go into here. Of course, the appointment of a unilingual Francophone judge would be equally deplorable, although highly

36 J-L Baudouin, '*Réflexions sur le processus de recodification du Code civil*' (1989) 30 *Cahiers de Droit* 817, 820–821.

37 Popovici (n17), 612.

38 As an illustration, in 2012, of 75 judgments rendered, two were private law cases. In 2011, of 66 judgments rendered, only one was a private law case.

39 Supreme Court Act, Revised Statutes of Canada 1985, c. S-26, s6.

40 Canadian Charter of Rights and Freedoms, part I of the Constitution Act of 1982, s16.

unlikely; in fact, to my knowledge, the unilingual justices of the Supreme Court have always been English-speakers. These latest appointments demonstrate that Quebec jurists must stay on the alert, as this situation concerns the whole of Quebec private law, which is largely in French for obvious reasons involving access to the legal *doctrine* and the body of case law.

This takes us back to the period in the past discussed above, to a time when some justices of the court (sometimes the majority of them) had no access to the *doctrine* and therefore to body of private law based on civil law principles because they did not understand the language. Jean-Louis Baudouin, who was very critical of the attitude of the Supreme Court of the time, wrote in 1985 the following about judicial bilingualism:

> For many years, with just a handful of notable exceptions, few judges from the common-law provinces could speak or even read French and few knew the basics of civil law. The change in recent years has been quite remarkable. [..] Thus the time when some jurists questioned the ability of the Court to hear and understand cases of pure civil law now seems to be over. The ideal of full bilingualism and possibly even 'bi-judicialization' is now not far from being reached and it probably will be reached one day if future governments respect certain basic requirements for access to the Court, including fluency in both official languages.[41]

I cannot help but point out that history repeats itself – and we can only hope that the mistakes of the past are not repeated.

Let us move on to another question. Focusing on the CCQ, many authors have emphasized the importance of comparative law to the development of the Code as it was being written. The CCQ is essentially concerned with private law and draws on laws taken from the CCLC, which were themselves rooted in French law, whether customary or codified. Other laws in the CCQ were inspired by French civil law or other systems of civil law. Finally, there are laws inspired by common law, a few from England and Wales, but mostly from other Canadian provinces and the US.[42] This eclecticism has marked Quebec private law[43] for many years, and the use of foreign sources as inspiration does not diminish the mixed nature of Quebec private law, in fact the opposite is true.[44] Scholars do not consider this recourse to foreign law to be a threat to Quebec's mixed legal system – which seems perfectly normal. With regard to civil law, the interpretation of these foreign elements should not be modelled on what has taken place in the past related to

---

41   Baudouin (n17) 125–130.

42   P-G Jobin, '*Le droit comparé dans la réforme du Code civil du Québec et sa première interprétation*' (1997) 38 *Cahiers de Droit* 477, 482.

43   Popovici (n24) 232–233.

44   Popovici ibid; Jobin (n42) 482.

common law, at the risk of returning to the past, as Professor Benoît Moore rightly points out:

> This fear of acculturation of the civil law by the common law is not new. In the past, that fear has been a cause of legal sclerosis in Quebec. That time is now over. The future of the *Civil Code of Québec* no longer raises questions of identity. It is no longer regarded as a Code under siege. The influences that the Code borrows – which are many and from diverse sources – are borrowed for reasons of efficiency and legal opportunity. Common sense travels: it is not an exclusive trait of any one legal system. What matters is that the borrowed concepts are useful and – beyond the national origin of any given borrowed institution – that we remain conscious of the identity and spirit of our system of civil law.[45]

Due to the identity, confidence and autonomy that the CCQ represents, it can show openness towards the wider legal world. The use of foreign sources, whether from systems of civil law or otherwise, is perceived as a strength, a characteristic feature of Quebec civil law. A feature which may ultimately be the *coup de grace* for the mixed nature of Quebec law, as traditionally understood from a civil-centrist point of view. At least, this is how the following words of Professor Benoît Moore's could be interpreted:

> The simple intermixing of sources is not a sign of acculturation or even of a mixed system, and it should not be seen as such. If the *Civil Code of Québec* can be said to be mixed, it has more to do with 'its constant openness to foreign sources of law', to use Professor Glenn's wonderful phrase, than with the borrowing of specific concepts. In this sense, not only does our Code – and, more broadly, North American codes – have a future, but it seems to me that it can and should play a role as a bridge between traditions, beyond sterile nationalism, with respect for the spirit of each system.[46]

In 1992, when the CCQ had been adopted but was not yet in effect, Professor H Patrick Glenn (who was cited by Professor Benoît Moore above) examined the place of comparative law in the interpretation of the CCQ. He wrote:

> All of this seems important in interpreting a Civil Code which requires broad and open methods of interpretation. To limit interpretation of the Code to an exegetical analysis would deny the fundamental and evolving nature of the Code. To limit the community involved in its interpretation to a single *communauté*

---

45   B Moore, '*Le droit civil et ses Codes – Parcours à travers l'Amérique: Rapport de synthèse*', in Andino Dorato, et al. (n33) 187, 211–212.

46   Moore ibid, 211–212.

étatique would restrict the available methods of interpretation to ensure the fundamental character of the Code.[47]

An optimist, Professor Glenn is far from seeing the mixed nature of the civil law element of the legal system as threatened, emphasizing again the strength provided by the CCQ:

> Thus the comparative law of the future may well disappear as a so-called scientific discipline, becoming just another way of thinking about the law. That is what seems to be indicated by current legal developments in the world. These developments appear full of promise for Quebec law and for the vigour and vitality of the modern code which the new Civil Code embodies. The openness of traditions is the best guarantee of their survival and well-being. It is by being closed that systems risk intellectual implosion, confrontation with other systems and the dominance of power relationships. Quebec jurists have never thought of the law in terms of closed systems. We are thus well prepared for the twenty-first century.[48]

With foreign sources of law, the mixed nature of Quebec private law takes on a different appearance from that of the past, but it is not in danger if the interpretative pitfalls of the past are avoided by judges and scholars. From this point of view, its own mixed nature is undeniably a distinctive feature of Quebec law, a feature which is now accepted and which will enable it to remain resilient over time. In effect therefore Quebec remains a mixed legal system in which the Civil Code has become a blend.

But when we speak of time, we are inevitably speaking of change. Up until now, the influence of the common law on the civil law of Quebec has attracted all the attention, the ultimate fear being 'acculturation' of the civil law by the common law. Today, one threat to the mixed nature of Quebec private law may well lie in the acculturation of the common law elements by the civil law elements, at least according to the thesis defended by Professor Daniel Jutras, who applies it to both public law and private law. Here is what he says about Quebec civil law:

> The idea that reference to common law sources is now either unnecessary or inappropriate is becoming commonplace. In short, the momentum of the *Civil Code of Québec* could end up pushing the notion of mixity out of Quebec private law – despite the latter's historical roots.[49]

---

47   HP Glenn, '*Le droit comparé et l'interprétation du Code civil du Québec*' in *Le nouveau Code civil: interprétation et application – Les Journées Maximilien-Caron 1992* (Éditions Thémis 1993) 176, 192.

48   Glenn ibid, 196.

49   D Jutras, '*Cartographie de la mixité: la common law et la complétude du droit civil au Québec*' (2009) 88 *Revue du Barreau Canadien* 247, 251.

The explanation offered by Professor Daniel Jutras is that of the 'completeness' of the civil law, an idea that currently suffuses the thinking of Quebec civil law jurists. This idea embraces identity, confidence and autonomy, which have been experienced and exhibited since the adoption of the CCQ.

> [..] in the period following the 1994 codification, a strengthened version of the notion of the completeness of Quebec civil law has appeared. Leaving behind defensive postures, this new discourse expresses a confidence that justifies autonomy and separation. It manifests itself in all areas, from civil procedure to the law of trusts, from federal legislation to codified law. According to this version of completeness, reference to the common law is not particularly relevant to comprehending and understanding the new civil law, which stands on its own. It is no longer a matter of simply avoiding the intrusion of concepts incompatible with the logic of civil law, but also of discouraging the continuous 'irrigation' of Quebec law by a practice that would confer persuasive value on foreign sources. In the areas of mixed law covered here, as in the wide-open field of comparative law, this attitude may result in close-mindedness that will impoverish Quebec civil law and deprive it of its uniqueness.[50]

But the threat described by Professor Daniel Jutras is the inverse of what is traditionally considered the greatest threat to civil law: if civil law cuts itself off from the influences of common law, civil law would ultimately be diminished and, in the process, lose its unique character. For Professor Jutras, the common law is not foreign to the Quebec legal system, nor to the private law within it.[51]

Another author, Michel Morin, shares similar views to Professor Jutras, clearly stating that mixed private law is weakened or may even disappear as a result of forgetting the roots of certain laws found in the CCQ. He writes:

> Although the common law remains the material source of several institutions of Quebec civil law, that origin is often veiled by the articles of the Civil Code or by the civil-law reasoning of judges. One may wonder whether the mixed nature of the civil law (or more accurately, its hybrid nature) is in danger of extinction or at least in a period of marked decline.[52]

These are a few of the evocations of danger that I was able to glean from the literature. I have chosen to quote extensively from these writings so that the views of these authors – concerning both the mixed nature of Quebec civil law and its status – would be revealed in their own words, free of any interpretation on my

---

50   ibid 270. See also B Moore, '*L'acculturation en droit de la consommation québécois*' in J-L Navarro and G Lefebvre (eds), *L'acculturation en droit des affaires* (Thémis 2007) 295, 326 *et seq.*

51   Jutras (n49) 248–249.

52   Morin (n6) 651.

part. Their views vary and suggest that contemporary concerns are substantially different from those of the past.

We can also see that the notion of mixity is nuanced. It would seem that, in this respect, Quebec private law is in the process of being redefined – perhaps because the mixed nature of Quebec private law dates from a time when cultural and societal dualities were exacerbated and when the development of the private law, in the name of preserving its integrity, was struck with paralysis. It is clear that Quebec jurists, at least those cited here, want to shed the past and look to the future, advocating for openness to other legal systems and sources. Thus, if the adoption of the CCQ did not mark a break with the past in substantive terms, it definitely marked a break in psychological terms.

Questioning the Mixity

Thus, we can see that the CCQ resulted in an established, affirmed and confirmed autonomy for private law. It seems that Quebec private law is in a phase of realizing its full potential or even reaching equilibrium. We can also see the variable importance given to the mixed nature of their legal system by the Quebec jurists who have written about it. The result is an equally variable appreciation of the specific elements that constitute a threat to that mixed nature, leading to the conclusion that threats are likely to take many forms, depending on your point of view.

So is the mixed nature of Quebec private law in danger? And if so how would this affect the mixed legal system of Quebec? Some people think so. But, unlike in the past, the threat would not come from the mixing itself, through the attraction that the common law elements or influences might exert on those drawn from the civil law. Rather the danger would result from the strength of Quebec private law itself, the CCQ being the culmination of a process of affirming and maturing 'a certain level' of mixing.

I return to the thought expressed by Professor Michel Morin who, regarding the origin anchored in the common law of some provisions in the Civil Code, notes that this origin disappears behind the 'civil law' style of the Code or the reasoning of judges, stating: 'One may wonder whether the mixed nature of civil law (or more accurately, its hybrid nature) is in danger of extinction or at least in a period of marked decline.'[53]

Once again, this seems to be a matter of perception. Or simply an understanding that the mixed nature of the legal system evolves over time: everything changes, nothing remains. The phenomenon described by Professor Michel Morin suggests that Quebec private law may have reached the consistency of a *purée*, to borrow a metaphor from Professor Esin Örücü. Quebec private law is a *purée* in that it is 'a blend so thorough that the constituent elements are indistinguishable

---

53   ibid 651.

and inseparable, the ingredients having been processed over a long period of time'.[54] However, is the fact that Quebec private law has reached a state of such 'homogeneity' (the word is used here with caution and in keeping with the metaphor) equivalent, as Professor Michel Morin suggests, to its mixed nature being in danger? If the state of mind embodied in the CCQ lasts for a significant period, will Quebec private law cease to be mixed? Is such a thing even possible? Of course, it cannot be – if we accept that all legal systems, even those called 'pure', are in fact mixed. Still, it may not be too far-fetched to ask whether mixity – once acquired and recognized, as is the case for Quebec private law – is a permanent condition?

I leave it to experts in the field to determine at what point it would be possible to consider that Quebec private law has *effectively* lost its mixed nature either through becoming so blended as to be indistinguishable or because the mixity has given rise to a new hybrid. This question, in fact, poses the same problem as that of determining at what point a legal system should be considered mixed – which is a far from simple task. But as an observer inside this system, I cannot help but notice that the mixed nature of Quebec's private law is ultimately, like any potential threats it may face, dependent on perceptions. As an illustration, I return to Professor Benoît Moore's assertion:

> Borrowing a concept does not imply borrowing its interpretation, if that interpretation is foreign to the policy of our law. The simple intermixing of sources is not a sign of acculturation or even of a mixed system, and it should not be seen as such.[55]

Some specialists in comparative law will doubtless disagree with Professor Moore's stand on what 'intermixing' or mixity are. While we probably should pay tribute to the past, in Quebec, that past and the mixed nature of our legal system have also meant a certain paralysis for private law.

Professor Benoît Moore's words however, provide evidence of the affirmation of the unique identity of Quebec private law. For my part, I wonder whether Quebec private law, through the process of codification and recodification, has fully appropriated its mixed nature, to the point that this aspect is overlooked by most people or taken for granted as simply a fixture in the landscape. This provokes the question, 'Can part of a mixed legal system such as the private law cease to be mixed despite its mixed origins?', In the end, the question of a threat to the mixed nature of Quebec private law is perhaps not the question we should be asking. The mixed nature of our private law is no longer seen as a weakness, an inadequacy or an area where identity is in play. Indeed, I would argue that the mixed nature of Quebec private law *is* the key to its legal identity. The problem may be that no one has yet found the right word to describe this new state of affairs.

---

54   Örücü (n7) 344.
55   Moore (n45) 211–212.

The mixed nature of Quebec private law derives from its different sources, even if today those sources are increasingly forgotten, victims of the passage of time and the daily practice of law which has no need to refer to those sources. Today, the mixed nature of this part of the law is perhaps only an issue for scholars and a handful of judges and lawyers. Is this mixity of one part enough to sustain the mixity of the system as a whole? The words of Joseph McKnight, written 35 years ago, remain pertinent for Quebec today:

> For the purpose of my definition of a mixed system I distinguish between what may be termed mixed and that which has already been blended to an extent that origins of rules are lost in ordinary legal practice. The distinction is therefore at once a practical and a psychological one, for whether a system is or is not a mixed one is in the minds of the Bench and Bar. To characterise a system as mixed is to recognise a prevailing state of the legal mind.[56]

Even if perceptions have never received good press in the legal profession (the law being supposedly an 'objective science'), I believe that it is impossible for those interested in Quebec as a mixed legal system to ignore the current views of Quebec jurists on this issue. I have confined my remarks to one part of that system, the private law, which is a major characteristic feature of Quebec law. The legal identity of Quebec private law is in a phase of maturation and expression. For me, as a private law jurist from Quebec, when I look at the history of my native land, I find the openness demonstrated and advocated by the authors cited here to be inspiring. For me, looking towards the future is natural, and the way we look at the mixed nature of Quebec's law must change, because the times and the signs have changed, and because the dominant influences in private and public law are entrenched.[57]

---

56   J McKnight, 'Some Historical Observations on Mixed Systems of Law' (1977) 22 Juridical Review 177, 178.

57   Thanks to Seán Donlan for his thoughful remark on this point.

Chapter 8

Saint Lucia

Although widely separated by climate and geography, the Caribbean island of Saint Lucia and the Canadian province of Quebec have intersecting colonial and legal histories. Nonetheless, as Seychelles in relation to Mauritius is not doing so well, so is Saint Lucia in relation to Quebec. Jane Matthews Glenn demonstrates this by considering a comparison between the two in three main phases: parallelism, convergence and divergence.

Both Quebec and Saint Lucia were established French colonies, endowed with similar administrative and judicial structures and subject to a similar body of law, when they were captured by the British in 1759 (Quebec) and 1803 (Saint Lucia), with British control being confirmed by treaty in 1763 and 1814 respectively. Both therefore became enclaves of French civil law in a British Empire in which the common law obviously dominated. Both came under similar pressures to assimilate – Anglicization of court structure, court procedure, court officials, areas of law, and so on; and both turned to codification as a way to resist these pressures. Their legal intersection was reinforced by the adoption of the Saint Lucia Civil Code, modelled on the 1866 Civil Code of Lower Canada, in 1879 and the Code of Civil Procedure, also based on its Quebec counterpart, in 1882.

As demonstrated by Matthews Glenn, subsequent events weakened the mixity of Saint Lucia to the extent that the Civil Code has been diluted by the insertion of common law concepts into it and the interpretation of the Civil Code has always been in the hands of judges trained in common law and unfamiliar with the civilian tradition. This 'intense intermingling', as she calls it, of civil and common law results in a 'hybrid' legal system.

Matthews Glenn looks in this chapter at these subsequent events with a view to determining whether or not Saint Lucia is an 'endangered' mixed jurisdiction. She asks whether the Quebec connection will continue to provide on-going protection to the island's civil law tradition in the future as it has in the past. She wonders what will be the effect on this tradition of having the Caribbean Court of Justice rather than the Privy Council as final court of appeals. At this point in time, Saint Lucia thus seems to be at a crossroads in protecting its civilian heritage.

Saint Lucia: 'The Quebec Connection – Parallelism, Convergence and Divergence'

Jane Matthews Glenn

Introduction

Mixed jurisdictions are the product of history, and this is notably so in the New World where France and Britain, in particular, struggled for dominance in the great imperial clashes of the seventeenth to early nineteenth centuries. These struggles produced a number of British 'colonies of conquest' which, under the doctrine of reception and British colonial practice, retained their existing laws and customs until subsequently changed. Quebec is the best known New World example, but lesser-known examples are found in the Caribbean basin, where the island colonies are evocatively described as having been 'visited, settled, abandoned, and resettled, handed about from one owner to another in the competition of nations, thrown first into one scale and then into the other, in order to adjust for the time being the claims of rival government'.[1] In fact, the leading English case on reception and continuation of law, *Campbell v Hall*,[2] arose in relation to the Caribbean colony of Grenada.

The doctrine of reception's presumption of continuity applies in principle to the whole body of law, public and private alike. But assimilation of public law usually occurs rapidly if not immediately after conquest, and it is really the continuation of the core of private law that marks the country as a mixed jurisdiction. Assimilation of private law arguably takes place in three stages: an informal stage, when local officials and judges ignore or change laws with which they disagree or do not understand; a piecemeal stage, when English law and procedure is introduced into a number of discrete areas (notably commercial law); and a wholesale stage, when the general corpus of the common law is introduced.[3] The difference between the

---

1   CP Lucas, *A Historical Geography of the British Colonies* (Clarendon Press 1888) vol ii, 14, quoted in CE Reis, 'Spanish Law in the British Empire' (1914) 14 Journal of the Society of Comparative Legislation (New Series) 24, 28.

2   (1774) Cowp 204, 98 ER 1045.

3   J Matthews Glenn, 'Mixed Jurisdictions in the Commonwealth Caribbean: Mixing, Unmixing, Remixing' in E Örücü (ed), *Mixed Legal Systems at New Frontiers*, JCL Studies in Comparative Law (Wildy, Simmonds and Hill 2010), 91–93. Various authors have identified differing patterns of piecemeal introduction: for example, RW Lee, 'The Civil

second and third stages is rather one of kind than degree, in that in the second stage, the ongoing civil law is the norm and the common law changes the exception to it, whereas in the third stage, the hierarchy between the two traditions is reversed, with the common law now being the general norm and the remaining civil law enclaves the exception. As RW Lee, writing in 1930, put it:

> What we call a system is in many respects a conglomeration. It is not so entirely one that great sections of it cannot be modified, or even replaced, without fatal results to the whole. Constitutional law depends on political allegiance, commercial law is peculiarly responsive to external influences, great changes in procedure may leave the substantive law unchanged. As compared with these, what we call specifically the civil law of a country is stubbornly unwilling to change. If this, the kernel of the legal system, retains its character substantially unaltered through successive ages, we shall say that the 'system' continues to exist.[4]

This suggests that a mixed jurisdiction becomes 'endangered' when its private law moves from the second to the third stage of assimilation.

Saint Lucia is the best known example of a mixed jurisdiction in the Commonwealth Caribbean today. This small island of some 238 square miles (617 sq km) – just slightly larger than the Isle of Man – located in the Windward chain of islands between the French *département* of Martinique to the north and the Commonwealth country of Saint Vincent and the Grenadines to the south, changed hands between the British and French some 14 times in all during the period of imperial conquest, before finally being taken by the British in 1803 as confirmed in the Treaty of Paris 1814. That it has survived as a mixed jurisdiction, despite almost overwhelming pressures to assimilate, is due in large measure to a fortuitous Quebec connection.

This chapter looks at the role the Quebec connection has played in preserving the ongoing character of Saint Lucia as a mixed jurisdiction. It asks whether this connection continues to protect the island's civil law tradition today, and

---

Law and the Common Law: A World Survey' (1915) 14 Michigan Law Review 89, 94–100; KD Anthony, 'The Reception of the Common Law System by the Civil Law Systems in the Commonwealth Caribbean' in M Doucet and J Vanderlinden (eds), *La réception des systèmes juridiques: Implantation et destin* (Bruylant 1994) 31–36; and MS Amos, 'The Common Law and the Civil Law in the British Commonwealth of Nations' (1937) 50 Harvard Law Review 1249, 1257 (suggesting that early introduction of English criminal and commercial law reflected the inadequacy of the civil law in these areas: 'The Roman law as received in the Middle Ages had little to offer in the shape of criminal law; and its commercial law, such as it was, proved quite inadequate to meet the vast demands of modern commerce').

4   RW Lee, 'What Has Become of Roman-Dutch Law?' (1930) 12 Journal of Comparative Legislation and International Law (Third Series) 33, 35.

divides this consideration into three main phases: Parallelism, Convergence and Divergence.

Parallelism

Saint Lucia and Quebec enjoyed parallel colonial histories, with minor moments of convergence, a parallelism which continued through the periods of colonization and conquest and extended into the post-conquest period.

Colonization

Both Saint Lucia and New France (as Quebec was called prior to conquest) were discovered by Europeans in the early sixteenth century and settled by the French in the early seventeenth century despite indigenous opposition.[5] Both were subject to periods of proprietary rule,[6] first by different privately owned companies and then by the same publicly owned company – the *Compagnie des Indes occidentales*, or West India Company – from 1664 to 1674.[7] Both then came under the direct control of the French Crown, with Saint Lucia comprising part of the colony of Martinique.

Both were thus endowed with similar administrative and judicial structures, with each being administered by a Governor and Intendant, and each having a *Conseil supérieur* as the highest tribunal. In Saint Lucia's case, this was the *Conseil supérieur de l'Ile Martinique*, composed of 12 counsellors selected from the influential merchants and planters of the colony, with the Chief Justice as president.[8] Like its New France counterpart, the *Conseil supérieur* performed not only judicial but also legislative and administrative functions.

5   French settlements in New France date from 1608 (Quebec City) and 1642 (Montreal). The situation in Saint Lucia is more complicated, as the English and French Crowns, as well as Carib Indians, claimed the right to grant the island to private individuals. French and English attempts at settlement, in 1605 and 1638 respectively, were defeated by the Caribs before a French settlement was successfully established in 1642: JH Pilgrim, *Snippets of St. Lucia's History* (2nd edn, Castries: Standard Publications 1960) 1–2.

6   The early English settlements have been described not as 'colonies', but rather as 'congeries of business ventures, hazarded by the monied English oligarchy in alliance with the throne': J Dupont, *The Common Law Abroad: Constitutional and Legal Legacy of the British Empire* (FB Rothman Publications 2001) xiii. The same can be said of the early French settlements.

7   These companies were intended to promote colonization, but were more interested in pursuing the more profitable trade in staples (furs in New France and sugar or tobacco in the West Indies). On the history of company rule in Saint Lucia, see Pilgrim (n5) and C Jesse, *Peeps into St. Lucia's Past* (Extra-mural Dept, U of the West Indies 1979).

8   NJO Liverpool, 'The History and Development of the Saint Lucia Civil Code' (1983) *Revue Générale de Droit* 373, 384 n34. Saint Lucia's court structure consisted of the

As French 'colonies of settlement', both Saint Lucia and New France were subject to similar bodies of laws. In Saint Lucia's case, this is described as consisting not only of local Ordinances and maritime and commercial law, but also of:

> nearly the whole body of the French Laws anterior to 1789, which are scattered over a great number of authorities, such as the *Coutume de Paris*, which is part of the ancient *'lex non scripta'* of France, the *Ordonnances*, Edicts and declarations of the French Monarchy, the *Code de la Martinique*, [and the works of such French writers as] Pothier, Merlin, Ferrière, Denisart, Domat, Pigeau, Jousse, and many others unnecessary to mention.[9]

The *Coutume de Paris*, in particular, was said to apply 'because the 33rd Article of the *arrêt* of the "*Conseil d'État du Roi*," of May, 1664, establishing the West India Company, expressly declares its obligatory effect in the West India Colonies, as it had been established in the French Colonies in the East'.[10] This *arrêt* has been carried forward and reprinted, in the original French, in the various compilations of the laws of Saint Lucia.[11] The list of civil law sources for New France is much the same.[12]

Conquest

Both Saint Lucia and New France were disputed by Britain and France during the global wars of the eighteenth and nineteenth centuries. Their fates were momentarily linked in the Seven Years War, which ended with the Treaty of Paris, 1763. Both colonies had been captured by the British during the war – New France in 1759[13] and Saint Lucia in 1762 – but in the ensuing peace negotiations, Britain elected to retain New France and return Guadeloupe and Martinique, including

---

Sénéchaussée, which exercised original civil and criminal jurisdiction and was presided over by the *Sénéchal*, with an appeal to the *Conseil supérieur*.

9   *Du Boulay v Du Boulay* (Windward Islands Court of Appeals) reported with Privy Council decision in [1869] 2 AC 430, 434 (Porter Atthill J). See also Liverpool (n8) 385, citing Colonial Office Doc 318/79 (also includes 'Roman law' in the list of sources).

10   *Du Boulay* ibid, 438 (Woodcock J).

11   See now Saint Lucia Revised Ordinances 1957, Appendix II ('Ancient French Law/*Ancien Droit Français*') No 1; see also W Renton, 'French Law within the British Empire' (1909) 10 Journal of the Society of Comparative Legislation (New Series) 93, 103–104 & 117–118.

12   See, for example, JEC Brierley and RA Macdonald (eds), *Quebec Civil Law: An Introduction to Quebec Private Law* (Emond-Montgomery 1993) 7–11.

13   Although Montreal did not fall into British hands until 1760, the key event was Britain's military success on the Plains of Abraham outside Quebec City in the fall of 1759.

Saint Lucia, to France.[14] In the result, Saint Lucia did not come under British control until it was recaptured in 1803. This control was ultimately confirmed by the Treaty of Paris 1814.[15]

What was the immediate effect of this change in sovereignty on the legal system of both countries? Did the various articles of capitulation, treaties, proclamations, instructions and so on reaffirm, supplement or vary the general presumption of continuity of law in colonies of conquest, and if so, to what extent? The response to this question is unclear for both countries, but it is more unclear for Quebec (as the conquered New France was renamed) than for Saint Lucia. As for Quebec, both the Articles of Capitulation and the 1763 Treaty were silent about the question, but the Royal Proclamation of 1763, issued by George III on the advice of the Privy Council to provide for the governance of the ceded colonies, called for the immediate application of English law and the eventual creation of English courts.[16] However, the military governor of Quebec prevaricated in this, which led to his recall in 1766. His position favouring the continuity of the civil law was eventually reflected in the Quebec Act of 1774, which provided for the ongoing application of civil law 'in all Matters of Controversy, relative to Property and Civil Rights'.[17]

Saint Lucia, for its part, was retained by France in 1763 and thus did not fall within the scope of the Royal Proclamation calling for application of English law.[18]

---

14   This choice met with strong criticism from a 'vociferous section' of the British public, who regarded the sugar islands as 'far more valuable than the frozen wastes of Canada': 'Treaty of Paris, 1763', *Encyclopaedia Britannica*, available at <www.britannica.com/EBchecked/topic/443764/Treaty-of-Paris> accessed 7 June 2013. A Burns, *History of the British West Indies* (Allen and Unwin 1954) 489.

15   The terms of the 1814 treaty were relatively generous to France (to support the restored Bourbon monarchy following the defeat of Napoleon), returning to France most of its overseas colonies taken in the war. However, Britain retained Saint Lucia and Tobago in the Caribbean and the Ile-de-France (now Mauritius) 'and its dependencies including the Seychelles' in the Indian Ocean: 'Treaties of Paris, 1814–15', *Encyclopaedia Britannica*, available at www.britannica.com/EBchecked/topic/443733/Treaties-of-Paris accessed 7 June 2013.

16   That is, it provided for the immediate 'Enjoyment of the Benefit of the Laws of Our Realm of England' and the eventual creation of 'Courts of Judicature and public Justice within Our said Colonies for hearing and determining all Causes, as well Criminal as Civil, according to Law and Equity, and as near as may be agreeable to the Laws of England': Royal Proclamation, Revised Statutes of Canada [RSC] 1985, Appendix II, No 1, art 4. The Proclamation is best known in Canada today for the protection it affords to aboriginal rights.

17   Quebec Act 1774 (UK) (14 Geo 3 c 83) s8. A main reason for this was to ensure the loyalty, or at least the neutrality, of the French inhabitants during the impending American Revolution.

18   The Proclamation of 1763 applied to all of the colonies ceded to or retained by Britain in the New World, which were organized into four governmental units: Quebec,

A first reassurance about the continuity of existing law was given by the military authorities in a Proclamation issued (in French) shortly after conquest, on 23 June 1803. It stipulated:

> Although the said Island was taken by storm and without a surrender or stipulation of any sort, nevertheless, to reassure the inhabitants and property owners about their present status pending a declaration of His Majesty, their Excellencies guarantee them full and complete enjoyment of all their property, under the laws existing in the Colony in the period immediately preceding the last cession.

All duly constituted authorities are charged to conform to this proclamation.[19]

The issuance of this Proclamation marks the generally accepted cut-off date for the continuity of French law.[20] The Treaty of Paris 1814 confirming British sovereignty over Saint Lucia was subsequently ratified under the express condition that French law continue in force on the island.[21] Concerns about continuity nevertheless remained, and less than a month after ratification the *Conseil supérieur* petitioned the Prince Regent (in French) that '[t]he sudden change of these laws would therefore be a source of trouble in the colony and confusion in all transactions. Their conservation is for us a measure that is as fair as it is beneficent; we therefore dare to beg it of your Royal Highness'.[22] In response the Governor of Saint Lucia issued an assurance in 1817 (also in French) that '[t]he laws, customs and

---

East and West Florida, and Grenada (comprising the Caribbean Islands of Grenada, the Grenadines, Dominica, Saint Vincent, and Tobago).

19   Entitled 'Proclamation of their Excellencies General Grinfield and Squadron Chief Samuel Hood, Commander of the Land and Sea Forces of His British Majesty, who accord to the Inhabitants of the Island of Saint Lucia the same Advantages as before the last Cession': reproduced (in French) in Saint Lucia Revised Ordinances 1957, Appendix II, No 4 [author's translation].

20   For example, Du Boulay (n9). However, its reference to 'the period immediately preceding the last cession [*l'époque immédiatement antérieure à la dernière cession*]' in fact pushes the cut-off date back to 1789 (thus protecting the law and legal system as it existed on the island prior to the French Revolution): NJO Liverpool, *The Influence of the Civil Code of Quebec on the Civil Code of St. Lucia* (unpublished MS on deposit at McGill, 1968) 10. But see W Renton (n11) 103–104.

21   Liverpool (n8) 378, citing *Du Boulay* (n9) 437–438. However, it is difficult to identify a relevant article of the Treaty, and none has been reproduced in the historical appendix to the Saint Lucia Revised Ordinances (n11) On the other hand, no treaty provision rebuts the presumption of continuity.

22   Anthony (n3) 30, quoting *David Graham & Co Ltd* v *Frank* (1921) Saint Lucia Gaz (De Freitas CJ) [author's translation].

regulations in force in the Colony at the time of publication of the present order will continue to be followed and enforced ...'.[23]

In sum, both colonies managed to retain their French civil law legal heritage during the transitional period following British conquest but, somewhat paradoxically in light of their present position, this heritage was more clearly and explicitly protected in Saint Lucia than in Quebec.

Post-conquest

Both Quebec and Saint Lucia faced ongoing post-conquest pressures to assimilate, which both resisted with varying degrees of success. Some Anglicization of substantive law was inevitable, of course, but procedural changes were as important as substantive changes at this time, with Anglicization of the administration of justice having pride of place in colonial policy. This affected court structure and procedure, judicial appointments, professional qualifications and language of proceedings.

Court structure and procedure

Anglicization of the court structure occurred almost immediately following conquest in Quebec, pursuant to instructions set out in the Royal Proclamation of 1763,[24] whereas in Saint Lucia the inherited French court structure, notably the *Conseil supérieur*, remained in place until 1831.[25] The Colonial Office championed this change in Saint Lucia and elsewhere, presumably with the understandable administrative goal of having some measure of uniformity in what had become an eclectic British Empire in the wake of the Napoleonic Wars.[26] The specific catalyst for change in Saint Lucia was the 1823 Colonial Office appointment of a Commission to enquire into the administration of criminal and civil justice in the West Indian and South American colonies. The Commission reported on Saint Lucia in 1830[27] and an Imperial Order-in-Council enacting a 'Charter of Justice' was adopted shortly thereafter; it set out 'widespread reforms ... to the legal infrastructure [and] the administration of justice' as well as to criminal law and procedure and certain aspects of the civil law in Saint Lucia and the other

---

23   As quoted in Liverpool (n8) 378 [author's translation]. The uncontested nature of the reference to 'the time of publication of the present order' suggests that few if any changes had then been made to the legal system by the British since conquest.

24   Above (n18).

25   In the interim period, the *Conseil supérieur* in both colonies was stripped of its legislative powers and its jurisdiction limited to judicial functions only.

26   As well as to simplify what Dupont (n6) 158 describes as 'a crazy quilt pattern of [court] jurisdictions' in all colonies, settled and conquered alike.

27   *Third Report of the Commissioners of Enquiry into the Administration of Criminal and Civil Justice in the West Indies and South American Colonies, Saint Lucia* (Colonial Office Doc 318/79, 1830).

Caribbean colonies.[28] In the result, the inherited courts were abolished by Imperial Order-in-Council in 1831 and replaced by a structure patterned on the English model, consisting of a Royal Court 'presided over by a Chief Justice and two Puisne Judges for the trial of civil causes, and by these three judges and three assessors for criminal trials',[29] with an appeal to the newly created Judicial Committee of the Privy Council.

Saint Lucia's court structure was also affected by a Colonial Office move towards regionalization. A regional structure was particularly favoured for the smaller islands in the Caribbean, and in 1838 the Colonial Office set up loose confederations of Leeward and Windward island colonies.[30] Saint Lucia was part of the Windward Island confederation administered by the Governor of Barbados (later the Governor of Grenada) and Lieutenant-Governors (renamed Administrators in 1856) of the individual colonies. The only common institution for the Windward Islands was a court of appeal (Court of Appeals for the Windward Islands) set up in 1859 and consisting of the Chief Justices of the various islands. Saint Lucia was the only civil law jurisdiction amongst the island colonies, and the court's judges 'treated the French law with scant courtesy'.[31] Saint Lucia has been part of a regional court structures since then,[32] and this has been identified as a principal reason for the weakening of the civil law tradition in Saint Lucia.[33]

Judicial appointments

Anglicization of the court structure and procedure in Saint Lucia brought with it Anglicization of the judiciary. To be sure, the Colonial Office appears to have made some effort to appoint justices familiar with the civil law both prior to Anglicization and after. The best known judicial appointment to the *Conseil supérieur* was a lawyer from the Channel Islands, Sir John Jeremie, who served as the *Conseil*'s President from 1825 until its abolition and replacement by the

---

28   See Anthony (n3) 35 and 56–58.

29   Liverpool (n8) 384, n34.

30   KW Patchett, 'The Legal Systems in the West Indies' in *Law in the West Indies: Some Recent Trends*, Commonwealth Law Series No 6 (British Institute of International and Comparative Law 1966) 73–76.

31   A Lewis, 'Official Opening of Conference' in RA Landry and E Caparros (eds), *Essays on the Civil Codes of Québec and St. Lucia* (University of Ottawa Press 1984).

32   The new court's jurisdiction included the larger colonies of Barbados, British Guyana and Trinidad and Tobago as well as the smaller colonies of the Leeward and Windward islands. However, the former court retained a limited appeal jurisdiction over interlocutory matters for the smaller colonies: Dupont (supra n 6) 159.

33   See, for example, KD Anthony, *The Mixed Legal System of Saint Lucia: Its Establishment and Decline*, PhD Thesis (University of Birmingham, 1988) 555f; and D White, 'Some Problems of a Hybrid Legal System: A Case Study of St. Lucia' (1981) 30 International and Comparative Law Quarterley 862, 863.

Royal Court in 1831;[34] and a well-known post-Anglicization appointment to the Royal Court was a lawyer from Quebec, James Armstrong, who served as Chief Justice from 1871 to 1881 and was principal author of Saint Lucia's Civil Code. Other appointments were less successful, and the composition of the Royal Court in the 1830s was described in somewhat unflattering terms: while one of the Puisne Judges was 'from his long experience, both as a lawyer and as *Procureur du Roi*, … the best selection that could have been made', the Chief Justice was less suitable – 'His qualifications for the Bar or the Bench might have ensured success in any *English* colony; but he was totally destitute of all knowledge of the French laws or language': as for the third member, he was 'a person utterly ignorant of the French language, without the slightest professional knowledge of the laws of the country, or indeed of any country …'.[35]

Professional qualifications
Anglicization of the court structure and the judiciary implied Anglicization of the legal profession for, as Anthony noted, 'it made little sense to cater for the admission of barristers, advocates, attorneys and solicitors who were not familiar with Common Law procedure and practice'.[36] Policies adopted throughout the Caribbean thus favoured British training for members of the legal profession, even in Saint Lucia where they provided for admission of those 'called to the bar in England or Ireland' as well as those who had 'kept six terms at any Inn or Court in England' or 'been admitted to practice at the bar of any British colony',[37] whilst nevertheless leaving the door open to admission of those with some measure of civil law training. This included not just those admitted to practise in British civil law colonies (such as Quebec) but also those who had been 'admitted as an Advocate in the United Kingdom and Ireland', had 'taken a degree in Civil Law at either of the Universities of Cambridge, Oxford, or Dublin' or had 'served as clerk to a [Saint Lucia] Procurer and such proof be held equivalent to any of the above qualifications'. In the result, many practitioners qualified locally during this period, serving a four-year period under articles and passing an examination based on the laws of Saint Lucia.

Language
Finally, Anglicization of the judiciary in Saint Lucia led inevitably to the adoption of English as the language of the courts, as it was felt that justice could hardly

---

34   Jeremie's suggestion to recruit judges from Martinique was not taken up (Liverpool (n8) 387), presumably because the Colonial Office did not want to appoint judges from outside the Empire.

35   HH Breen, *St. Lucia, Historical, Statistical and Descriptive* (Longman, Brown, Green and Longmans 1844; reprinted Frank Cass and Co Ltd 1970) 333–334 [emphasis in original].

36   Anthony (n3) 60.

37   ibid, 61.

be expected from judges who were not conversant in the language of pleadings.[38] Pressure from the Colonial Office to introduce English began in earnest in 1832 and, in spite of considerable opposition in Saint Lucia, it was adopted as the language of the courts as of 1 January 1842.[39] Legislation continued to be bilingual for some time, but 'the French version inevitably got more inaccurate'.[40] Moreover, the adoption of English as the official language of the courts led to its more frequent use in other areas, a not unintended result. In pressing for the change to English, the Secretary of State for the Colonies had written: 'I suppose it is now too late to retreat; in fact it never could be made at all, if we were to wait till English had become the vernacular tongue. One of the main objects of the measure is to promote that change …'.[41]

In the face of all of this movement towards the common law, it is surprising that the civil law tradition survived in Saint Lucia, as it did in Quebec, in the core private law area of 'Property and Civil Rights'.[42] A main reason it did so is the Quebec connection.

Convergence

The key event was the 1879 adoption of a Civil Code for Saint Lucia modelled on the 1866 Civil Code of Lower Canada[43] (as Quebec was referred to at that time), but the scene had been set in the years prior to that event.

----

38   Liverpool (n8) 393, citing Colonial Office Doc 243/46.

39   See generally Anthony (n3) 62–65. English had been introduced as the language of the administration in 1818, over the objection that this would lead ultimately to a change in the laws, which were in French, and was thus contrary to the guarantee of their continued use contained in the Treaty of Paris, 1814: Liverpool (n8) 384.

40   Liverpool ibid, 396. He indicates, without further precision, that printing in both languages continued 'for a long time afterwards'.

41   As quoted in Liverpool ibid, 395. Anthony (n3) 31, emphasizes the gradualism of the Colonial Office approach, under which English law was to be introduced only after the groundwork had been laid for its acceptance, with Anglicization of the population being an important factor.

42   To use the term consecrated in the Quebec Act 1774 (n19) and echoed in the provincial jurisdiction section (s92) of the British North America Act 1867 (UK) (30 & 31 Vict, c 3) [renamed Constitution Act 1867 by the Canada Act 1982 (UK) 1982, c 11].

43   The Saint Lucia Code is sometimes said to be based on the Napoleonic Code. However, the Napoleonic Code never applied in Saint Lucia, as the island came under British control in 1803, a year prior to the adoption of the Napoleonic Code. The Civil Code of Lower Canada was a codification of French customary law although it adopted the style of the Napoleonic Code: Brierley and Macdonald (supra n12) 25, 35; see also HP Glenn, 'Napoleon's Civil Code *Outre-Mer*: A Quebec perspective' in D Fairgrieve (ed), *The Influence of the French Civil Code on the Common Law and Beyond* (British Institute of International and Comparative Law 2007).

Pre-codification

The need for some sort of compilation of the 'Ancient French Law' in force in Saint Lucia had been felt for some time. Problems arising from the diversity of civil law sources and the difficulty of understanding the language in which they were written were compounded in Saint Lucia by the destruction of those very sources in a fire in 1796, in which the principal city, Castries, was razed to the ground and all official and private documents and records destroyed.[44] Lack of cooperation of Saint Lucia's French legal community added to the problem: 'Not only were the laws unobtainable, but it would seem that early attempts by the British to obtain them were not encouraged by the French law officers who saw in the absence of a written set of laws, a greater dependence by the British on the learning of those who professed to know what those laws were.'[45] Consolidation or codification of the laws of Saint Lucia was thus a priority, and a number of attempts were made, particularly following Anglicization of the court structure.

An initial suggestion was made in the 1830s by the first Chief Justice of the Royal Court, who proposed to undertake the task of consolidating and amending the laws of the colony himself. Breen, writing in 1844, described this proposal as

> ... a scheme which, strange to say, received the sanction and encouragement of the Governor and Council. That ... the codification of the entire body of the laws should have been resolved upon, will appear no less credible, than that such an undertaking should have been entrusted to one who was ignorant even of the 'titles' of those laws, and, if pointed out to him, incapable of comprehending them in the only language in which they were written. ... Happily the prompt interposition of Viscount Goderich spared the Colony the exhibition of a piece of Utopian Legislation unparalleled in colonial history.[46]

A more serious attempt at codification was made in the 1840s, largely at the instigation of the then Governor of Barbados and the Windward Islands, Sir Robert Torrens, who underlined the difficulties facing the administration of justice in the colony in his address to the Legislative Council of Saint Lucia in 1845:

> The Head of the Local Government, the Judge on the Bench, the Law Officer, the Barrister, the Special Magistrate and Justice of the Peace are each unprovided with an entire manual of the laws, which, in their various spheres, they are to administer and enforce, and which it is their duty to know: and her Majesty's

---

44   FJ Carasco in JH Pilgrim (ed), *Historical Review of the Castries Municipality from 1785 to 1967* (Castries City Council 1967) 25.

45   Liverpool (n8) 385.

46   Breen (n35) 334–336.

subjects in St. Lucia have no means of general acquaintance with the laws under which they live save by hearsay, custom and such uncertain means.[47]

A committee of local legal notables was thus struck shortly thereafter to collect, translate, revise and print the laws of the island. To assist it, Governor Torrens enquired about codification efforts in Lower Canada and was advised by the Canadian Governor, Cathcart, that an English edition of the Code was being printed. Cathcart was mistaken about this, however, as the work of codification did not begin in Quebec until 1857.[48] The committee also seemed to place considerable reliance on receiving a translation of the *Coutume de Paris* from Canada, which did not arrive.[49] In the end, the then Governor, Darling, '... took the matter into my own hands and ... completed a collection of all the St. Lucia laws, ordinances, Orders-in-Council, Orders of Government and proclamations since the island came under British rule', together with a selection of laws from the *Code de la Martinique* 'to be printed in French leaving it to the Government interpreter of the court to translate it as and when necessary', which collection the Colonial Office somewhat reluctantly approved in 1851.[50]

Another local attempt at codification also failed,[51] but these various attempts set the stage for the adoption in 1879 of the Saint Lucia Civil Code based on the Civil Code of Lower Canada adopted in 1866.

---

47   Liverpool (n8) 396–397, quoting Colonial Office Doc 321/22.

48   Cathcart might have been referring to the 1845 publication of the Revised Acts and Ordinances of Lower Canada, a consolidation of the public acts of the colony prior to its union with Upper Canada in 1841. (Upper and Lower Canada were created by the Constitutional Act 1791 (UK) (31 Geo 3, c 31) and correspond to the present-day provinces of Ontario and Quebec.)

49   Liverpool (n8) 398. The committee could not have realized that a publication which was sent to them – *Fundamental Principles of the Laws of Canada* (Duvernay 1832–1833) – contained an English translation of the *Coutume*. Or alternatively they were expecting to receive a publication entitled *An Abstract of Those Parts of the Custom ... of Paris Which Were Received and Practised in the Province of Quebec in the Time of the French Government* (Eyre and Strahan 1772–1773; Quebec 1775) which, despite its English title, was in French.

50   Liverpool ibid, 399, quoting Colonial Office Doc 253/107. Governor Darling's task was not a simple one. The Chief Justice of the near-by island of Dominica described his own similar efforts at compilation as follows: 'It was not a trifling task I had to perform. The original Acts in the Secretary's Office were fast travelling to eternal oblivion. The climate and vermin had bereft the greater part of their seals; many of their titles were effaced, and others so mutilated as to be nearly illegible': quoted in OR Marshall, 'Legal Education for the West Indies' in *Law in the West Indies Some Recent Trends*, Commonwealth Law Series No 6 (British Institute of International and Comparative Law 1966) 143.

51   Liverpool (n8) 400.

Codification

Saint Lucia's adoption of a code modelled on that of Lower Canada came about largely through the efforts of two men, William Des Voeux, a member of the colonial civil service with some legal training who had been appointed Administrator of Saint Lucia in 1869, and James Armstrong, a practicing Quebec lawyer of considerable experience who had been named Chief Justice of Saint Lucia in 1872.

When Des Voeux and Armstrong arrived in Saint Lucia, the need for codification was more pressing than ever. Both were aware of this, and both favoured the adoption of a code based on the recently adopted Civil Code of Lower Canada. While their relative age, education and experience would suggest that Armstrong was the principal author,[52] the two men undertook the project together and worked at it assiduously from 1872 to 1876. And while Armstrong might have played the leading role in drafting the Code, it was Des Voeux who succeeded in getting it enacted.[53] As Liverpool rightly observed, 'their combined efforts … still stands as a monument to the industry and conscientiousness of civil servants of their day'.[54]

In the end, the Saint Lucia Civil Code appeared, in English only,[55] as a schedule to the Civil Code Ordinance 1876,[56] which provided for the appointment of Commissioners to examine and report on the draft Code and for its coming into force, with such changes as the Legislative Council had adopted in the interim, 'when it shall have been approved by Her Majesty'. This Ordinance was proclaimed

---

52   Writing in 1934, the Acting Chief Justice of Saint Lucia at the time of codification described the Code as 'principally the work' of Armstrong, and went on to say that whenever the Code differed from its Canadian model, 'the change is generally due to Judge Armstrong's local judicial experience and the needs of the colony as he understood them.' JEM Salmon, *Ex parte Monsignor William Floissac, D.D.* (1934) Saint Lucia Gaz 184, as quoted in Liverpool (n8) 402, n88.

53   See Anthony (n3) 54.

54   Liverpool (n8) 401. In 1872, the Legislative Council appointed at three-man committee to consult with the Chief Justice on codification, but their efforts 'were not productive': ibid, n84.

55   Des Voeux was very critical in his memoirs of the English version of the Civil Code of Lower Canada, writing that 'all but the commercial chapters … must have been prepared by those to whom English was not a familiar language': *My Colonial Service* (John Murray 1903) vol 2, 210. But see Brierley and Macdonald (n12) 29: 'Perhaps the most singular success of the Canadian Code was its generally satisfactory rendering of the Civil law tradition into English, in which respect it marked a noticeable improvement over previous statutory style in this sector'; and, more generally, JEC Brierley, 'Quebec's Civil Law Codification: Viewed and reviewed' (1968) 14 McGill Law Journal 521. Des Voeux concluded that he did not wish to print both versions, not only for reasons of economy but because this 'would tend to perpetuate the French language in the island, which was for many reasons undesirable'.

56   Ordinance No 16 of 1876.

in force on 8 October 1877; the Commissioners reported on 6 February 1878; the Code (with minor Colonial Office changes) was adopted by the Legislative Council on 20 December 1878; and it was assented to by Her Majesty and thus became law on 20 October 1879.[57] Adoption of the accompanying Code of Civil Procedure, also based on its Quebec counterpart, followed shortly thereafter.

Both Quebec and Saint Lucia, therefore, were governed by substantially similar Codes which had been adopted in each jurisdiction for essentially the same reason, to provide 'a technical reordering of a complex body of norms ... to make this private law more accessible in both its language and substance to legal professionals'.[58] The similarity of the two Codes meant that Saint Lucia had a body of jurisprudence to which it could look when applying its Code. The Court House library included Quebec court reports and works by French and Canadian commentators; as well, the English court reports included decisions of the Privy Council from Quebec, and the fact that they were reported in the English language enhanced their utility.

The adoption of a Civil Code based on Quebec's Code was an important moment of convergence, even overlap, of the legal regimes of the two jurisdictions, and did much to curb the erosion of the civil law in Saint Lucia. However, changes in both jurisdictions since the adoptions of the Codes means that the two civil law regimes are no longer converging, or even developing along parallel paths, but rather are diverging.

Divergence

The divergence of the legal regimes of Saint Lucia and Quebec can be explained by the fact that Saint Lucia has been less vigilant than Quebec in carving out a special place for its distinct civilian heritage. In Saint Lucia, unlike Quebec,[59] the Civil Code never took on the larger role of defining its society. As Kenny Anthony, a leading scholar of Saint Lucia's legal tradition – and its present Prime Minister – put it:

---

57   This way of proceeding deflected criticism from certain provisions relating to marriage, although Des Voeux was recalled to England before he could assent to the Ordinance. See generally Liverpool (n8) 402–407.

58   Brierley and Macdonald (n12) 25. The preamble to the Saint Lucia Civil Code Ordinance, 1876, begins: 'WHEREAS uncertainty, causing serious inconvenience to the public, has for a long time existed with respect to the Law relating to many civil matters, and it is expedient that such uncertainty should be removed; and it is also expedient that the Civil Law should be consolidated and amended; ....'

59   See, for example, S Normand, '*Le Code civil et l'identité*', in *Du Code civil du Québec: Contributions à l'histoire immédiate d'une recodification réussie* (Éditions Thémis, c2005).

In St. Lucia's case, there was never any demonstrated anxiety to ensure protection of its civilian heritage. The tendency has been to accept changes in its substantive law to satisfy the political imperatives of regional cooperation. Special safeguards to protect the island's mixed legal identity do not exist and have never been sought.[60]

One reason for this is that the Code was an 'elitist affair', largely divorced from a black population with no political rights.[61] Another might be that for much of its history Saint Lucia was under the control of the Colonial Office, for whom protection of the colony's legal specificity was hardly a priority.[62] In the result, Saint Lucia's civil law heritage faced post-codification pressures similar to those it had faced pre-codification, and these eventually led to a recodification introducing large areas of common law into the Code. These pressures had as their source the Colonial Office's penchant for a regional form of government in the British Caribbean.

Post-codification

The movement towards regional government of the smaller islands, begun tentatively in the pre-codification period, continued in the post-codification period, affecting not only court structure, professional qualifications and other procedural matters, as in the earlier period, but ultimately the substance of the Civil Code itself.

Court structure

At the intermediate appeal level, Saint Lucia remained part of the Windward Island Court of Appeals until this court was replaced first by a West Indian Court of Appeal (composed, like its predecessor, of the Chief Justices of all the islands) in 1920[63] and then by a combined Windward Islands and Leeward Islands Court of Appeal in 1940. Perhaps more significantly, regionalization also occurred at the trial level in this same period, and Saint Lucia became without its own court when the Royal Court of Saint Lucia was abolished in 1940 and replaced by a tribunal

---

60   Anthony (n33) 574. See also KD Anthony, 'The Viability of the Civilist Tradition in St. Lucia: A Tentative Appraisal' in Landry and Caparros (n31) 58–59.

61   Anthony (n3) 54.

62   The colony achieved limited representative government in 1924 (extended in 1936), and full independence in 1979.

63   The new court's jurisdiction included Barbados, British Guyana, Trinidad and Tobago as well as the smaller colonies of the Leeward and Windward islands. However, the former court retained a limited appeal jurisdiction over interlocutory matters for the smaller colonies: Dupont (n6) 159.

shared with the other smaller, common law, islands (the Windward Islands and Leeward Islands Supreme Court).[64]

Professional qualifications
Regionalization of the court structure brought with it further movement towards similarity of the requirements for qualification for the practice of law. As has been seen, Saint Lucia, like the other Caribbean jurisdictions, has long admitted practitioners with UK qualifications who enjoy considerable ease of movement within the region.[65] However, the earlier practice of also admitting locally trained barristers ended in 1946 when the Legal Practitioners Ordinance[66] was amended to require that even such locally trained barristers pass the examinations of the Law Society of England rather than local examinations based on Saint Lucia law. This dealt an 'overt blow' to the civil law, as the previous system had

> produced a cadre of lawyers who knew their law well, understood the French–Canadian system on which the law was based, and came to the practice of the profession with a practical knowledge acquired through constant attendance on their masters. They upheld the supremacy of the Code and resisted any attempt by English trained judges to apply English law in the decision of cases.[67]

Resources
The availability of French civil law legal material was seriously affected by a fire in 1948, in which much of Castries, including the Court House and its library collection, was again destroyed. The civil law materials in the collection were not replaced, thereby compounding the losses similarly caused in 1796. This was 'another blow to our French legal system', as predominantly British-trained 'Bench and Bar experienced difficulty in ascertaining with certainty how the law had developed'.[68]

The Colonial Office's drive towards regionalization accelerated after the Second World War, not so much for Imperial efficiency reasons as in the past, but rather in anticipation of decolonization. The high point of this drive was the creation of the West Indies Federation in 1956, and part of the preparation for it to revise Saint Lucia's Civil Code so as to 'assimilate the Code to the Law of England where they differ, in the light of the present needs of the Colony …'.[69]

---

64   Patchett, 'Legal Systems' (n30) 73. Further court restructuring reflecting broader regional government changes followed recodification.
65   See NJO Liverpool and KW Patchett, 'The Legal Profession in the West Indies' in *Law in the West Indies* (n30) 131.
66   Now Saint Lucia Revised Ordinances 1957, c 116.
67   Lewis (n31) 13.
68   ibid.
69   Laws of Saint Lucia (Reform and Revision) Ordinance, No 21 of 1954, s4 (3).

Recodification

The divergence between the civil law regimes of Saint Lucia and Quebec increased substantially as a result of reforms made to their codes in 1956 (Saint Lucia) and 1994 (Quebec). While the Quebec reforms were directed at reinforcing the civil law tradition,[70] those in Saint Lucia represented a direct threat to its continuation. This is clear from the way the need for reform was presented to the Legislative Council:

> It has long been recognised that it is necessary to bring up to date the whole body of the Civil law and align it with current thought and practice in the West Indies. In this connection *the value of the French civil law as the basic law of the colony requires reassessing* and it is probable that a larger infusion of English law is necessary if the law of St. Lucia is to be put on a more satisfactory footing. This is of particular importance having regard to the possibility of West Indian Federation.[71]

The task of reform was given to Allen Montgomery Lewis (later Sir Allen), a leading Saint Lucian lawyer trained in both civil and common law,[72] who acted in consultation with a committee consisting of the Crown Attorney and two barristers appointed by the Governor. Reform of the Code began in 1954; the revised Code was adopted in 1956;[73] and it came into force on 30 June 1957.

The main technique of reform was to retain the existing provisions of the Code but to engraft upon them, by open reception clauses, large areas of the common law – particularly in the substantive areas of matrimonial relations, tutorship, trusts, contracts and torts, contract and agency as well as in the procedural area of evidence.[74] The style of reception varies from article to article, with a few referring

---

70   Quebec's reform (which, coincidentally, began in 1955 – almost the same time as Saint Lucia's) restated rather than reformed the law, removing the overarching references to French law and specific references to English law included in the 1866 Code or added subsequently. The new Code has been described as 'free-standing and autonomous; it exists on its own, exclusively, without apparent reference to its own bijural antecedents or its own historical or socio-political context. It is the Code of a new nation-state'. JEC Brierley, 'The Renewal of Quebec's Distinct Legal Culture: The New *Civil Code of Quebec*' (1992) 42 University of Toronto Law Journal 484, 498–499.

71   Saint Lucia, Legislative Council Meeting [undated], as quoted in Anthony (n31) 58 [emphasis added]. A general review of Saint Lucian laws was timely, as there had been no review since the 1916 consolidation: Lewis (n31) 12–13.

72   Lewis had been called to the Saint Lucia Bar in 1931 (that is, prior to the 1946 examination changes) and then qualified as an English barrister after the Second World War.

73   Civil Code (Amendment) Ordinance, Saint Lucia Ordinance No 34 of 1956.

74   Arts 145(2), 160A, 216, 916A, 917A, 1608A and 1137, respectively, of the revised Code (reproduced in VF Floissac, 'The Interpretation of the Civil Code of Saint Lucia' (1983) 14 *Revue Générale de Droit* 409, 425f, and KD Anthony, 'The Courts and

simply to 'the law of England' in a given domain – as in article 145(2), which provides that where parties 'have mutually agreed to live separate and apart from each other, such agreement has the same effect as it has by the law of England' – and most referring more broadly to the law of England 'for the time being' – as in article 1608A, which provides that 'the law of England for the time being relating to the contract of agency shall extend to and apply in the Colony' and that the relevant articles of the Code 'shall as far as practicable be construed accordingly'. And one – article 917A, dealing with the key areas of contractual and extra-contractual obligations – is more sweeping still, in that it couples a broad 'for the time being' incorporation of English law with a categorical rejection of recourse to civil law sources to interpret that law:

> (1) Subject to the provisions of this Article,[75] ... the law of England for the time being relating to contracts, quasi-contracts and torts shall *mutatis mutandis* extend to this Colony, and provisions of [the relevant articles of the Code][76] shall as far as practicable be construed accordingly; and the said Articles shall cease to be construed in accordance with the law of Lower Canada or the 'Coutume de Paris'.

On the other hand, a number of these articles qualify the scope of reception of English law by what might be called 'paramountcy' clauses, making reception '[s]ubject to the provisions of this Code or any other statute' (or some such similar phrase). And here again, article 917A is most explicit about this:

> (3) Where a conflict exists between the law of England and the express provisions of this Code or of any other statute, the provisions of the Code or of such statute shall prevail.

---

the Interpretation of a Civil Code in a Mixed Legal System: Saint Lucia Revisited' (1995) 5 Caribbean Law Review 144, 195f. Other than introducing the trust, property law went largely untouched. As Floissac observed (429): 'It would be lamentable if the complicated English law of real property were ever substituted for the simple system which we inherited from France through Quebec. The fundamental right called ownership and the owner's liberty to burden his radical title with emphyteuses, leases, servitudes, usufructs, hypothecs and other encumbrances are concepts intelligible to the simplest layman.'

75   The several provisos (1) exclude the English doctrine of 'consideration' in favour of the civilian notion of 'cause'; (2) preserve the civil law's more generous approach to third party rights under a contract; and (3) protect provisions of the 1879 Code relating to 'proof of obligations' as well as those relating to 'specific' (that is, special or nominative) contracts.

76   The mentioned articles include the basic article governing fault-based responsibility (art 985) and two specific articles varying the burden of proof for things under a person's care (arts 986 and 987). For a discussion of the interpretation of these articles, see Anthony (n74) 207–213.

This recodification technique results in an intense intermingling of the common and civil law, and the Saint Lucian legal system is sometimes described as 'hybrid' for this reason.[77] It raises interesting questions of interpretation, which are discussed below.

Post-recodification

What pressures does Saint Lucia's civil law tradition now face as a result of this recodification, and more generally? The question of interpretation of the Code in the post-recodification era is an obvious issue, but others are similar to those faced in earlier eras: resources, professional qualifications and court structure.

Interpretation

All mixed jurisdictions in the British Commonwealth face similar general concerns about the interpretation of the civil law by courts which are fundamentally common law in structure and approach.[78] One such concern is that courts ignore the difference between a code and a simple statute, and thus fail to interpret the Code as an organic whole. The Privy Council has been strongly criticized in this regard.[79] Another is that courts follow common law rather than civil law methodology by preferring precedent over doctrine when deciding cases. But it is hard to see how it could be otherwise, at least in a country like Saint Lucia where doctrinal sources are few. In any event, *stare decisis* is no longer applied as rigorously as previously, even in common law jurisdictions, and looking to precedent simply reflects a more general notion of fairness that 'like cases should be decided alike'.[80] And yet another is that courts apply common law precedents to interpret civil law provisions which they regard as similar to the common law.[81]

But what of specific Saint Lucian concerns about the interpretation of its revised Code? One is whether the phrase 'the laws of England for the time being' has an 'ambulatory' effect, incorporating English statute law as it stands at the date of adjudication rather than simply as it stood at the date of adoption of the revised Code. Judicial opinions seem to be divided on this issue. While a 1974 trial decision

77   For example, White (n33); A Huxley, 'How Hybrid is Saint Lucian Law?' in Landry and Caparros (n31).

78   See generally JL Friesen, 'When Common Law Courts Interpret Civil Codes' (1996–1997) 15 Wisconsin International Law Journal 1.

79   See generally A Bisson, 'A Comparison between Statutory Law and a Civil Code' in Landry and Caparros (n31). For Saint Lucia see Floissac (n74) 410 and 418f and Anthony (n74) 176f.

80   On the Caribbean generally see AD Burgess, 'Judicial Precedent in the West Indies' (1978) 7 Anglo-American Law Review 113; on Saint Lucia see Anthony (n74)166–168 and 180f.

81   Anthony, ibid, 180f.

interpreted the phrase as ambulatory,[82] a 2009 decision of the Privy Council held the contrary,[83] citing a 2007 decision of the Eastern Caribbean Court of Appeal in support. However, the Court of Appeal in that case had in fact specifically declined to decide which of the two opposing views was correct, holding that it was unnecessary to do so as the matter was more clearly decided by applying a 'paramountcy' clause (article 917A(3) in this instance).[84] The court described the argument based on paramountcy as 'a formidable argument' as 'there is here a clear conflict between the present law of England and article 609 of the Code. The 1982 Act made the law of England directly the opposite of what it had been before and, hence, the opposite of article 609 of the Code'.[85]

Another interpretation concern is thus the effect of the various paramountcy clauses in the Saint Lucia Code. Such clauses make the received English law 'subject' to the provisions of the Code and other statute law, and their effect is conveyed most explicitly in article 917A(3) of the Code which provides that where 'a conflict' exists between English and Saint Lucia law, the latter 'shall prevail'. As we have seen, the Court of Appeal of Eastern Caribbean States decided in 2007 that such paramountcy clauses preclude an ambulatory effect in provisions incorporating English law 'for the time being'. The same court also suggested in a 1992 case, *Northrock Ltd v Jardine*,[86] that paramountcy clauses play an even broader role in protecting Saint Lucia's civil law heritage. *Northrock* involved an action by property owners against the operators of a near-by quarry for compensation for structural damage to their houses. The issue was identification of the appropriate cause of action, which affected the location of the burden of proof. In the court's view, a common law action would be framed in negligence and the plaintiffs would have to prove fault.[87] However, while a civil law action brought under the general delictual article 985 also requires the plaintiffs to prove fault, an action brought under the more specific delictual article 986 (relating to responsibility for damage caused by things under the defendant's care) reverses the burden of proof and requires the defendant to disprove fault. Floissac CJ, speaking for the court, set out the paramountcy consequences: 'To the extent to which our article 986 is a rule of

---

82   *Cools v Saint Lucia Agriculturists Association Ltd* (1974, unreported) cited in Floissac (n74) 428 and Anthony (n74) 199 (re ambulatory effect of UK Occupiers' Liability Act 1957).

83   *George (Administratrix of the Estate of) v Eagle Air Services Ltd* (2009) UKPC 34, para 3 (re UK Administration of Justice Act 1982).

84   *Mathurin v Augustin (Administer of the Estate of)* HCVAP 2007/041 (2007) paras 9–10 and 16 (also re UK Administration of Justice Act 1982).

85   Para 11.

86   (1992) 44 West Indian Reports 160 (ECS CA).

87   It excluded recourse to the rule in *Rylands v Fletcher* (1868) LR 3 HL 330, citing (at 166) the Privy Council's decision in *Quebec Railway, Light, Heat and Power Co v Vandry* (1920) AC 662 in this regard.

law, it conflicts with the law of England and prevails over the latter by virtue of article 917A(3). To the extent to which our article 986 is a rule of evidence, it excludes contradictory English rules of evidence the importation of which would otherwise have been authorized by our article 1137.'[88] In the end, the court decided the damage was caused by a person and not a thing, which brought it under article 985 and required the plaintiff to prove fault. This meant, the court held, that it was required by the applicable paramountcy clauses 'to interpret ... article 985 by reference to the English law of tort and to prove liability under [it] by reference to the English law of evidence'.[89] In other words, it follows from the court's analysis in *Northrock* that where the civil and common law rules are in conflict, the civil law rule is paramount and applies, and it is only where the two sets of rules are not in conflict that the common law rule applies. Pushing this analysis slightly, one might suggest that since the common law rule applies only because it does not conflict with the civil law rule, it is really the civil law rule that is applied – albeit circuitously – in this case as well. Pushing this argument still further, one might even be tempted to question the utility of canvassing the common law rules at all, since they apply only if they accord with the civil law rules. In short, the various 'paramountcy' clauses could prove to be a Trojan Horse in regard to the 1956 infusion of English law into large areas of the Saint Lucia Civil Code.[90]

A final, overarching, concern is therefore the extent to which courts may have recourse to civil law sources in interpreting the revised Civil Code. The 1956 revisions undoubtedly reinforced the tendency, already strong in the common law-trained Bench and Bar, to have what Anthony has described as 'uninhibited recourse'[91] to English authorities in deciding cases. But to what extent is such recourse required by the terms of revised Code itself? Logic suggests that civil law should continue to be applied in cases dealing with those areas of the law, notably property law, left untouched in the 1954 recodification. And *Northrock* points to the need to refer to civil law sources in interpreting the paramountcy clauses – if not more broadly – in those areas of the Code, such as the law of obligations, most affected by the importation of English law, and to do so notwithstanding the Code's admonition that they 'shall cease to be construed' in accordance with Quebec and French law. And finally, that courts should continue to seek guidance from Quebec

---

88   Art 1137 provides: 'Any question relating to evidence, *which is not covered by any provision of this Code or any other statute*, must be decided by the rules of evidence as established by the law of England' [emphasis added].

89   ibid.

90   Floissac (n74) 428–429 suggests that applying their 'natural and ordinary meaning', art 917A(3) (and presumably the other paramountcy clauses) and the other articles in the Code 'may find themselves uncomfortably juxtaposed', and their juxtaposition presents 'an enigma peculiar to our civil law'.

91   Anthony (n74) 146.

and French civil law sources has been reaffirmed by the Privy Council as recently as 2007:

> Their Lordships consider that anyone attempting to interpret the Civil Code must bear in mind that it is derived, in most cases word for word, from the Quebec Civil Code of 1865 [sic], which in turn was derived from the Code Civil of France. In adopting the St Lucia Civil Code, the legislature must in their Lordships' view have intended that its terms should be construed with due regard to what they had been understood to mean in Quebec and France. The jurisprudence which has been attached to the provisions of the Code by the courts and legal writers of those countries must at the very least have considerable persuasive authority.[92]

Resources

A tendency to rely on common law sources is probably inevitable given the paucity of civil law resources in Saint Lucia, both in the Court House library and in the library of the Eastern Caribbean Supreme Court; and while the library of the Law Faculty of the University of the West Indies contains an encouraging amount of Quebec materials, it is located in Barbados and is thus not readily accessible. However, the English law reports housed in the Saint Lucia libraries include Privy Council decisions, and Saint Lucia jurists continue to cite its Quebec decisions (although they are now somewhat dated, as Canada abolished appeals to the Privy Council in 1948). And past and present decisions of Quebec courts (including the Supreme Court of Canada) are now readily available online.[93] In general, however, usefulness of the old French material as well as of Quebec sources, which are increasingly in French,[94] is diminishing with the loss of fluency of Saint Lucia lawyers in the French language.[95] And recent Quebec decisions, even when available in English, are arguably less useful because of the combined effect of the revision of the two codes.

Local civil law sources are similarly wanting. The number of cases is limited, as Saint Lucia's population of some 180,000 persons is 'only

---

92   *Prospere (nee Madore) v Prospere et al* (2007) UKPC 2 (a matrimonial property case) para 15, quoting *Polinere v Felicien* (2000) UKPC 2. See also *National Insurance Corporation v Winmark Limited* (2009) UKPC 9 (includes references to Quebec's new Code, not just to the 1866 Code).

93   Notably on the Canadian Legal Information Institute's open-access site, available at <http://www.canlii.org/>.

94   Although all judgments of the Supreme Court of Canada are published, side-by-side, in both French and English.

95   Floissac (n74) 417 ('Even if there were such [French] books or judgments, they would be of no value to us without a qualified interpreter. The truth is that even if we purported to write or speak in the French language, we would be better understood in Martinique, Haiti or Mauritius than in France or Quebec.').

averagely litigious'[96] and few can afford sustained litigation.[97] Moreover, few cases are reported: the West Indian Reports date only from 1958, and the economies of publication are such that judgments from small countries such as Saint Lucia must compete for space with those from the larger jurisdictions;[98] judgments prior to 1958 and unreported judgments since then are published in the Saint Lucia Gazette, but the lack of an indexing system limits their accessibility.[99] Codifiers' reports are of marginal usefulness, as the report of the Commissioners appointed in 1877 to review the draft Code is too limited in scope to be useful, and printed copies of the Quebec codifiers' reports have been difficult if not impossible to find in Saint Lucia (although they are now readily available online);[100] moreover, Saint Lucia jurists are conscious of the Privy Council's disapproval of the use of such sources.[101] Finally, local doctrinal writing is sparse, although it is difficult to see how this could be otherwise: the pool of authors is small, as the number of lawyers is limited[102] and civilian academics are rare; and a scholarly journal, the University of the West Indies' *Caribbean Law Review*, has existed only since 1991. But electronic access to many academic journals from around the world, although costly, is now available; a renewed interest in mixed jurisdictions globally has seen publication of articles in a wide variety of journals.

Professional qualifications
The tendency for Saint Lucia lawyers to qualify for practice in England has continued apace, with the rest obtaining 'the certificate awarded by the Council of Legal Education established by the Caribbean Legal Education Agreement', a

---

96   Huxley (n73) 372.

97   Floissac (n74) 417.

98   For example, the Consolidated Index to Vols 1–80 of the West Indies Rep shows only 22 reported cases dealing with the Saint Lucia Civil Code in the 54-year period 1958–2012.

99   Anthony (n74) 194. Floissac (n74) 417 speaks of unreported judgments 'lie[ing] in oblivion in issues of the St. Lucia Gazette hidden in the recesses of the Registry and unknown places', and Patchett locates them in 'government *Gazettes*, Court Judgment Books, Court Registries and perhaps in practitioners' notebooks': KW Patchett, 'Introduction' in *Law in the West Indies* (n30) 60.

100   Notably on the Hathi Trust Digital Library's open-access site <http://catalog.hathitrust.org/Record/010475994?type%5B%5D=all&lookfor%5B%5D=code%20civil%20du%20Bas%20Canada%20&ft=ft>. The extensive background reports commissioned by Quebec's Civil Code Revision Office are similarly available online on McGill University's open-access site http://digital.library.mcgill.ca/ccro/index.php> accessed 22 October 2013.

101   See *Despatie* v *Tremblay* (1921) AC 702 (JCPC), as mentioned in Anthony (n74) 160–161.

102   Moreover, West Indian lawyers do not specialize to the same extent as North American and English lawyers do: Patchett, 'Introduction' (n30) 60.

provision added to the Legal Practitioners Ordinance[103] in 1975 to take account of the establishment of a Law Faculty at the University of the West Indies in 1970. The Law Faculty is a common law institution, and does not have the resources necessary to accommodate the needs of the limited number of Saint Lucia students who attend.[104]

What possibilities are there for Saint Lucians to receive a civil law education? 'Notaries Royal' are still locally trained and examined, but because barristers have the right to act as notaries, very few notaries qualify separately.[105] Scottish advocates and law agents are still admissible to the practice of law, but few if any Saint Lucia lawyers choose this route. The Saint Lucia Legal Practitioners Ordinance also provides for the admission of '[a]ny barrister or advocate of any of the Superior Courts of any British Possession where similar privileges are accorded to barristers of the Supreme Court'.[106] This could serve as a vehicle for the admission of Quebec-trained lawyers but for the fact that the Quebec Bar regulations would probably exclude the recognition of 'similar privileges' to Saint Lucia-trained lawyers,[107] thereby precluding the necessary reciprocity for Saint Lucia recognition. Finally, the Ordinance makes no provision for admission of students educated in civil law jurisdictions, notably Quebec, but not called to the bar of that jurisdiction. One possibility might be for students of the University of the West Indies to attend a Quebec law faculty, either as graduate students or as visiting undergraduate students for a semester or a year.[108] This would introduce them to the civil law tradition without sacrificing the advantages of a West Indian education.

Court structure
Regionalization of the court structure continued after recodification as it had before, with the much anticipated but short-lived Federation of the West Indies

---

103   (n66).

104   Rose-Marie Belle Antoine, *Commonwealth Caribbean Law and Legal Systems* (2nd edn, Routledge-Cavendish 2008) 60 (common law emphasis in UWI legal education 'exerts pressure on law students and practitioners from St Lucia who, by and large, have to educate themselves on the civil law aspects of the legal system').

105   Liverpool and Patchett (n68) 127–128; see also VA Cooper, 'The Notarial System in St. Lucia' in Landry and Caparros (n30).

106   (n66) s2(b).

107   As it is unlikely that the common law degrees of Saint Lucia's English- and UWI-trained lawyers would be assessed as equivalent to Quebec's civil law degrees by Quebec Bar or Chamber of Notaries: Regulations respecting the standards for equivalence of diplomas and training of the Barreau du Québec, Compilation of Québec Laws and Regulations [CQLR], chapter B-1, regulation 16, section 6 ff.

108   The recently created 'Canada-CARICOM Leadership Scholarships Program' might be available to facilitate this. Available at http://www.scholarships-bourses.gc.ca/scholarships-bourses/can/institutions/cclsp-pblcc.aspx. accessed 6 November 2013.

(1958 to 1962) engendering the creation of a bi-level (that is, trial and appeal) Federal Supreme Court in place of the region's existing courts including those of the Windward Islands and Leeward Islands. Other regional arrangements followed in the post-Federation period,[109] and Saint Lucia eventually came under the jurisdiction of the present Eastern Caribbean Supreme Court, established in 1981.[110] This court consists of a High Court (with resident judges in each of the Member States) and a Court of Appeal headquartered in Saint Lucia (consisting of the Chief Justice and three Justices of Appeal). The Saint Lucia resident High Court judge need not be a member of the Saint Lucia legal profession, nor is Saint Lucia guaranteed an appointment to the Court of Appeal.[111] This means that interpretation of the Saint Lucia Civil Code by judges trained in the common law and unfamiliar with the civilian tradition is still the norm.

The Privy Council remains the final court of appeal for Saint Lucia and most other Commonwealth Caribbean countries, although this seems about to change as a result of the inauguration of the Caribbean Court of Justice (CCJ) in 2005.[112] The CCJ was established in the context of the Caribbean Community and Common Market (CARICOM) with a dual mandate of deciding disputes arising from the regional relationship (its 'original' jurisdiction) and – particularly important in the present context – of serving as the final court of appeal from the domestic tribunals of Member States (its 'appellate' jurisdiction).[113] The CCJ is thus intended to supplant the Privy Council in this role, for reasons of both principle (for example,

109   See Dupont (n6) 159.

110   On the OECS generally see WC Gilmour, 'Legal and Institutional Aspects of the Organisation of Eastern Caribbean States' (1985) 11 Review of International Studies 311.

111   In contrast, Quebec, like all other Canadian provinces, has its own trial and intermediate appeal courts. As well, three of the nine judges of the Supreme Court of Canada must be from Quebec (more precisely, appointed 'from among the judges of the Court of Appeal or of the Superior Court of the Province of Quebec or from among the advocates of that Province'): Supreme Court of Canada Act, RSC 1985, c S-26, s 6. The importance of this provision in ensuring 'that the Court has civil law expertise and that Quebec's legal traditions and social values are represented on the Court' was recently recognized by the Supreme Court in *Reference re Supreme Court Act, ss. 5 and 6*, 2014 SCC 21.

112   See generally DDE Pollard, *The Caribbean Court of Justice: Closing the Circle of Independence* (Caribbean Law Publishing 2004), and Antoine (n104) chapters 16 and 17.

113   Some have expressed doubts about this wide mandate and the ability of a single Bench to 'juggle original and appellate jurisdiction, domestic and international law and even civil and common law': O Jones and C Ononaiwu, 'Smoothing the Way: The Privy Council and Jamaican Accession to the Caribbean Court of Appeal' (2006) 16 Caribbean Law Review 183, 183; see also L Birdsong, 'The Formation of the Caribbean Court of Justice: The Sunset of British Colonial Rule in the English Speaking Caribbean' (2004) 36 University of Miami Inter-American Law Review 197, 221–223.

national sovereignty,[114] regional solidarity) and practicality (for example, access to justice).[115]

Saint Lucia has now decided to make this change[116] and it is difficult to judge the effect this might have on its civil law tradition. On the one hand, the presence of the former French and Dutch colonies of Haiti and Suriname amongst the members of the enlarged CARICOM means that the mixed jurisdictions of Saint Lucia and Guyana would be less isolated than previously in the essentially common law Caribbean Commonwealth. The CCJ judges would thus have more occasion to hear civil law cases, and the civilian and mixed jurisdictions such as Saint Lucia would have more chance of having their appeals heard by a court composed of at least some civil law judges. On the other hand, it is not certain that many States – particularly the non-Commonwealth, civil law States of Haiti and Suriname – will elect to have the CCJ as their final court of appeal, in which case the 'advantage in numbers' would be minimal.[117] Nor are any of the nine judicial positions reserved for civil law judges[118] (although qualified judges, practitioners or teachers of law

---

114   See, for example, D Simmons, 'The Caribbean Court of Justice: A Unique Institution of Caribbean Creativity' (2004–2005) 29 Nova Law Review 171, 182 ('Our statute laws are no longer made for us in the United Kingdom; our Cabinets, exercising executive authority, no longer receive dictates of policy from the United Kingdom. Why should our law continue to be interpreted and fashioned in Downing Street? The third arm of government, the judicial, requires repatriation. Continuation of appeals to the JCPC is an affront to sovereignty and inconsistent with independence.').

115   The Privy Council's disapproval of capital punishment is undoubtedly another reason for some: for example, V Ettori, 'A Comparative Analysis of the Canadian and Caribbean Progressions towards Judicial Independence: Perspectives on the Caribbean Court of Justice' (2002) 12 Caribbean Law Review 100, 107f.

116   In an opinion issued at the request of the Government, the Eastern Caribbean Court of Appeal has advised that this can be accomplished by simple legislation, without the need for a national referendum: Caribbean Community (CARICOM) Secretariat, 'Eastern Caribbean Court Opinion on CCJ for Saint Lucia', Press Release 112/2012 (31 May 2013), available at http://www.caricom.org/jsp/pressreleases/press_releases_2013/pres112_13.jsp accessed 19 December 2013; and legislation is expected to be tabled soon: 'St Lucia pressing ahead with plans to make CCJ final court', *The Gleaner* (Jamaica, 3 July 2013), available at <http://jamaica-gleaner.com/latest/article.php?id=46177> accessed 10 January 2014.

117   While most countries have signed on to the CCJ's original jurisdiction, only Barbados, Belize and Guyana have so far accepted its appellate jurisdiction: 'PM Wants Full Support for St Lucia's Move to CCJ', *Antigua Observer* (Antigua, 2 July 2013), available at http://www.antiguaobserver.com/st-lucia-court-pm-wants-full-support-for-st-lucias-move-to-ccj/ accessed 10 January 2014. The delay is due mainly to the fact that in most countries, ending appeals to the Privy Council ('de-linking') requires a constitutional amendment, which sometimes means a special legislative majority and sometimes a popular referendum). See Birdsong (n113) 298f; Jones and Onanaiwu (n113).

118   Although 'at least three' positions are reserved for experts 'in international law including international trade law' (reflecting the court's original jurisdiction): Agreement

from civil law as well as Caribbean or Commonwealth jurisdictions are eligible for appointment,[119] and Commonwealth appointments could include those from mixed jurisdictions). As well, Saint Lucia's hybrid Code has been treated surprisingly sympathetically by the Privy Council, and it is not sure that it will receive similar treatment by a court lacking historical experience with mixed jurisdictions.

Conclusion

A mixed jurisdiction becomes endangered when its private law – 'the kernel of the legal system' – no longer retains its character substantially unaltered.[120] This occurs when the new law is no longer introduced in a piecemeal manner to discrete areas of the law but in a wholesale manner to the general body of private law. In Saint Lucia, the 1879 adoption of a Civil Code modelled on the 1866 Civil Code of Lower Canada protected the civilian private law kernel of its legal system, in the face of almost overwhelming odds, for almost a century: 'codified law *is* "tough law"'.[121] However, large-scale infusion of the common law into the Civil Code itself moved Saint Lucia further along the path to change. Saint Lucia is now at a crossroads in protecting its civilian heritage.

Saint Lucia thus faces what might be called 'intrinsic' challenges to its civilian heritage, affecting the content of the law that is administered. But it also faces, now as in the past, substantial 'extrinsic' challenges affecting the manner in which the law is administered. A major challenge has been the Colonial Office's policy of Anglicization of both Bench and Bar.[122] And its policy of regionalization has meant that Saint Lucia's legal specificity has been progressively diluted with each change in court structure, from the Windward Islands to the Windward and Leeward Islands to the British Caribbean a whole. What will be the effect of the

---

establishing the Caribbean Court of Justice, 14 February 2001, available at <http://www.caricom.org/ccjagrmnt.htm> accessed 10 January 2013 art IV(1).

119   Agreement, art IV(10). As Simmons (Chief Justice of Barbados and President of the independent Commission charged with appointing CCJ judges) explains (n129) 192: 'The Agreement has deliberately cast a wide net for the judges of the court in order to capture the best available talent in common law and civil law jurisdictions and to invest the court with the kind of diversity that a final court deserves.' The Commission advertised widely and received some 90 applications from around the world: Birdsong (n113) 214.

120   Lee (n4).

121   White (n33) 881 [emphasis in original]; see also Antoine (n119) 42: 'Codified law is ... "hard law", being of enduring quality by the mere fact that it is enshrined in statute. This ... is one of the reasons that ... St Lucia ... still retains the Romano-Germanic tradition ... originally brought to the island by the French centuries ago. The judge-made "soft law" of England could not entirely replace it.'

122   Antoine (n104) 65 ('The most damaging weapon of the common law, however, was the training of lawyers and judges in the common law tradition.').

proposed substitution of the Caribbean Court of Justice for the Privy Council? Will it strengthen or weaken Saint Lucia's civil law tradition?

TB Smith once observed that the struggle to maintain the civilian tradition in a number of mixed jurisdictions 'is a damn close fought business'.[123] In Saint Lucia's case, it is too damn close to call.

---

123   TB Smith 'The Preservation of the Civilian Tradition in Mixed Jurisdictions' in AN Yiannopoulos (ed), *Civil Law in the Modern World* 1965 (Louisiana State University Press 1965) 4, as quoted in Antoine (n104) 71–72.

Chapter 9
Cyprus

Cyprus embraces a robust pragmatic approach to mixing its system and eludes classical forms of mixedness to illustrate the reverse: a civil law influenced public law and a common law influenced private law, while at the same time taking from both traditions those aspects that suit it, for example a substantially codified legal system under which it applies common law principles where there is no Cypriot legislation in force and in so far as existing Cypriot legislation is not contradicted.

Embracing the principles of common law and equity alongside the regular citation of decisions of the Greek Symvoulio tis Epikrateias and the French Conseil d' Etat by the Supreme Court of Cyprus in constitutional and administrative law matters, it can be argued that Cypriot constitutional justice forms an idiosyncratic osmosis between Continental and common law. Cypriot administrative law in particular is similar to Greek, French and German Continental administrative law, and not to English administrative law; as a result, Greek and French authorities and jurisprudence have guided the evolution of Cypriot administrative law. With respect to human rights, the Supreme Court is regularly guided by the case law of the European Court of Human Rights and of Continental countries.

In private law a similarly idiosyncratic mix applies. Continental legal thinking is influential in some areas, such as family law (where also religious laws apply), and in some areas such as succession a combination of civil and common law principles apply, while in the case of land law there is no application of common law principles.

In this chapter, Achilles Emilianides addresses the rich diversity of the Cypriot legal system demonstrating – perhaps in contrast to Quebec, the lively awareness of the contribution of mixtures to the development of the current legal system and the various ideologies surrounding the debate as to how to classify it. Although there are challenges and potential constraints being imposed on the system following the accession of the Republic of Cyprus to the EU, present developments, particularly in the field of legal education, suggest that this mixed legal system is far from endangered and open to the possibility of potential changes in the mixture.

Here, laws from different origins seem to co-exist, but also blend with university degree courses in law unusually offering a mixture of Greek, English and Cypriot content in both English and Greek. This contributes to the future strength of the legal system of Cyprus.

Cyprus: 'Everything Changes and Nothing Remains Still'

Achilles C. Emilianides

Historical Development of the System

Prior to British rule

The history of Cyprus begins with the early Neolithic period, when the Achaean-Mycenaean Greeks arrived at the island at around 1,600 BC and Achaean civilization was introduced into Cyprus.[1] Extensive Greek colonization continued in subsequent years and by 1,000 BC the island had adopted the Greek city–state system of government, as well as the Greek civilization, culture and way of living.[2] The island's predominantly Greek character therefore dates from that period. Despite successive conquests by Assyria, Egypt and Persia, the Greek element remained dominant in the island. Cyprus was once again brought under Greek rule by Alexander the Great and came under the rule of the Ptolemies for about two and a half centuries.

In 58 BC Cyprus became a province of the Roman Empire. During the early period of the Roman rule, Christianity was introduced in Cyprus. The Orthodox Church of Cyprus is considered to be apostolic, since it was founded by Apostle Barnabas, who is considered as the Church's first Archbishop.[3] The conversion of Cypriots to Christianity had been completed by the beginning of the fifth century. With the exception of sporadic Arab invasions, Cyprus remained for more than eight and a half centuries, between 325 and 1191, a province of the Byzantine

---

1 For an extensive history of Cyprus see, inter alia, G Hill, *A History of Cyprus* (Cambridge University Press1940–1952) v. 1–4.

2 F Colotas, 'Study of the State and Legal Institutions of the Ancient Cypriot Kingdoms' (1988) 21 Cyprus Law Review 3267 (in Greek).

3 For a history of the Orthodox Church of Cyprus see J Hackett, *A History of the Orthodox Church of Cyprus* (Methuen and Co 1901).

Empire.[4] Thus, Christianity was the State religion of the island, similar to other parts of the Byzantine Empire.[5]

The period of the Byzantine rule in Cyprus ended in 1191, when Cyprus came within the same year under the rule of then King of England, Richard the Coeur de Lion, the Order of the Knight Templars and eventually the King of Jerusalem, Guy de Lusignan. The island remained under the rule of the Lusignans for nearly 300 years, from 1191 until 1489, which is considered to be the period of the Frankish rule of Cyprus. During the period of Frankish rule, Catholicism became the official religion of the island. However, the great majority of the population adhered to the Orthodox Christian religion and were Greeks.

The legislation during the Lusignan period was the one contained in the Assizes of Cyprus, which were modelled after the Assizes of Jerusalem.[6] However, the ecclesiastical courts of the Greek Orthodox Church applied, with respect to the family affairs of members of the Orthodox Church, the so-called 'Hellenic laws' of Cyprus, which essentially consisted of a codification of Byzantine law.[7] It could be argued that the family law provisions of the Assizes were somewhat influenced by the Hellenic laws of Cyprus, as evidenced by provisions for divorce. During the Venetian rule from 1489–1571, the Assizes continued to be the governing legislation.[8] Thus, in the period of Frankish and Venetian rule of the island, some elements of pluralistic conception of the Cypriot legal system can be identified.[9]

The period of Ottoman rule of Cyprus lasted for more than 300 years, from the conquest of the island by the Ottomans in 1571 until 1878; during this period adherents of the Islamic faith first appeared in Cyprus. The Sharia law was not only the personal

---

4   JHA Lokin, 'Administration and Jurisdiction in Cyprus in the 6th Century A.D' in *Proceedings of the Second International Cyprological Conference*, v. II (Society for Cypriot Studies 1986) 1.

5   C Tornaritis, *The Ecclesiastical Courts Especially in Cyprus* (1976) 15; D Seremetis, 'The Administration of Justice in Cyprus during the Byzantine and Post-Byzantine Era' in *Proceedings of the First International Cyprological Conference*, v. III (Society for Cypriot Studies 1973) (in Greek) 309ff.

6   N Coureas, *The Assizes of the Lusignan Kingdom of Cyprus* (Cyprus Research Centre 2002); A Emilianides, 'Polyarchy in the Frankish Rule of Cyprus' in *Mélanges à la mémoire de Michel Dendias* (1978) 7; J Richard, 'The Law of the Medieval Kingdom' in T Papadopoulos (ed), *History of Cyprus*, v. IV (Foundation of Archbishop Makarios III 1995) (in Greek) 375.

7   A Emilianides, 'The Hellenic Laws of Cyprus during Frankish Rule' (2004) 25 Yearbook of the Cyprus Research Centre 51 (in Greek); A Emilianides, 'The Hellenic Laws of Cyprus and the Hexabiblos of Armenopoulos' (1951) Yearbook of the Faculty of Law of the Aristotle University of Thessaloniki 33.

8   E Aristeidou, 'Assizes in Cyprus during the Venetian Rule' (2001) 22 Yearbook of the Cyprus Research Centre 95 (in Greek).

9   I adopt Griffith's definition of pluralism as the presence or interaction of two or more kinds of laws in legal traditions within the same system or social field. J Griffith, 'What is Legal Pluralism' (1986) 24 Journal of Legal Pluralism and Unofficial Law 1.

law of the Muslims of Cyprus, but also the State law, thus replacing the law of the Assizes. The Sharia law was applied by the Sharia courts, which were the competent courts for the legal affairs of all people living in the island, irrespective of their religion.[10] Furthermore, during this period foreigners living in Cyprus could take advantage of the system of capitulations prevailing in Cyprus, on the basis of capitulatory conventions between the Ottoman Empire and various European countries.[11]

The only exception to such exclusive competence of the Sharia courts was the law of personal status and family relations of members of the Orthodox Church. The ecclesiastical courts of the Orthodox Church continued to be the only competent courts with regard to the family relations of their members and continued to apply the Byzantine law. During that period the Orthodox Church was considered to have the primary role in the preservation of faith, national identity and traditions of the Greek Cypriots.[12] The right of all Christian communities to administer their religious and family affairs was eventually recognized, following the *Tanzimat* reform, by the Ottoman Imperial rescript, *Hatt-ı-Humayun* of 18 February 1856 which also applied in Cyprus.[13] The *Hatt-ı-Humayun* granted spiritual advantages and exemptions, as well as a form of religious autonomy to the various Christian and non-Muslim religious communities living within the boundaries of the Ottoman Empire. Pluralistic legal elements can therefore also be identified during this period.

The period of British rule

The Ottoman Empire assigned to the UK the rights of possession and administration of Cyprus, by signing the Convention of Defence Alliance on 4 June 1878 in Constantinople.[14] With the signing of the Treaty, the period of British rule in Cyprus

---

10   G Grivaud, 'Law and Economy' in T Papadopoulos (ed), *History of Cyprus*, v. VI (Foundation of Archbishop Makarios III 2011) (in Greek) 269; M Zekia, 'A Short Historical Survey of the Laws Administered by the Ottoman Civil and Criminal Courts and of the Constitution of such Courts during the Ottoman Era in Cyprus During 1571-1878' in *Proceedings of the First International Cyprological Conference*, v. III (Society for Cypriot Studies 1973) 457 and T Haycraft, 'Ottoman Law in Cyprus' (1908) 24 Law Quarterly Review 279.

11   A Emilianides, 'Capitulations and Privileges of Foreigners in Cyprus' (1937) 1 Cypriot Studies 1 (in Greek).

12   T Papadopoulos, *The History of the Greek Church and People under Turkish Domination* (2nd edn Variorum 1990); H Luke, *Cyprus under the Turks 1571–1878: A Record Based on the Archives of the English Consulate in Cyprus* (Oxford University Press 1921).

13   G Dionyssiou, 'The Ottoman Administration of Cyprus and the Tanzimat Reforms' (1994) 20 Yearbook of the Cyprus Research Centre 361; *Parapano v Happaz* (1893) 3 CLR 69; *Tano v Tano* (1910) 9 CLR 94; G Serghides, *Internal and External Conflict of Laws in Regard to Family Relations in Cyprus* (1988) 32ff.

14   See G Georgallides, *A Political and Administrative History of Cyprus 1918–1926* (Cyprus Research Centre 1979) 3ff.

officially began. While Cyprus still theoretically belonged to the Ottoman Empire and could eventually return on the fulfilment of certain conditions, in effect the real and only sovereign of Cyprus was the UK, which exercised the administration of the island and was granted the power to enact laws and conventions for the island of Cyprus and to regulate its commercial and consular relations and affairs.[15]

It was held that the position of Cyprus during that period was analogous to that of a protectorate, in the sense that it fell within the designation of a country under the protection of the UK, which in fact governed the island.[16] This peculiar situation ceased in 1914, when, immediately after the outbreak of the First World War, the UK unilaterally annexed Cyprus by Order in Council of 5 November 1914;[17] the annexation was eventually recognized by Turkey in 1923 by Article 20 of the Treaty of Lausanne. In accordance with Article 16 of the Treaty of Lausanne, Turkey renounced all rights and titles whatsoever over Cyprus. The island was proclaimed as a Crown Colony on 10 March 1925.[18]

The administration of Cyprus by the UK was a colonial one, without genuine involvement by the native population. The objective of the colonial administration was to equalize the influence of the votes of the Greek Cypriots in the Legislative Council, who were the majority of the population, with the combined votes of the British and the Turkish Cypriots. The colonial Government further had the right to decline to enforce any decision.[19] Eventually, the Legislative Council was itself abolished, as a response to the disturbances of 1931, which culminated in the burning down of the Government House in Nicosia.[20] In a referendum held on 15 January 1950 and organized by the Church, more than 95 per cent of the indigenous Greek population voted in favour of the Union (*Enosis*) of the island with Greece; however, the British colonial Government rejected the Greek position, with the then Minister of State for Colonial Affairs, Henry Hopkinson, eventually declaring that Cyprus should never be allowed full independence.[21]

On 1 April 1955 the National Organisation of Cypriot Fighters (EOKA), led by George Grivas (alias Dhigenis), a Greek Cypriot who was a colonel in the Greek army, declared an armed insurrection against the British, demanding the Union

---

15   G Tenekides, '*La condition internationale de la République de Chypre*' (1960) 6 *Annuaire Francais de Droit International* 133.

16   *Parounakian* v *The Turkish Government*, Annual Digest 1929–1930, Case N. 11, which was a judgment of the Anglo-Turkish Mixed Arbitral Tribunal.

17   Cyprus Annexation Order in Council of 5 November 1914; C Orr, *Cyprus under British Rule* (Robert Scott 1918) 175.

18   *Cyprus Gazette* 1 May 1925, Notification No. 266.

19   A Emilianides, 'Justice and Human Rights during British Rule in Cyprus' (2006) 3 Cyprus Law Tribune 66 (in Greek).

20   P Stylianou, *The Movement of October of 1931 in Cyprus* (1984) (in Greek); V Livadas, Y Spanos and P Papapolyviou, *The Insurrection of October 1931* (2004) (in Greek).

21   House of Commons Minutes, 28 July 1954, 552.

(*Enosis*) of the island with Greece.[22] Turkey, with the encouragement of the UK, became involved in Cyprus and negotiations ensued between the UK, Greece and Turkey.[23] On 11 February 1959 the Zurich Agreement was concluded between Greece and Turkey. The Agreement, which was in fact imposed on the people of Cyprus, was then signed in London by the leaders of the two communities of Cyprus, Archbishop Makarios and Fazil Küçük.[24] The Republic of Cyprus was established as an independent and sovereign republic on 16 August 1960, when its Constitution came into force and British sovereignty over Cyprus, as a Crown colony, ceased.[25]

The introduction of common law in Cyprus was gradual. Until 1927 a dualistic system of administration of justice was retained; when the defendant was an Ottoman subject[26] the courts applied Ottoman law, whereas in the remaining cases they applied English law. Ottoman cases were renamed Cypriot cases after 1914, when Cypriots became British citizens.[27] Ottoman law thus remained dominant in the island until 1935, to the extent that it had not been substituted or amended by subsequent legislation based on English law. It could well be argued that it was during this period that Cyprus first showed signs of becoming a mixed legal system in the conventional sense of interrelationship and contention between common law and civil doctrines. Until the British period the hybrid character of the Cypriot legal system amounted to a co-existence of the official State law with religious personal laws. However, during the British rule common law conflicted with the Ottoman legislation, which had been directly influenced by the codifications of civil law countries, and which contended for supremacy (and survival) with the common law.[28]

---

22   SIMAE (Council for the Preservation of Historical Memory of the EOKA Struggle), *Fifty Years on from the EOKA Struggle* (Ministry of Education 2006) (in Greek); R Holland, *Britain and the Revolt in Cyprus: 1954–1959* (Clarendon Press 1998); A Emilianides, *The Reports of the European Commission of Human Rights with Respect to Cyprus. App. 176/1956 & 299/1957* (Ministry of Education and Culture 2008) (in Greek).

23   See E Hatzivassiliou, *The Cyprus Question 1878–1960: The Constitutional Aspect* (University of Minnesota 2002).

24   A Emilianides, 'The Zurich and London Agreements and the Cyprus Republic' v. II (*Melanges Seferiades* 1961) 629; G Vlachos, '*L'organisation constitutionelle de la Republique de Chypre*' (1961) 3 *Revue International de Droit Comparé* 526.

25   Cyprus Act, 1960, s1, Republic of Cyprus Order in Council 1960 S.I. 1960 No. 1368.

26   The term 'Ottoman' also included Cypriots. *Papa Nicola v Louca* (1883) 1 CLR 6 ; *Frangoudi v Michaelides* (1895) 3 CLR 221.

27   A Emilianides, 'The Private International Law in Cyprus' in *Symposium on Cypriot Legal Issues* (Aristotle University of Thessaloniki 1974) (in Greek) 88; A Emilianides, 'The Question of Citizenship of Cypriots from the British Rule until Today' in *Symmeikta Streit* (1939) 299 (in Greek).

28   E Vassilakakis and S Papasavvas, *Elements of Cypriot Law* (Sakkoulas 2002) (in Greek) 24.

British judges were therefore called upon to interpret and apply a variation of civil private law, as this was transformed into Ottoman law embodying Ottoman religious beliefs and culture.[29] As correctly noted by Symeonides and others, however, with the introduction of English procedural law in Cypriot courts, the Ottoman law had lost all hope of survival.[30] The courts were composed mainly of British judges who applied English common law and the rules of equity as subsidiary sources of law.[31] Furthermore, judgments of the Cypriot Supreme Court were subject to appeal before the Privy Council, which, despite being situated outside of Cyprus, was the supreme judicial authority of the island.[32]

British common law eventually substituted Ottoman law as the dominant law of the island, following the enactment of the Courts of Justice Law 38/1935, s. 49 of which explicitly provided that any court, during the exercise of its civil or criminal jurisdiction, would apply the laws of the colony of Cyprus, the common law and the rules of equity, as well as laws of the British Empire and Orders in Council having general application. From 1935 onwards Cyprus has joined the family of common law countries, although this does not mean that Ottoman law was altogether abolished: the Ottoman Civil Code was abolished in 1945, but some of its provisions remained in effect until 1953; the Ottoman Land Code was abolished in 1946, but the Transfer of Land Law of 1890 which was partly influenced by Ottoman legislation, remained in effect until 1965,[33] and the Ottoman Naval Code was only abolished in 1960, following Independence, despite the undeniable supremacy of British naval law when compared to the respective Ottoman law.

Cyprus and Common Law

Cyprus has often been described as an essentially 'common law country'.[34] Even the Supreme Court has stated in an otherwise obiter comment that 'Cyprus is a

---

29   A Emilianides, 'Conflict of Laws during the British Rule of Cyprus' in *Proceedings of the Fourth International Cyprological Conference* v. III (Society for Cypriot Studies 2012) 67 (in Greek).

30   S Symeonides, 'Introduction to Cypriot Law' in F Frantzeskakis, D Evrigenis and S Symeonides, *Comparative Law* (Sakkoulas 1978) (in Greek) 380ff.

31   *Karageorghiades v Haji Pavlo* (1900) 5 CLR 39.

32   *Parapano v Happaz* (1893) 3 CLR 69; A Emilianides, 'The Parapano Judgment: Conflict of Laws for the Recognition of Children and Succession in Cyprus during British Rule' in A. Emilianides, *Five Studies on the History of Cypriot Law* (Dikaionomia 2007) (in Greek) 67.

33   G Stavrinakis, 'Immovable Property in Cyprus' in *Symposium on Cypriot Legal Issues* (Aristotle University of Thessaloniki 1974) (in Greek) 161.

34   More recently A Neocleous and C Christoforou, 'Cyprus' in *International Agency and Distribution Law* (2nd edn Juris Publishing 2012).

common law country'.[35] The importance of common law for the legal system of the Republic of Cyprus should definitely not be underestimated.[36] By virtue of Article 188 of the Constitution, the laws which were in force during the British rule of Cyprus remained in force to the extent that they are not subsequently repealed or modified and to the extent that they are not contrary to or inconsistent with the Constitution. The Laws of Cyprus in force on 1 April 1959, immediately prior to Independence, were compiled by former Attorney-General of the Republic, Criton Tornaritis, and were published in six volumes and 354 Chapters (Caps),[37] each Chapter corresponding to a single law. Laws that continue to be in force after Independence are referred to by their respective Cap in the 1959 edition.[38]

The decision to maintain in effect the legislation previously in force, even following Independence, was unavoidable. The aim of Greek Cypriots for *Enosis* had not been realized and the new constitution provided for a bi-communal structure which required a neutral legal system; accordingly, the incorporation of Greek legislation into the Cypriot legal system, as most Greek Cypriots would wish for, was not a realistic option. Furthermore, it would be practically impossible for Cyprus to establish an autochthonous legal system; Cyprus had been under foreign rule for several centuries and local customary law was not considered as a significant source of law, much less as having the potential to contribute to the establishment of a distinct 'Cypriot' legal system.[39]

The Cypriot legislator, however, went even further than the constitutional text dictated. Section 29(c) of the Courts of Justice Law 14/1960 provides that common law and the principles of equity are to be considered as a source of law, in so far as they are not inconsistent with or contrary to the Constitution, provisions of International Treaties or Convention promulgated in accordance with Article 169 s3 of the Constitution, or legislation enacted in accordance with the Constitution, or legislation which remains in force in accordance with Article 188 of the Constitution. It was further provided in section 29(e) of Law 14/60 that laws of the Parliament of the United Kingdom of Great Britain and Northern Ireland which were in force in Cyprus on the day prior to Independence would also be maintained as a source of law, to the extent that they were not inconsistent with or contrary to the Constitution, or International Treaties or Conventions, or legislation enacted in accordance with the Constitution; the latter provision covering those laws of the UK which were of general application to the colonies.

---

35   *Kolokasides* v *Republic* (1992) 2 CLR 252 (in Greek).

36   C Tornaritis, *The Legal System of the Republic of Cyprus* (1984) (in Greek); A Iacovides, 'An Introduction to the Law in Force as Applied in Cyprus' (1988) 24 Cyprus Law Review 3745 (in Greek).

37   *The Statute Laws of Cyprus in force on 1 April 1959*, v. I–VI.

38   For example, Interpretation Law is Cap. 1, Advocates Law is Cap. 2.

39   Symeonides (n30); L Loucaides, 'Sources and Methods of Cypriot Law' in *Topics of Cypriot Law* (1982) (in Greek) 18.

This essentially meant that Cyprus would continue to apply the common law after independence and that English cases would continue to be considered as precedent for Cypriot courts. The decision to adopt the common law en masse, both with regards to judgments prior to independence and post-independence, was a rather rushed decision. As Symeonides correctly notes the decision of the legislator to characterize the English common law as a source of law restricted significantly the power of the Cypriot citizen to know the law of his country[40] and even more importantly might lead to cases where the Cypriot courts are bound to follow the common law despite the fact that this may have been abolished by statute in England.[41]

In addition to the maintenance of post-independence common law as a source of law, some of the most important pieces of legislation remain in force since the British rule with minor amendments and effectively refer to common law rules (or sometimes English law as it was in force in 1959), often as influenced by the Indian codifications. These include: Contract Law, Cap. 149; the Law of Torts, Cap. 148; Company Law, Cap. 113; Trusts Law, Cap. 191; Criminal Law, Cap. 195; Civil Procedure Rules; Criminal Procedure Law, Cap. 155 and the Law of Evidence, Cap. 9. The aforementioned legislation remain in force, despite the fact that in England the respective legislation might in the meantime have been repealed or amended.

English academic publications, such as those found in the Sweet & Maxwell's Common Law Library[42] are regularly cited before Cypriot courts as authority for the determination of the common law rules in a given field, whereas advocates and judges routinely refer to the English *White Book* in order to interpret the rules of civil procedure.[43] However, since Cypriot Civil Procedure rules have not adopted the amendments which have taken place in the meantime in England, litigants have to refer to versions of the English *White Book* published prior to independence and in particular between the period 1954–1959. This is understandably rather awkward. Furthermore, other common law jurisdictions might be taken into consideration

---

40   Symeonides (n30). I do not agree with the approach of G Pikis, *The English Common Law, The Rules of Equity and their Application in Cyprus* (1981) (in Greek) 2ff, who argues that the adoption of English common law was due to the common belief of Greeks and Turks that the law as applied in Cyprus gave comfort and security to the people and their property rights. On the contrary English law was at the time viewed as an integral part of the colonial system of Government against which the Greek Cypriots had revolted.

41   L Loucaides, 'The Dependence of Cypriot Law from Common Law' in *Topics of Cypriot Law* (1982) (in Greek) 36; C Savva, 'The Unconstitutionality of Section 29, Paragraph 1 of the Courts of Justice Law establishing Case-Law as a Source of Law' (1989) 3 Cyprus Law Tribune 32 (in Greek).

42   Published by Sweet & Maxwell this is widely considered as the leading collection of common law textbooks, such as Phipson on *Evidence*, Chitty on *Contracts*, Clerk & Lindsell on *Torts* and so on.

43   *The White Book* is an authoritative textbook interpreting the English rules on Civil Procedure, published by Sweet & Maxwell.

when appropriate. Two of the main Cypriot statutes: the Criminal Law, Cap. 154 and the Contract Law, Cap. 149, were based on the respective Indian legislation and as a result Indian textbooks might well be referred to by the courts.[44]

Major Deviations from Common Law

Public law

The Constitution of Cyprus is unique in its perplexity and in the multiplicity of safeguards that it provides for the principal numerical minority of the island, namely the Turkish community.[45] The principle of bi-communality permeates the whole constitutional structure, according, in many respects, an equal status to the Greek community representing 82 per cent of the population, with the Turkish community representing 18 per cent. The structure provided by the Constitution aimed at ensuring that each Community would enjoy partial administrative autonomy, while at the same time the numerically smaller Turkish Community would effectively participate in the exercise and functions of Government in such a way so as to avoid the supremacy of the larger Community.

De Smith noted that the 1960 Constitution is a tragic and occasionally an almost ludicrous document and noted that it is possibly the most rigid, detailed and complicated Constitution in the world.[46] Not surprisingly, the Zurich Agreement[47] failed to establish cooperation between the Greek and Turkish communities of the island[48] and proved to be unworkable in practice.[49] In 1963 there was an outbreak of violence in the island, which led to a constitutional breakdown.[50] In 1964 a United Nations Peacekeeping operation came to the island and has remained there since.[51] Inter-communal talks began with the aim of achieving a satisfactory solution to the

---

44   *Eliades* v *Petrides* (1972) 1 CLR 5.

45   A Emilianides, *Constitutional Law in Cyprus* (Kluwer 2014).

46   A S De Smith, *The New Commonwealth and its Constitutions* (Stevens and Sons 1964) 282.

47   See paragraph 1.2. and footnote 24 above.

48   A Emilianides, *The Parliamentary Co - Existence of Greeks and Turks in Cyprus* (Epiphaniou 2003) (in Greek).

49   A Emilianides, *Beyond the Constitution of Cyprus* (Sakkoulas 2006) (in Greek); C Tornaritis, *Peculiarities of the Constitution of Cyprus and Effect on the Normal Function of the State* (1980) (in Greek); TW Adams, 'The First Republic of Cyprus: Review of an Unworkable Constitution' (1966) 19 Western Political Quarterly 475.

50   S Kyriakides, *Cyprus: Constitutionalism and Crisis Government* (University of Pennsylvania Press 1968).

51   A Emilianides, 'The United Nations Forces Function, its International Conflicts and Civil Strifes' in *Melanges Bridel* (1968) 147.

'Cyprus Problem'.[52] However, in July 1974, the Republic of Turkey invaded the country with its armed forces and occupied the northern part of the island.[53] As a result of the Turkish invasion, the Greeks and other Christians of the region were displaced to the southern part of the island, whereas the Turks of the southern part of the island were forced to move to the north.

On 15 November 1983, the Turkish-occupied area declared itself to be the 'Turkish Republic of Northern Cyprus' ('TRNC'), although that entity is recognized only by Turkey. The Turkish occupation in Cyprus continues to the present day and therefore the Republic of Cyprus is prevented from exercising its powers over the occupied territory. The Republic of Cyprus remains, however, the only internationally recognized entity of the island and the occupied areas continue to form part of the Republic of Cyprus. Consequently, the de facto legal system of the 'TRNC' does not enjoy recognition,[54] although it continues to function in practice.[55]

As a result of the 'Cyprus Problem' and the abnormal constitutional situation prevailing in the island, a significant number of constitutional provisions which refer to the Turkish Cypriot community have not been in force for 50 years, even though they are considered to be fundamental and thus not subject to modification. A doctrine of necessity has been accepted by the Supreme Court of Cyprus, so that the House of Representatives may enact laws, even contrary to those provisions of the Constitution which are temporarily not in force because of the Cyprus Problem. This has resulted in a fundamental differentiation between the written form of the 1960 Constitution and the living Constitution as applied in Cypriot case law and practice since 1964. No analysis of the constitutional order of Cyprus would be complete, without an understanding of the importance of the doctrine of necessity in the perseverance, interpretation and function of the Constitution.[56]

---

52   P Polyviou, *Cyprus in Search of a Constitution: Constitutional Negotiations and Proposals* (1976).

53   The invasion was considered as inconsistent with international law. I Brownlie, 'The Prohibition of the Use of Armed Force for the Solution of International Differences with Particular Reference to the Affairs of the Republic of Cyprus' in *International Law Conference on Cyprus* (Cyprus Bar Council 1979) 198–213; R McDonald, 'International Law and the Conflict in Cyprus' (1981) 19 Canadian Yearbook of International Law 3.

54   *Loizidou* v *Turkey*, Judgment of 23/3/1995 and 18/12/1996; *Cyprus* v *Turkey*, Judgment of 10/5/2001; L Loucaides, 'The Judgment of the European Court of Human Rights in the Case of Cyprus v Turkey' (2002) 15 Leiden Journal of International Law 225; C Paraskeva, *The Relationship between Domestic Implementation of the European Convention on Human Rights and the Ongoing Reforms of the European Court of Human Rights, with a Case Study on Cyprus and Turkey* (Intersentia 2010), *Orams* v *Apostolides* (2009) ECR I-3571.

55   The analysis of this chapter will not take into account the de facto legal system functioning in the occupied areas.

56   A Emilianides, 'Accession of the Republic of Cyprus to the EU, the Constitution and the Cypriot Doctrine of Necessity' (2007) Cyprus Yearbook of International Relations 65.

With respect to constitutional law interpretation, the Supreme Court has often cited judgments of civil law courts, such as the Greek *Symvoulio tis Epikrateias* and the French *Conseil d'Etat*.[57] In addition the Supreme Court has been at times guided by the case law of the Supreme Court of the United States of America; for example, the Supreme Court has formulated certain general principles which govern the constitutional review of legislation which effectively derive from the early twentieth century jurisprudence of the Supreme Court of the United States.[58] The Supreme Court of Cyprus does not apply common law with regards to the interpretation of the Constitution; however, it often applies certain common law principles, such as stare decisis even in constitutional law cases. It could therefore be argued that Cypriot constitutional justice forms an idiosyncratic osmosis between civil and common law.[59]

The same osmosis occurs in Cypriot administrative law. Article 146 of the Constitution introduced for the first time the judicial review of administrative action,[60] a jurisdiction which was unknown to English and Cypriot law at the time of Cyprus' independence. As a result, common law did not have any influence in the development of Cypriot administrative law. The structure of judicial control of administrative action in Cyprus is founded on the principles of civil administrative law. For the brief period of time before 1963, when the Supreme Constitutional Court was functioning under the Chairmanship of the German Ernst Forsthoff, the development of administrative law was primarily founded on German law and secondarily on Greek and French administrative law; however, due to linguistic barriers (since very few Cypriots are German speaking), Greek and, secondarily, French case law and textbooks proved to have a more lasting influence on the development of Cypriot administrative law since 1963.

Accordingly, the development of Cypriot administrative law is mainly based on the case law of the Greek *Symvoulion tis Epikrateias* and the *French Conseil d'Etat*.[61] In *Morsis* the Supreme Court held that it would be reasonable to apply

---

57   S Papasavvas, *La Justice Constitutionelle à Chypre* (Presses Universitaires d' Aix-Marseilles 1998); E Nicolaou, *The Constitutional Review of Laws and the Distribution of Competences of the Organs of the State in Cyprus* (Sakkoulas 2000) (in Greek).

58   These were stated in the leading case *The Board of Registration for Architects and Civil Engineers* v *Kyriakides* (1966) 3 CLR 640 and have been adopted by the case law of the Supreme Court ever since.

59   S Papasavvas, 'The Osmosis of Continental Public Law and Common Law in Cyprus' (2002) 28 *To Syntagma* 693 (in Greek).

60   N Charalambous, *The Action and Control of Public Administration* (2nd edn 2004) (in Greek); A Angelides and S Angelides, *Administrative Procedural Law* (Cyprus Bar Association 2011) (in Greek).

61   L Clerides, 'The Influence of Greek Administrative Law in the Development of Administrative Law applicable in Cyprus' (1974) 1 Cyprus Law Tribune 7 (in Greek).

principles of administrative law adopted in civil law countries such as Greece, France or Germany, not as foreign law, but as Cypriot law.[62]

Part II of the Constitution of Cyprus which guarantees fundamental rights and liberties is modelled on the European Convention on Human Rights; however, the provisions of the European Convention have been extended and enlarged in some respects with a number of social and economic rights added in order to meet the basic requirements of a modern society.[63] As a result the Cypriot courts are invoking the case law of the European Court of Human Rights, not only with respect to the interpretation of the Convention, but also with respect to the interpretation of the corresponding constitutional articles. Therefore, the courts will try, wherever possible, to interpret the relevant constitutional provisions in a manner which is consistent with the interpretation adopted by the European Court of Human Rights.[64]

The complicated inter-relationship between civil and common law in the field of administrative law is further highlighted in cases where the Supreme Court is called upon to interpret statutes while adjudicating administrative law cases. Similar cases might lead to a situation where the Supreme Court applies rules of procedure deriving from civil law principles, as well as civil administrative law principles, while at the same time applying the common law rules for the construction of a statute.[65]

The leading judgment of the Supreme Court in *Yiallouros* v *Nicolaou*[66] is a solid example of the difficulties associated with common law educated judges applying civil law notions. In *Yiallouros* the Supreme Court effectively adopted the legal concept of *drittwirkung*, in accordance with which an individual plaintiff can rely directly on the constitutional provisions safeguarding fundamental rights in order to sue another individual or the government for the violation of those rights. The Supreme Court held that the violation of constitutional rights vests in the victim the right to invoke legal remedies for the vindication of his rights, including compensation for any damage suffered because of the violation. Consequently, the violation of constitutional rights is directly actionable before

---

62   *Morsis* v *The Republic* (1965) 3 CLR 1. Also M Triantafyllides, 'A Tabulation of Cases in which the Supreme Court of Cyprus when Deciding them Referred to Principles of Greek Administrative Law' in *Proceedings of the First International Cyprological Conference*, v. III (Society for Cypriot Studies 1973) 393.

63   *Attorney-General* v *Ibrahim* (1964) CLR 195, 225; *Attorney-General* v *Afamis* 1 RSCC 121, 125–126; A Emilianides, *Constitutional Law in Cyprus* (Kluwer 2013), C Tornaritis, *The State Law of the Republic of Cyprus* (Cyprus Research Centre 1982); P Evangelides, *The Republic of Cyprus and its Constitution with special regard to Constitutional Rights* (Difo-Druck GmbH 1996).

64   A Loizou, *Cyprus and the European Convention on Human Rights* (Sakkoulas 2003) (in Greek); C Tornaritis, 'The Operation of the European Convention for the Protection of Human Rights in the Republic of Cyprus' (1983) 3 Cyprus Law Review 455.

65   For example, *Krishna Pillay* v *Republic* (1988) 3 CLR 112.

66   (2001) 1 CLR 558 (in Greek).

Cypriot Courts. However, the Supreme Court, instead of expressly relying on the notion of *drittwirkung*, or analysing the general theory associated with the notion, opted to justify its judgment on the doctrine of equity, a doctrine unrelated to the protection of constitutional rights as understood in the civil law tradition.[67]

Private law

The Land Law, Cap. 224, although enacted during the period of British rule, expressly excludes the application of common law principles and the rules of equity. The system is based on rules which have very few similarities with English land law and are a mixture of elements deriving from various sources. It has been held that the application of the common law doctrine would be contrary to the philosophy of the Cypriot legislation governing land.[68] However, it has also been held that the common law rules on trusts apply with regards to immovable property. It should be further noted that Cap. 224 does not have retrospective effect and as a result the division of categories of immovable property in accordance with Ottoman law might still be relevant for the determination of rights of specific individuals.[69]

The system of compulsory acquisition of immovable property prescribed by Article 23 of the Constitution is based on the civilian legal tradition.[70] Furthermore, an amendment regarding common property is directly influenced by the corresponding provisions of Greek civil law. Similarly, the Associations and Foundations Law 57/1972 was enacted on the basis of the corresponding provisions of the Greek Civil Code and it is grounded on principles drawn from the civil law of Europe.[71]

With respect to succession law, the Wills and Succession Law 20/1895 was enacted during the British rule and remained in force until 1946 when the current Wills and Succession Law, Cap. 195, was enacted. The 1895 Law and its successor, the 1946 law, governed the succession of non-Muslims. Law 20/1895 had constituted a curious mixture of elements drawn not only from English and Ottoman law, but also from the Italian Civil Code and therefore indirectly from Roman law. These Italian influenced provisions were taken from sections

---

67   S Papasavvas, 'There is Drittwirkung of Human Rights in the Cypriot Legal Order: Comments and Thoughts on the Judgment of the Supreme Court in Civil Appeal 9931 Yiallouros v Nicolaou' (2002) 15 *Dikaiomata tou Anthropou* 837 (in Greek).

68   *Millington Ward* v *Roubina* (1970) 1 CLR 88; *Ayios Andronicos Development Ltd* v *Republic* (1985) 1 CLR 2362.

69   I Boyiadjis, 'Law in Rem' *Corpus de Jure Cyprii* (Council of Legal Studies 1987) 57 (in Greek); G Stavrinakis, 'Immovable Property in Cyprus' in *Symposium on Cypriot Legal Issues* (Aristotle University of Thessaloniki 1974) 157 (in Greek).

70   A Symeou, *The Safeguard of Property and its Compulsory Acquisition in Cyprus* (2003) (in Greek).

71   A Emilianides, 'Certain Problems of Interpretation of the Associations and Foundations Law' (2008) 8 Cyprus and European Law Review 329 (in Greek).

720–1049 of the Italian Civil Code, which were first translated into Greek and subsequently into English to form the basis of an original Cypriot legislation.[72]

The current law, the Wills and Succession Law, Cap. 195, which was also enacted during the British rule, is also very mixed.[73] Intestacy and the rules of disposable portion are governed mainly by civil law principles drawn from the Italian Civil Code the main lines of which are themselves derived from Roman law. In testate succession however, wills and their construction are governed exclusively by common law principles.[74] Furthermore, the Administration of Estates Law, Cap. 189, introduces the common law system of administration of estates as an integral part of Cypriot succession law. Under this regime the estate of the deceased is not directly acquired by the heirs or the legatees; rather, the rights and liabilities attaching to the estate of the deceased, including the statutory portion and the undisposed portion, are vested in the personal representative of the deceased and not the heirs.

Family law

Family law will be considered separately, because of its significance for the hybridity of the system. The Constitution provides for two communal chambers: a Greek Communal Chamber and a Turkish Communal Chamber, which shall have legislative power in educational, cultural, religious and other matters of purely communal nature, including matters of personal status. Following the self-dissolution of the Greek Communal Chamber, Law 12/1965 transferred the competences of the Greek Communal Chamber to the newly established Ministry of Education and Culture, the House of Representatives and the Council of Ministers. The Turkish Communal Chamber no longer functions in the areas controlled by the Republic due to the inter-communal crisis.[75]

According to Article 111 of the Constitution, matters of marriage and divorce of the members of the Greek Orthodox Church were governed by the law of the Greek Orthodox Church and were cognizable by a tribunal of the Church. All the aforementioned rights of the Orthodox Church were also granted to the ecclesiastical groups of the three other religious groups of the Republic: the Maronites, the Armenians and the Roman Catholics. Furthermore, Article 111 provided for the competence of the ecclesiastical courts of the Greek Orthodox

---

72   A Bertram, 'The Law of Wills and Succession in Cyprus: A Study in Comparative Legislation' (1911) 12 Journal of Comparative Legislation and International Law 324, 326.

73   *Charalambous* v *Demetriou* (1961) CLR 30.

74   A Emilianides, *Cypriot Succession Law* (2nd edn Hippassus 2014) (in Greek); A Emilianides, *Family and Succession Law* (Kluwer 2012).

75   For the family law of the Turkish Cypriot Community see A Emilianides, 'The Case for Amending the Current Legal Framework' (2011) 11 Cyprus and European Law Review 135; G Serghides, 'Reflection on Some Aspects of the Family Law of the Turkish Community in Cyprus' (2011) 11 Cyprus and European Law Review 156.

Church or the ecclesiastical courts of the three religious groups in family law matters.

The compulsory character of religious marriage and the jurisdiction of ecclesiastical law were criticized as being inconsistent with contemporary legal principles and social perceptions. The need to adjust all matters relating to personal institutions to the commitments of the Republic of Cyprus towards international conventions led to the First Amendment of the Constitution (Law 95/1989), which amended article 111 of the Constitution.[76] According to the provisions of Law 95/1989 all matters relating to divorce, judicial separation or restitution of conjugal rights or to family relations of the members of the Orthodox Church, came under the jurisdiction of a Family Court, whereas all matters relating to divorce, judicial separation or restitution of conjugal rights or to family relations of the members of the three religious groups, came under the jurisdiction of the Family Courts of the religious groups. Members of the Greek Community were given the option to perform a civil marriage instead of a religious one.

The 1989 amendment of the Constitution has modernized Cypriot family law and has diminished its religious character. However, church membership is still important not only with respect to the application of the provisions of Article 111 of the Constitution, but also with respect to the interpretation of the Cypriot law of marriage and divorce. Furthermore, matters relating to betrothal, religious marriage and nullity of religious marriage continue to be governed by the law of the Greek Orthodox Church or the Church of the corresponding religious group as the case may be, despite the fact that the dispute will be adjudicated by the Family Court or by the Family Court of the respective religious group. Canon law thus retains some importance in family law.

Nearly all legislation relevant to family law was enacted following the 1989 constitutional amendment and reflects changing social structures and policy in the regulation of family law affairs.[77] Civil law influences in Greek law are obvious in all family law institutions. Judges of Family Courts regularly cite the textbooks of Greek professors of family law as authorities, in the same manner that District Court judges cite leading common law academic authorities when adjudicating cases concerning contract law or tort law. It is therefore well settled that Cypriot family law adheres predominantly to the civil law tradition.[78]

However, it would be wrong to consider that common law has no influence in family law institutions. The Marriage Law, Cap. 279 was, until its substitution with the Marriage Law 104(I)/2003, a legal instrument governing the marriage of persons who were not members of the Greek Orthodox Church, or one of the three

---

76 A Emilianides, *The Cypriot Law of Marriage and Divorce* (Sakkoulas 2006) (in Greek) 145ff.

77 A Emilianides, *Family and Succession Law in Cyprus* (Kluwer 2012).

78 Society of Lawyers of Northern Greece, *Grounds for Divorce in accordance with Greek and Cypriot Law* (Sakkoulas 1993) (in Greek); G Serghides, *Grounds for Divorce* (2007) v. I—I (in Greek).

religious groups or the Turkish Community. Its provisions were mainly based on common law principles. The English marriage legislation and common law as they applied prior to independence still govern the validity of certain categories of marriages, celebrated in Cyprus, as well as all marriages celebrated abroad.[79] Furthermore, the provisions of the English Matrimonial Causes Act, 1950 (which applied in Cyprus prior to independence) and common law principles, apply in divorce proceedings of members of the Turkish Cypriot Community whose marriages were celebrated in Cyprus.[80] There is admittedly no rational justification why such an anachronistic English law of 1950 ought to apply to divorce proceedings which are adjudicated more than 60 years later or to nullity proceedings of marriages which were not celebrated in accordance with English law.

There is currently no law governing cohabitation without marriage in Cyprus, since Cypriot family law refers exclusively to married couples.[81] It is therefore accepted that the common law of equity concerning constructive trusts applies to cohabitants.[82] There is, however, debate as to whether the rules of equity governing the creation of a trust between the spouses where property exclusively belonged to one of the spouses,[83] could apply after the enactment of the Matrimonial Property of the Spouses Law 232/1991 which derives from civil law principles. Section 14 of Law 232/91 provides that if the property of either spouse has increased during the duration of the marriage and the other spouse has contributed to such increase, then the other spouse may file a matrimonial property petition before the Court and claim the part of the property which has been increased due to his/her contribution. In *Orphanides* it was held that the rules of Law 232/91 exclusively govern the distribution of matrimonial property between the spouses, in such a way that it is not possible to also apply the principles of the English law of equity.[84] Contrary to the aforementioned case law, however, subsequent case law of the Supreme Court has held that the Family Court may apply the common law principles of equity in matrimonial property disputes.[85] This is a highly problematic approach as the rules

---

79   Emilianides (n77).

80   G Serghides, 'Civil Substantive Law with respect to the Dissolution of Marriage' (1989) 8 *Kypriaki Martyria* 54 (in Greek).

81   S Loizidou, 'The Witch's Brew: Cohabitation and its Property Implications on Relationship Breakdown in Cyprus' in G Serghides, *Matrimonial Property of the Spouses and Partners and Various Legal Issues* (2010) 30.

82   *Clerides* v *Stavrides* (1998) 1 CLR 521 (in Greek); *Reckendorfer v Reckendorfer* (2004) 1 CLR 1132 (in Greek).

83   *Pentafkas v Pentafka* (1991) 1 CLR 547 (in Greek).

84   *Orphanides v Orphanides* (1998) 1 CLR 179 (in Greek), adopted in *Christoforou v Christoforou* (1998) 1 CLR 1551 (in Greek); *Papaioannou v Papaioannou* (2000) 1 CLR 656 (in Greek).

85   *Logginos v Logginou* (2000) 1 CLR 1347 (in Greek); *Michael v Yiangou* (2001) 1 CLR 1643 (in Greek); *Philippou v Philippou* (2003) 1 CLR 1343 (in Greek).

of equity should never be contrary to statutory provisions, much less provisions of a mandatory character.[86]

Specific Issues

The significance of language

Article 3 of the Constitution provides that the official languages of the Republic are Greek and Turkish. Furthermore, both the Greek and Turkish texts of the Constitution are originals and have the same authenticity and legal force, although the English text of the Constitution shall guide the Supreme Court in reaching an authoritative interpretation of the text of the Constitution in any case where there is conflict between the two original texts.[87] Article 189 of the Constitution, however, provided that for a period of five years after the coming into operation of the Constitution in 1960 all laws which continue to be in force under Article 188 of the Constitution (that is, legislation enacted during the British rule) may continue to be in the English language and the English language might continue to be used in any court proceedings. This was intended to be a transitional provision; however, translation of the legislation proved to be a daunting task and Law 51/1965 provided, contrary to the constitutional provisions, for a further extension of the use of the English language in both legislation and court proceedings.[88]

This anomalous situation whereby the legislation and the court proceedings were in a language different from either of the official ones, eventually ended following social pressure with the enactment of Law 67/88 which held that court proceedings should be conducted in one of the official languages of the Republic and not in English.[89] All the judgments of the Supreme Court of Cyprus until 1989 were published in English; it is only since 1989 that they have been published in Greek. It should be further noted that whereas legislation enacted prior to independence has been translated into Greek, such translation is still considered as an unofficial version, the official text of the legislation being the English one; thus, in case of conflict between the two texts, the English text will prevail. Post-independence legislation is not published in English, but in Greek only.

This resistance of legal and social elites to translate the legislation into the official language and to abolish English as the working language of the courts was mainly due to the fact that many lawyers and judges were educated in Britain and

---

86   G Serghides, 'Matrimonial Property of the Spouses according to Cypriot Law' in Serghides (n81) 11ff; *Pericleous v Egglezou and Another* Appeal 5/10, 9/6/11.

87   *Rodosthenous* (1961) CLR 127; *Ramadan v The Electricity Authority of Cyprus* (1961) 1 RSCC 49; *Stademos Hotels Ltd v Improvement Board of Amathous* (1991) 4 CLR 2537 (in Greek).

88   *Koumi v Kortari* (1983) 1 CLR 856.

89   *Sofocleous v Stylianou* (1992) 1 CLR 81 (in Greek).

were accustomed to the English common law. It was therefore considered that the maintenance of the English language in courts was consistent with the status of Cyprus as a 'common law country'. It comes as no surprise that the most loyal supporters of the introduction of the Greek language in courts were lawyers and judges who had graduated from Greek universities.[90]

The Bar and the justice system

In Cyprus there is no distinction between barristers and solicitors such as the one found in England, nor is there a distinction between advocates and notaries as found in most civil law systems; indeed the concept of notaries does not exist in the Cypriot legal order. Cypriot advocates may therefore handle either judicial or extra-judicial work, on the basis of their preferences; the conception of the Bar in Cyprus is a unitary one, where the advocate, once admitted to the Bar, may undertake any kind of legal work.[91] The Cyprus Bar Association is the professional association of advocates and it exercises disciplinary control over its members, without interference by public authorities; indeed, the Cyprus Bar Association is considered as a legal person under private law and not under public law.[92]

Until fairly recently Cypriot lawyers studied exclusively outside of Cyprus, mainly in the UK and Greece. It is understandable that advocates who were educated in the UK normally were in favour of maintaining the special links between Cyprus and the common law, whereas advocates who were Greek-educated supported the introduction of civil law thinking in the Cypriot legal system. In 2007 the State recognized and accredited the first University Law Department; this was the Law Department of the University of Nicosia, a private university, which soon became the first University to offer a fully-fledged Cypriot law degree and to have its graduates admitted in the Bar.[93] The State University of Cyprus followed suit, as did other private universities.

---

90   L Papaphilippou, 'Language and Justice' *Corpus de Jure Cypri* v I, v 1 (Council of Legal Studies 1987,) 135 (in Greek); F Nicolaides, 'Language and Courts' (1992) 39–40 Cyprus Law Review 5871 (in Greek). I do not agree with D Karoulla-Vrikki, 'English or Greek Language? State or Ethnic Identity: The Case of the Courts in Cyprus' (2001) 25 Language Problems and Language Planning 259, that the dominant role of English in court until 1988 reflected Cyprocentric State identity associations, or that the introduction of the Greek language was the outcome of Hellenocentric tendencies with the ultimate aim to foster ethnic identity. It would be indeed paradoxical if Cyprocentric identity was associated with the language of another State and in particular the former ruler of Cyprus.

91   A Emilianides, *Professional Law of Advocates* (Dikaionomia 2007) (in Greek).

92   *Emilianides v Board of the Cyprus Bar Association* (1992) 3 CLR 174 (in Greek).

93   K Ebeku, 'Developing Legal Education in the Commonwealth: The Case of the Republic of Cyprus' (2005) 5 Journal of Commonwealth Law and Legal Education 145; and by the same author, 'An Introduction to the Law Department of the University of Nicosia' (2009) 9 Cyprus and European Law Review 445.

The lack of PhD holders and Cypriot legal academics has led the newly established university departments of law to seek faculty members from Greece. It is therefore interesting to note that the majority of members of full-time faculty in Cypriot law departments are Greek academics and not Cypriots. Furthermore, Cypriot private universities have focused on offering not only a Cypriot law curriculum, but also a Greek law curriculum and, sometimes, an English law curriculum, in an attempt to attract students from Greece, as well as other countries. This has led to a rather unique co-existence of Cypriot, Greek and English law curriculum. Although the State University of Cyprus offers a Cypriot law curriculum, it purports to offer Cypriot law within a comparative environment. Three other private universities, the European University, Cyprus, the Neapolis University, Paphos, and Frederick University, offer both Cypriot and Greek law concentrations, whereas the University of Central Lancashire (Cyprus Campus) offers an English law curriculum.

One university in particular, the University of Nicosia, offers all three concentrations (Cypriot, Greek and English) to potential students, with students being able to study either one concentration only, or a mix of concentrations by studying some courses of Cypriot law, some courses of Greek law and some courses of English law. Whereas, courses of Cypriot and Greek law are in the Greek language, courses of English law are offered in the English language.[94] Perhaps, even more importantly, academics might teach courses in both languages and in any of the concentrations.[95] The course of European Comparative Law has further been introduced as a required course at LLM level.

It is considered that the introduction of Cypriot law schools, combined with the experiment of mixing legal traditions at the level of legal education, might prove to be beneficial for the further development of the mixed character of the Cypriot legal system.

The justice system and the role of the Supreme Court

In light of the maintenance of English common law as a source of law, English cases may be cited before Cypriot courts and indeed they are often used as guidelines, where there is no relevant Cypriot case law. Cyprus adopts the doctrine of precedent; as a result, previous judgments of the Supreme Court are binding on lower courts. The Supreme Court itself may depart from its earlier decisions whenever it concludes that a previous decision is founded on an indisputably wrong principle of law, or a principle leading to manifest injustice or a principle which

---

94   It is noted that the mother tongue of all Greek Cypriots is Greek and that high-school courses are taught in Greek in public schools; however, private high-schools normally teach in English, rather than Greek.

95   For instance during the past five years I have personally taught English, Cypriot and Greek Private International Law and Family Law, as well as Cypriot and English Tort Law and Cypriot and Greek Succession Law.

cannot be reconciled to changed legal or social circumstances. It is thus noted that previous case law is only binding so far as a subsequent law with different content has not been enacted. The legal rule which must be applied is the ratio decidendi, or the legal principle on which the previous decision was founded. The ratio of the case is distinguishable from obiter dicta, which are statements on principles of law made in the course of a decision, but on which the decision does not depend.

Case law is therefore of great significance with regard to the interpretation of legal provisions.[96] However, Cyprus has developed a substantially codified legal system, which somewhat restricts the dependence of Cypriot law on English common law. Cypriot courts have further asserted their right to subject the application of the English common law to the condition that it be suitable for Cyprus, a fact which has contributed to the conclusion that 'the danger of further Anglicization of Cypriot law does not seem to have materialized'.[97] Cypriot courts will therefore apply common law principles where there is no Cypriot legislation in force and in so far as existing Cypriot legislation is not contradicted. A field where legislation reflects almost entirely common law rules is Private International Law or Conflict of Laws, which remains the most striking omission from the Cypriot legislative corpus. The gradual Europeanization of private international law rules has, however, significantly restricted the importance of the application of common law rules in this area.

The system is effectively a two-tier system, with the Supreme Court acting as the highest appellate court of the land. More often than not, District Court judgments which consider difficult questions of law are appealed before the Supreme Court. Judgments of the Supreme Court are published officially in annual volumes separated into three main Parts.[98] Part 1 contains Civil Law cases, whereas Part 2 contains Criminal Law cases and Part 3 contains Administrative Law cases. Since 1991 Part 1 has further contained the Judgments of the Appellate Family Court.[99]

Judges are appointed from the legal profession; there is no school for judges as in many civil law countries. Judges at first instance (District Court Judges) are called to hear and determine both civil and criminal law cases; however, there are also four specialized courts, namely Family Courts, the Industrial Disputes

---

96   C Artemides 'The Principle of Commitment of Courts to Case-Law in English Common Law' in *Aspects of Cypriot Law* v I (Asselia 1981) (in Greek) 219; S Nikitas, 'The Principle of Judicial Precedent in English Common Law' *Corpus de Jure Cyprii* v I (Legal Studies Council 1987) (in Greek) 119.

97   S Symeonides, 'The Mixed Legal System of the Republic of Cyprus' (2003) 78 Tulane Law Review 441, 450.

98   Since 1992 important first instance administrative law judgments of the Supreme Court have been collected separately in Part 4.

99   Although comprised of Supreme Court judges, this is a separate court established in accordance with Art.111 of the Constitution, as amended by Law 95/1989: *Nicolaou* (1991) 1 CLR 1045 (in Greek).

Tribunal, the Rent Control Tribunal and the Military Tribunal. Cases before the District Courts are heard by a single judge, who may be, depending on the value of the dispute, a District Court Judge, a Senior District Court Judge, or a President of a District Court. A person may be appointed as President of a District Court or Senior District Court Judge if he is an advocate who has practiced law for ten years and is of a high moral standard and as a District Court Judge if he is an advocate who has practiced for six years and is of a high moral standard.

The Supreme Court has exclusive jurisdiction for the appointment and promotion of judges, with the exception of Supreme Court judges themselves; these are appointed by the President of the Republic amongst lawyers of high professional and moral standards, who have practised for at least 12 years. Whereas, the President has seemingly unlimited power to choose any lawyer who has the appropriate high professional and moral standard as a judge of the Supreme Court, a practice has emerged in accordance with which the President of the Republic seeks and follows the advice of the Supreme Court and, more recently, of the Cyprus Bar Association, prior to the appointment of a new member of the Court. With one exception[100] all Presidents of the Republic have appointed Supreme Court justices from amongst Presidents of the District Courts, a practice which safeguards the political neutrality of the judges, but at the same time is dependent almost exclusively upon seniority and years of service.

Since 1964 the Supreme Court has exercised the jurisdiction and powers of both the Supreme Constitutional Court and the High Court by virtue of the Administration of Justice (Miscellaneous Provisions) Law, 33/1964, which was enacted in accordance with the doctrine of necessity. Consequently, the Supreme Court is not only the highest appellate court of the Republic, having jurisdiction to hear and determine all civil and criminal law cases, but it also exercises exclusive jurisdiction as both a first instance and appellate administrative court by virtue of Article 146 of the Constitution. In addition Article 155 s4 of the Constitution stipulates that the Supreme Court shall have exclusive jurisdiction to issue orders in the nature of habeas corpus, mandamus, prohibition, quo warranto and certiorari;[101] such writs are collectively referred to as prerogative orders and have their origin in English common law.

This situation results in judges who have been practising civil and commercial law, which is common law oriented, for all of their professional careers, suddenly being called to adjudicate civil law oriented administrative law cases, both at first instance and at appellate level. Some of these judges might have never studied civil law or practised administrative law before their appointment to the Supreme Court. In practice, this often leads to newly appointed judges of the Supreme Court trying to apply common law reasoning and conceptions to administrative law

---

100   In 1997 former President of the Republic, Glafkos Clerides, appointed Justice Rallis Gavrielides, a senior member of the legal service of the Republic.

101   P Artemis, *Prerogative Orders* (2004) (in Greek); C Clerides, 'Prerogative Orders' (1994) 3 Cyprus Law Tribune 297 (in Greek).

cases which ought to have been decided on the basis of civil law principles. This frequently results in misconceptions about the role of the Supreme Court when acting as an administrative court; because, whereas in administrative proceedings the role of the judge ought to be of an inquisitorial nature, most Supreme Court judges treat the administrative proceedings as if they were civil law proceedings to be governed by common law oriented civil procedure rules which are adversarial.

The influence of EU law

Following the accession of the Republic of Cyprus to the EU in 2004, questions arose as to the need for an amendment to the Constitution, so as to reflect the post-accession framework of the Republic, as well as the position of EU law within the Cypriot legal order.[102] The Constitution was amended with the Fifth Constitutional Amendment of 2006, Law 127(I)/2006, which aimed at facilitating the exercise of the rights and obligations of the Republic of Cyprus as a member state of the EU. As a result EU law now has an intra-constitutional effect, in the sense that this is considered to be an integral part of the Constitution and no constitutional provision may invalidate any provision of a binding nature of EU law. EU law is therefore accorded constitutional status by the Constitution itself, in the sense that no other provision of the Constitution may be invoked so as to declare the provisions of EU law unconstitutional.[103]

The introduction of EU law in the Cypriot legal system is gradually further transforming Cypriot private law. Cypriot private international law, once a field dominated by common law principles, has been strikingly affected by the harmonization of European private international law rules; the new rules following pre-dominantly the civil law tradition. The same is true with respect to fields which were previously only governed by common law principles, such as consumer law or intellectual property law, competition law, public procurement and so on. The EU itself is sometimes described as a mixed supranational system,[104] and even

---

102   A Emilianides, 'The Constitution of Cyprus post-Accession' in A Emilianides (ed), *Policy Proposals* (Power Publishing 2005) (in Greek) 81; S Laulhé-Shaelou, *The EU and Cyprus: Principles and Strategies of Full Integration* (Brill 2010); *Attorney-General v Constantinou* (2005) 1 CLR 1356 (in Greek).

103   C Lycourgos, 'Cyprus Public Law as Affected by Accession to the European Union' in C Kombos (ed), *Studies in European Public Law* (Sakkoulas 2010) 101ff. C Lycourgos, 'The Application of EU Law in Cyprus: Selected Aspects' (2012) The Cyprus Yearbook of International Law 43ff; S Laulhe-Shaelou, 'Back to Reality: The Implications of EU Membership in the Constitutional Legal Order of Cyprus' in A Lazowski (ed), *Brave New World. Application of EU Law in the New Member States* (TMC Asser Press 2010) 471.

104   H Kötz, 'The Value of Mixed Jurisdictions' (2003) 78 Tulane Law Review 435, 439.

English law is increasingly labeled as becoming a 'mixed' system through the incorporation of EU law and the adoption of doctrines of civil law reasoning.[105]

The application of EU law to a system that was already a mixed one, has led to an increase in the extent and intensity of the hybridity of the legal system; while the effect of EU law on the system is gradual, its catalytic effect is undeniable. The actual experience of EU participation, however, has not so far verified the hypothesis that mixed systems would enjoy a special place in the process of European integration, since they could provide inspiration and valuable lessons for cross fertilization throughout the EU.[106] Cyprus remains a small State and its experience with legal hybridity is mostly ignored during negotiations for harmonization at a European level, where Member States are mainly anxious to safeguard the continuation of their national legal rules within the context of a harmonized European legislation, rather than with achieving legal hybridity or with academic discussions over finding the 'best' solution.[107]

Is the Mixed Legal System of Cyprus an Endangered One?

Since the early 2000s, Cyprus has been constantly characterized as a mixed legal system.[108] In 2000 Alecos Markides, then Attorney-General of the Republic of Cyprus, accurately stated that the study of the legal evolution of Cyprus 'provides an exceptional example for comparative law of the possibilities of harmonious co-existence and sometimes even the blending of legal systems' and that 'at present two different systems of law, the Anglo-Saxon and the Continental, apply in peaceful co-existence in different spheres'.[109] More recently Vernon Palmer categorized Cyprus within the set of jurisdictions having a mixed system of civil and common law.[110]

---

105 JE Levitsky, 'The Europeanisation of the British Legal Style' (1994) 42 American Journal of Comparative Law 347; X Lewis, 'A Common Law Fortress under Attack: Is English Law being Europeanised' (1995) 2 Columbia Journal of European Law 1; T Bingham, 'There is World Elsewhere: The Changing Perceptions of English Law' (1992) 41 International and Comparative Law Quarterley 513.

106 As expressed, for example, in JM Smits (ed), *The Contribution of Mixed Legal Systems to European Private Law* (Intersentia 2001).

107 I refer here also to my personal experience as a legal expert of the Republic of Cyprus with respect to the negotiation of European Community private law instruments from 2006–2013.

108 Symeonides (n97); N Hatzimichail, 'Cyprus as a Mixed Legal System' (2013) 3 Journal of Civil Law Studies 38; D Kyprianou, *The Role of the Cyprus Attorney-General's Office in Prosecutions: Rhetoric, Ideology and Practice* (Springer 2010) 48.

109 Foreword to the first edition (2000) of Neocleous' *Introduction to Cyprus Law* (Center for International Legal Studies 2000) vii.

110 V Palmer, 'Two Rival Theories of Mixed Legal Systems' (2008) 3 Journal of Comparative Law 7, Appendix A.

It has been recently argued that Cyprus fulfils the criteria set out by Vernon Palmer in his 'Third Legal Family' project as the 'lowest common denominator' of a mixed jurisdiction, that is, that the legal system must be built upon dual foundations of common law and civil law materials, that the duality must be obvious to an ordinary observer and that there should be structural allocation of content.[111] However, it should not be underestimated that Palmer described systems where 'in every case the civil law will be cordoned off within the field of private law, thus creating the distinction between private continental law and public Anglo-American law. This structural allocation is invariable in the family'.[112] Palmer further argues that 'so far we have no example of a reverse allocation of these respective spheres. One vainly searches for a system where continental law predominates in the public sphere, while Anglo-American law dominates in the private'.[113]

However, as I have tried to show, this is the case of the Cypriot legal system; common law dominates in the field of private law (with the major exception of family law and some other minor exceptions), whereas civil law dominates in the field of public law.[114] Therefore, if one is to adopt the definition of a 'third legal family',[115] Cyprus should be included as an indicative example of the 'reverse' category of such legal family.

The question arises whether this hybridity of the Cypriot legal system is under threat.[116] On the basis of the preceding analysis I would argue that this does not seem likely. As Symeonides correctly notes 'the diverse elements that compose the law of Cyprus owe their origin and survival to its troubled political history; they are accidents of history'.[117] Extra-legal considerations ought to be taken into account when hypothesizing on the potential vulnerability of the system.

It would seem that the demand of Greek Cypriots for Union with Greece has been completely abandoned following the 1974 Turkish invasion. The 1960 Constitution, a Constitution that never functioned in its entirety even for a single day, and which collapsed after three years of malfunction, became, after 1974, the legal and political basis of Greek Cypriots. Greek Cypriots became the guarantors of the Constitution, by using it in order to resist the effects of the Turkish invasion.[118]

---

111   Hatzimichail (n108) 94.

112   V Palmer (ed), *Mixed Jurisdictions Worldwide: The Third Legal Family* (2nd edn Cambridge University Press 2012) 9.

113   Palmer (n112) fn 24.

114   This uniqueness of the Cypriot legal system is also hinted by Hatzimichail (n108) 40–41.

115   I share many of the concerns of E Örücü, 'What is a Mixed Legal System: Exclusion or Expansion' (2008) 1 Electronic Journal of Comparative Law 1.

116   I use the term without any value judgment as to whether hybridity of a legal system is 'better' or 'more desirable' than an alleged purity.

117   Symeonides (n97) 454.

118   A Emilianides, 'The International System and the Constitution of Cyprus' in P Papapolyviou et al. (eds), *The Cyprus Question and the International System: 1945–1974* (Patakis 2013) 229 (in Greek).

As a result the Constitution became autochthonous, even though this was neither the intention of its drafters, nor the spirit of its provisions.

Despite Greece's geographical proximity and the fact that most Cypriots consider themselves Greek, Cyprus has for the past half century a distinct legal and political system, completely unrelated to Greece. Merging the Cypriot system to the Greek one does not seem currently a desirable solution for the majority of the political and social elites of the island. The continuing negotiations for the solution of the 'Cyprus Problem' and the desire to effect neutral solutions as to the identity of the legal system, seem, as in 1960, to exclude the substitution of common law by Greek civil law.

Furthermore, the majority of Cypriot lawyers and judges remain faithful to common law; a Cypriot lawyer thinks and acts like a common lawyer, rather than as a civil law one. Even in fields which are clearly of a civil law nature, such as family law or administrative law, Cypriot lawyers and judges still reason in terms of precedents and the distinction between ratio and obiter just like their common law counterparts; a Cypriot lawyer applying civil law is unlike a Greek lawyer applying the exact same provisions because he interprets these provisions with a somewhat differentiated mind-set. In light of the fact that common law seems firmly entrenched in the Cypriot legal system, it would be extremely premature to predict its demise.

On the other hand, the continuing application of civil law seems equally secure. The Government of the Republic of Cyprus has announced its intention to establish distinct administrative courts of first instance which will be composed by specialized judges who will focus on civil law principles; there are no voices suggesting a substitution of civil law based administrative or family law with their common law counterparts. Furthermore, the establishment of Cypriot law schools having Greek academics as members of faculty enables comparative research and the opportunity to approach Cypriot law through the lens of civil law lawyers. It is characteristic that all law departments in Cyprus seem to agree on the significance of comparative law for the proper teaching of Cypriot law. The teaching of Cypriot law in Greek and the preparation of legal textbooks and materials in Greek is further instrumental in enabling legal practitioners to appreciate the hybridity of Cypriot law, instead of resorting to English legal textbooks as the only sources of authenticity.

There is little doubt that Cypriot law needs modernization. Much of the legislation is dated, enacted during a different era and without the people of Cyprus having the opportunity to consider the implications of such legislation. Whereas, common law could always serve as guidance for the Cypriot lawyer, there is absolutely no justification in retaining post-independence common law as a source of law more than 50 years after Independence. Uncritical deference to the judicial system has sometimes hindered the undertaking of a serious and comprehensive effort to modernize Cypriot legislation, although the contribution of the judiciary to the development and smooth functioning of the system should not be underestimated. EU law has also proved to be an enormous challenge for

Cypriot lawyers but might provide the necessary impetus for the modernization of the system.

As Heraclitus famously noted, everything changes and nothing remains still, as you cannot step twice into the same stream. The water of the legal stream of Cyprus is constantly changing; however, it seems that the new water will most likely remain blended rather than pure.

Endnote to Mixed Legal Systems:
Endangered, Entrenched, Blended or
Muddled?

Introduction

In this concluding chapter, we draw together a number of threads suggested by our contributors, as well as adding our own suggestions for future developments. Language, legal education, legal writing, the size of the jurisdiction, the wider world, uncodified but even codified law tempered by judges, difficulty in getting to original sources, the international financial picture, the impact of globalization, changing style and mentality are all factors impacting mixed legal systems and changing the equilibrium between the constituent parts. These appear mostly as negative factors. Other factors such as the strength of tradition, the search for coherence, nationalism, heritage, culture, seeking for identity and the influence of champions supporting distinctiveness, appear to be positive factors in maintaining the mixedness of a legal system.

General Issues

The study of 'mixed legal systems', both conceptually and in its many contexts, is a complex task, but one that may make significant contributions to comparative study. Similar to our jurisdictions, our comparative terminology and taxonomies are products of history rather than science. The language of comparative law, for example, 'circles', 'families', 'systems' and so on, lump together broadly-linked traditions, at both national and pan-national levels. These are blunt tools for understanding ever-changing and open legal traditions. The crude classifications of much contemporary comparative scholarship remains rooted in a rather shallow positivism of the past, in flawed assumptions about legal centralism and monism. Classification as 'mixed' is too often a mere catch-all category that effectively marks the failure of orthodox taxonomies to capture global legal reality.[1] It may

---

1 LG Baxter, 'Pure Comparative Law and Legal Science in a Mixed Legal System' (1983) 16 Comparative and International Law Journal of Southern Africa 84, 93. For example, Joseph Dainow calls Louisiana, a mixed jurisdiction, a '*systeme juridique sui generis*'. See '*Le droit civil de la Louisiane*' (1954) 6 *Revue de Droit International et de Droit Comparé* 19 at 32.

also suggest an inability or unwillingness among Western scholars to engage in the study of more complex mixes, especially those involving religious and customary law. Some comparative lawyers even treat 'mixed legal systems' or its correlates as a meaningful 'family'.[2] Of course, the creation of new taxonomies brings its own perils: the more complicated the classifications, the more confusion is created, defeating the goal of simplifying our analyses.

One of the difficulties is defining a 'mixed legal system'.[3] There have been many attempts to define various instances of mixing: historical or contemporary, overt or covert, structured or unstructured, complex or simple, blended or unblended and different authorities adopt different definitions, as indeed have our authors. Suggesting that mixed systems are those at points of contact or confluence (in the sense of osmosis) between different legal traditions assumes that existing taxonomies are accurate and meaningful. For instance, Joseph McKnight speaks of mixed systems as 'those having substantive attributes (and those of method) derived from two or more systems generally recognised as independent of others'.[4] In describing South Africa, Tom Bennett states that a mixed system describes the co-existence of two regimes 'which, although both applicable to the same persons, did not necessarily create contradictions, since they were confined to specific subject areas, for example, common law was used for commercial transactions and procedure, and civil law for family law and property'.[5]

In current comparative research the term, 'mixed legal systems' is used for those jurisdictions that contain significant and explicitly segregated, but non-overlapping elements of different legal traditions. In practice, it is a residual category for systems that cannot be assigned elsewhere. It can cover any mix, whether Western or non-Western. The phrase 'mixed jurisdictions' may sometimes be used in this general manner or more narrowly for mixtures of Anglo-American and Continental laws. The phrase is most often applied to the Western mixes

---

2   See M Rheinstein, 'Legal Systems: Comparative Law and Legal Systems' in (1968) *International Encyclopaedia of the Social Sciences* (IX edn, DL Sils ed., The Macmillan Company, New York) 204. More recently, see VV Palmer, *Mixed Jurisdictions Worldwide: The Third Legal Family* (2nd edn Cambridge University Press 2012). JM du Plessis also supports the view that there must be an 'independent recognition of a separate family' JM du Plessis, 'Comparative Law and the Study of Mixed Legal Systems' in M Reimann and R Zimmermann (eds), *Oxford Handbook of Comparative Law* (Oxford University Press 2006) 477, 510.

3   See, for example, KCJ Reid, 'The Idea of Mixed Legal Systems' (2008) 78 Tulane Law Review 5. As he points out, the striking characteristic of mixed systems historically was their mutual isolation.

4   J McKnight, 'Some Historical Observations on Mixed Systems of Law' (1977) 22 Juridical Review (ns) 177, 186.

5   WT Bennett. 'Legal Anthropology and Comparative Law: A Disciplinary Compromise' (2010) Stellenbosch Law Review 5–6.

that have dominated comparative scholarship.[6] Building on the work of earlier comparatists, Palmer has added the 'third legal family' as another 'term-of-art' for those mixed systems – many classical mixed jurisdictions – that share 'profound generalizable resemblances'.[7] Unfortunately, these different phrases – 'mixed legal systems', 'mixed jurisdictions' and the 'third legal family' – are used very casually in the broader scholarly literature. The result is often confusion rather than clarity. As William Tetley has written, '[f]acetiously, one might ... define a mixed jurisdiction as a place where debate over the subject takes place.'[8]

However defined, there are many mixed systems of law around the world. In fact, overt mixes arguably make up the majority of the legal traditions in the world. The ubiquity of mixity, both overt and covert, reflects the important paths in which legal ideas and institutions have travelled around the globe. Both for nominally pure and so-called mixed systems, the 'transfrontier mobility of laws' is significant.[9] Indeed, the subjects of 'reception' and 'transplantation', of 'contamination', and 'diffusion', and so on, are central to comparative law.[10] The Italian comparatist Michele Graziadei has even suggested that comparative law can be characterized as the 'study of legal transplants and receptions'.[11] Viewing comparative study in this way puts mixed legal systems at the centre of comparative law. The fact that laws and peoples are not static lies at the bottom of all mixed systems. But understanding this mobility reminds us that transplants and receptions have affected all modern traditions.

With respect to mixed systems, the mobility of law takes various forms with diverse paths. Some European jurisdictions, such as the Channel Islands, Cyprus, Malta and Scotland, are explicitly and obviously mixed. They still bear clear traces

---

6   'Classical mixed jurisdictions', as used by Vernon Palmer, are roughly the same, referring to specific jurisdictions, such as Louisiana, Puerto Rico, Quebec, Scotland, and South Africa, about which there is a considerable body of scholarly writing. See V Palmer, 'Mixed Legal Systems: The Origin of the Species' (2013) 28 Tulane European and Civil Law Forum 103.

7   V Palmer *Mixed Jurisdictions Worldwide: The Third Legal Family* (Cambridge University Press 2001), 4.

8   W Tetley, 'Mixed Jurisdictions: Common Law v Civil Law (Codified and Uncodified)' 60 (2000) Louisiana Law Review 677, 680 n3.

9   See, for example, E Örücü, 'A Theoretical Framework for Transfrontier Mobility of Law' in AJ De Roo, E. Örücü and RW Jagtenberg (eds), *Transfrontier Mobility of Law* (Kluwer Law International 1995).

10   The concept of 'legal transplants' remains controversial. See, for example, R Cotterrell 'Is There a Logic of Legal Transplants?' in D Nelken and J Fest (eds), *Adapting Legal Cultures* (Ashgate 2001) 71. Cf W Twining, 'Diffusion of law: a global perspective' (2004) 49 Journal of Legal Pluralism 1, in which his use of 'diffusion' builds on the use of that term in the social sciences and includes both laws and norms.

11   M Graziadei, 'Comparative Law as the Study of Transplants and Receptions' in M Reimann and R Zimmermann (eds), *The Oxford Handbook of Comparative Law* (Oxford University Press 2008).

of their plural pasts. Such mixity is even more easily seen in those colonies where Western laws were imposed, including transfers from one Western sovereign to another. In this way, Western laws came into contact with numerous other legal and normative traditions: Asian, Hindu, Islamic and a wider variety of customary traditions. Some of these were already complex hybrids. The addition of Western laws further complicated the normative-legal spaces of much of the world. Even where such impositions did not occur, Western political, economic and military dominance has ensured that its laws were frequently borrowed.

Indeed, no modern legal system, nominally pure or mixed, is immune from these influences. Unlike the conviction, accurate or merely ideological, of originality and unity in the nominally pure traditions, for example Anglo-American and Continental law, those in mixed systems appear to be merely liminal, bipolar half-breeds at the margins of existing, presumably natural, classifications. This particular balance may become entrenched or the system may tilt towards one or other of the traditions. At least in theory, the constituent elements can blend to such an extent that the mixed nature of the system faces the danger of extinction. The result globally is a number of coherent and connected, though never closed, legal traditions. Indeed, far-flung jurisdictions, including many post-colonial States, continue to look to their mother tradition for guidance.

The maintenance and preservation of mixed systems is due to a number of different factors, either singly or in combination. The work of its jurists, either scholars or judges, may be important. TB Smith, for example, championed Scotland's mix. William Howard Taft, later President of the United States, earlier served as Civil Governor of the Philippines. A more general political will, such as that which brought about the revised Civil Code in Quebec can also be significant. Perhaps most importantly, shifts in global power can be critical. In many of the jurisdictions discussed here, it is the increasing dominance of the common law that endangers present mixes. As our contributors note, the reasons have as much to do with Anglo-American cultural, military and economic hegemony as reason.[12] In fact, discussion of equilibrium in the mixed systems is often shorthand for the maintenance of existing civilian elements in the face of this hegemony. Some mixed systems will flourish because of these changes, for example, Mauritius. Others, such as Saint Lucia and Guyana, will struggle to maintain a working balance between their different component parts. It is these latter which might be referred to as 'endangered'. Other systems, like perhaps Mauritius and Cyprus, will strike a working balance. Entrenchment and endangerment is related to strength or weakness of these types of factors.

---

12   On wider themes of legal hegemony, see, for example U Mattei, 'A Theory of Imperial Law: A study on US Hegemony and the Latin Resistance' (2003) 10 Indiana Journal of Global Legal Studies 383.

Concluding Remarks

Our aim has been to evaluate a selection of mixed legal systems. One of the lessons of this collection is that mixing may take many forms and reflect a wide range of cultural, geographical and political contexts. It is also clear from the contributions in this collection that the ways in which mixed legal systems have evolved, survived or find their mixedness threatened are unique. No single dominant culture is represented by mixed legal systems. Indeed, the elements that combine to produce a mixed legal system are themselves a unique cultural form: 'mixedness is itself the culture'.

Our chapters reveal the multiplicity of approaches to mixed legal systems. Those working on mixtures of common law and civil law, as in many of our chapters, continue to produce valuable work with ever-greater influence. Other scholars have examined more complex mixes.[13] Building on this work, still others have suggested that mixed legal systems and 'legal pluralism' could usefully be studied together.[14] Of course, any research into mixed legal systems must acknowledge these existing debates and assess their continuing relevance. Ideally, our understanding of the manner in which mixes are created and evolve is also broadened. In addition, both existing and new terminology used in analysing individual instances of mixity – including the term 'endangered' introduced here – must be clarified.[15] New mixes, ongoing mixes, legal systems in transition and endangered systems must then be re-evaluated with the knowledge gained.

This collection provides new and valuable information for the study of mixed systems, as well as for the understanding of legal mixtures and movements more generally. There has arguably been an increase in 'mixing' at all legal levels – subnational, national, transnational. With the criss-crossing of influences, there are unprecedented 'contaminations' or indeed 'inspirations' throughout our present globalized legal environment. The relevance of mixed systems, both established and exotic, to this new legal complexity is increasingly obvious.

The chapters collected here face a twofold challenge. First, they illustrate the difficulty of arriving at satisfactory definitions of 'mixed legal systems'. Second, they provoke a question of two parts: does a mixed legal system have any inherent

---

13   See especially E Örücü, 'What is a Mixed Legal System: Exclusion or Expansion? in in E Örücü (ed), *Mixed Legal Systems at New Frontiers* (Wildy, Simmonds and Hill 2010). See also E Örücü, 'Turkey's Synthetic Civilian Tradition in a "Covert" Mix with Islam's Tradition: A Novel Hybridity?' and S Farran, 'Pacific Punch: Tropical Flavours of Mixedness in the Island Republic of Vanuatu', both in M Mattar, V Palmer and A Koppel (eds), *Mixed Legal Systems, East and West* (Ashgate 2014 TBC).

14   See, for example, SP Donlan, 'To Hybridity and Beyond: Reflections on Legal and Normative Complexity' in Mattar, Palmer and Koppel ibid..

15   Note that not all contributors subscribed to the term 'endangered', and in the chapters alternative terms and concepts have been used such as, 'at risk', 'exposed to harm' 'threatened', 'in danger', 'smothered', 'diluted' and so on.

value distinct from other legal systems; if not, does it matter that some mixed legal systems appear to be endangered? For some it might, for others it is not seen as very important – change happens. What the chapters in this collection do suggest is how difficult it is to pinpoint the moment when that system became endangered. This is rarely a single event. Instead, gradual change slowly directs the evolution of the system. The passage from bilingualism to monolingualism, both in legal language and in the wider population, may be critical, as in the Philippines and Guyana. Shifts in the focus and form of legal education and training may also be important, as in Jersey, Seychelles and the Philippines. Other factors, such as geographic proximity to different influences, are also relevant. Scotland's physical and political affinity with England was, and remains, critical to its changes as does its place in Europe. Similarly, the political link between the Philippines and the US was, and remains, important. In an increasingly international or transnational arena, affiliation with regional legal organizations may also play a role. Cyprus' place in the EU and the place of Seychelles and Mauritius in COMESA (the Common Market for Eastern and Southern Africa) or SADC (Southern African Development Community) are important influences.

It might also be asked whether the comparatist can draw any firm conclusions about what makes mixed systems endangered and if this knowledge is useful for such systems. The answer seems to be a qualified 'Yes'. For example, Quebec's popularization of the revised Code Civil might be advocated as a strategy for developing a sense of jurisdictional ownership of their system. Pedagogical initiatives in Cyprus and Mauritius might ensure that future lawyers and judges receive a trans-systemic legal education that allows them to protect, or at least to consciously and conscientiously change, their current mix. Similarly the establishment of the Institute of Law on Jersey serves as a reminder of what can be done with limited resources and a clear focus.

However, an understanding of the law and legal institutions is not enough. There was general consensus among contributors that a wide area of knowledge is required for understanding legal traditions. While context is important, looking at positive law is not enough. Comparative legal scholarship, both on nominally pure and mixed systems, must go beyond black letter law to a deeper analysis of legal practice that draws on legal history, sociology and anthropology of law, and indeed that anthropology of law and comparative law must work together.[16] Much more could, of course, be added: economics, political science, international

16   Tom Bennett claims that one of the reasons why comparative lawyers have ignored African customary law in the South African mixture is because the former was regarded to be in the province of legal anthropology, while research into its Roman–Dutch and English legal heritage was seen to fall within comparative law and the study of 'mixed legal systems'. He urges a compromise between the two fields for a more meaningful understanding of such a system. Bennett (n5). For a similar argument, see SP Donlan, 'The Mediterranean Hybridity Project: At the Boundaries of Law and Culture' (2011) 4 Journal of Civil Law Studies 355.

law, law and development, and so on. Cultural studies of different types have also brought a deeper awareness of multiculturalism, legal pluralism and identity. However difficult it may be to master, this trans-disciplinarity is more essential than ever. The study of mixed systems, freed from the illusion of pure types, may be especially important in exploring the complex relationship between laws and cultures. While we are aware that we have only scratched the surface in this collection, the contributions here are an important addition to our knowledge in this area and a platform on which future studies can be built.

Index

Italic page numbers indicate tables